A MIDSUMMER DRIVE THROUGH THE PYRENEES • DIX, EDWIN ASA

ILLUSTRATIONS.

MAP.

Publisher's Note

Note: This is an historic book. Pages numbers, where present in the text, refer to the first edition of the book and may also be in indexes.

If you have any questions, could you please be so kind as to consult our Frequently Asked Questions page at www. rarebooksclub.com/faqs.cfm? You are also welcome to contact us there.
Publisher: General Books LLC™, Memphis, TN, USA, 2012. ISBN: 9781770459694.

Proofreading: pgdp.net

❊ ❊ ❊ ❊ ❊ ❊ ❊ ❊

from images generously made available by the
Bibliothèque nationale de France (BnF/ Gallica) at http://gallica.bnf.fr

A DIFFICULT BIT ON THE ROUTE THERMALE.

A MIDSUMMER DRIVE THROUGH THE PYRENEES

BY

EDWIN ASA DIX, M.A.

EX-FELLOW IN HISTORY OF THE COLLEGE OF NEW JERSEY AT PRINCETON

ILLUSTRATED

New York & London
G. P. Putnam's Sons
The Knickerbocker Press

1890

"How comes it to pass," wondered a traveler, over twenty years ago, "that, when the American people think it worth while to pay a visit to Europe almost exclusively to see Switzerland and Italy; when in 1860 twenty-one thousand Americans visited Rome and only seven thousand English; so few should think it worth while to visit the Pyrenees? It is certainly the only civilized country we have visited without finding Americans there before us. Is it accident or caprice, or part of a system of leaving it to the last,—which 'last' never comes? The feast is provided,—where are the guests? The French Pyrenees form one of the loveliest gardens in Europe and a perfect place for a summer holiday. 'La beauté ici est sereine et le plaisir est pur.'"

The query is still unanswered to-day. The stream of summer journeyings to Europe has swollen to a river; it has overflowed to the Arctic Ocean, to the Baltic, to the Black Sea and the Mediterranean. The Pyrenees—a garden not only, but a land of sterner scenery as well,—almost alone remain by our nation of travelers unvisited and unknown.

A MIDSUMMER DRIVE THROUGH THE PYRENEES

CHAPTER I.

IN PERSPECTIVE.

"In fortune's empire blindly thus we go;
We wander after pathless destiny,
Whose dark resorts since prudence cannot know,
In vain it would provide for what shall be."

A trip to the Pyrenees is not in the Grand Tour. It is not even in any southerly extension of the Grand Tour. A proposition to exploit them meets a dubious reception. Pictures arise of desolate gorges; of lonely roads and dangerous trails; of dismal roadside inns, where, when you halt for the night, a "repulsive-looking landlord receives the unhappy man, exchanges a look of ferocious intelligence with the driver,"—and the usual melodramatic midnight carnage probably ensues. The Pyrenees seem to echo the motto of their old counts, "*Touches-y, si tu l'oses*!" the name seems to stand vaguely for untested discomforts, for clouds and chasms, and Spanish banditti in blood-red *capas*; to be, in a word, a symbol of an undiscovered country which would but doubtfully reward a resolve to discover.

Yet there is a fascination in the project, as we discuss a summer tour. There, we know, are mountains whose sides are nearly Alpine, whose shoulders are of snow and glacier, whose heads rise to ten and eleven thousand feet above the sea. There, we know, must be savage scenery,—ravines, cliffs, ice-rivers, as in the Alps; valleys and streams and fair pastures as well, and a richer southern sunlight over the uplands; besides a people less warped by tourists, intensely tenacious of the past, and still tingling with their old local love of country,—a people with whom, "to be a Béarnais is greater than to be a Frenchman."

To visit the Pyrenees, too, will be almost to live again in the Middle Ages. The Roman, the Moor, the Paladin, Froissart, Henry of Navarre, have marked the region both in romance and in soberer fact. Its valleys have individual histories; its aged towns and castles, stirring biographies. The provinces on its northern flanks, once a centre, a nucleus, of old French chivalry, are saturated with mediæval adventure. One visits the Alps to be in the tide of travel, to find health in the air, to feel the religion of noble mountains. In the Pyrenees is all this, and more,—the present and the past as well. As we call down the shades of old chroniclers from the dust of upper library tiers, we grow more and more in desire of a closer acquaintance. Cæsar, Charlemagne, Roland, the Black Prince, Gaston Phoebus, Montgomery and knightly King Henry stand in ghostly armor and beckon us on.

II.

Facts of detail prove farther to seek. We inquire almost in vain for travelers' notes on the Pyrenees. Those who had written on Spanish travel spoke of the range admiringly. But these authors, we find, invariably, only passed by the eastern extremity, or the western, of the great mountain wall; the mountains themselves they did not visit. Search in the large libraries brings out a few scant volumes of Pyrenean travel, but all, with two or three exceptions, bear date within the first three-fifths of the century. It is with books, often, as with the *Furançon*, the wine of the Pyrenees, and with certain other vintages: age improves them only up to a certain limit; when put away longer than a generation, they lose value.

Taine's glowing *Tour*, itself made nearly thirty years ago, is a delight, almost a marvel; the style, the torrent of simile, the vivid thought, rank it as a classic. But M. Taine's is less a book of travel than a work of art; in the iridescence of the descriptions, you lose the reflection of the things described. Even hand-books, the way-clearing lictors of travel, prove, as to the Pyrenees region, first scarce and then scanty. The few we unearth in the stores are armed only with the usual perfunctory fasces of facts,—cording information into stiff, labeled bunches, marshaling details into cramped and characterless order, scrutinizing the ground with a microscope, never surveying it in bird's-eye view. Two recent novels we eagerly buy, hearing that their scenes are laid in that vicinity; but each merely speaks, in easy omniscience, of the "distant chain of blue mountains," or of the "far-off snow-peaks outlined against the horizon," and the fiction proves hardly worth sifting for so little fact. Plainly the Pyrenees lack the voluminous literature of the Alps. Plainly we shall have, in part, to grope our way. The grooves of Anglo-Saxon travel are many and deep, lined increasingly with English speech and customs; but they have not yet been cut into these Spanish mountains.

The search enlarges the horizon, however. The lonely roads we learn to qualify in thought with occasional branches of railway; the dangerous trails, with certain cultivated highways; the dismal road-side inns, with spasmodic hotels, some even named confidently as "palatial." We read of spas and springs and French society, more than of chasms and banditti. We realize in surprise that over all the past of these mountains flows now in bracing contrast the easy, laughing tide of modern French fashion,—life so different in detail, so like in kind, to the day of trapping and tourney.

It is enough:
"Now are we fix'd, and now we will depart,
Never to come again till what we seek
Be found."

III.

Difficulties always lessen after a decision. I casually question a doughty Colonel, who has been an indefatigable traveler; he has twice girdled the earth, and has many times cross-hatched Spain; he has not been to the Pyrenees, but heartily urges the trip. He assures me that the banditti there have become, he believes, comparatively few; that they now rarely slit their captives' ears, and that present quotations for ransoms, so he hears, are ruling very low, much lower than at any previous epoch. Thus comforted, we interview other traveled friends; but our goal is to all an unvisited district. We find no kindly Old Travelers returned from Pyrenees soil, to counsel us, advise us, and inflict well-meant and inordinate itineraries upon us. At least, then, we are not alone in our ignorance; it is evident that our knowledge of the region is not blamably less than that of others, and that the Pyrenees are in literal fact a land untrodden by Americans.

Questions of accessibility now arise. It seems a far cry from Paris to the doors of Spain. The Pyrenees are not on the way to Italy, as are the Alps. They are not on the way around the world, as are the Mountains of Lebanon and the Sierras. They are not strictly on the way even to Spain. But we consider. Our country men are streaming to Europe, quick-eyed for unhackneyed routes, throwing over the continent new and endless net-works of silver trails. They travel three full days to reach the Norway fjords, and five in addition to see the high noon of midnight. They journey a day and night to Berlin, and forty-two hours consecutively after, without wayside interest, to visit the City of the Great Czar; if they persevere toward the Kremlin, and around by "Warsaw's waste of ruin," they will have counted a week in a railway compartment. Constantinople and Athens lie two thousand miles away, Naples and Granada nearly as far; all sought, even in summer, though quivering in the tropics' livid heat. We came round to our Pyrenees: it needs from Paris but nine hours to Bordeaux, with coigns of vantage between; in four hours from Bordeaux, you are by the waters of the Bay of Biscay, or in six, in the centre of the Pyrenees chain.

IV.

And so *La Champagne* leaves its long wake across the Atlantic, and we journey down from Paris to the little city of the Maid of Orleans; wander to Tours, the approximate scene of the great Saracenic defeat; drive along the quays of Bordeaux, and visit its vineyards and finally come on, in the luxurious cars of the *Midi* line, to the shores of Cantabria and the popular watering-place of Biarritz.

CHAPTER II.

A BISCAYAN BEACH.

Clearly we are in advance of the summer season at Biarritz. It is the latter part of June. The air is soft and warm, the billows lap the shore enticingly. But fashion has not yet transferred its court; the van of the column only has arrived. A few adventurous bathers test the cool surf; the table-d'hôte is slimly attended;

the liverymen confidentially assure us, as an inducement for drives, that their prices are now crouching low, for a prodigious leap to follow.

But everything has a pleasing air of anticipation. Since we are to be out of the season at all, we are glad we are in advance of it. This is the youth of the summer, not its old age. People are looking forward; events are approaching, instead of receding; the coming months seem big with indefinite promise of benefit and pleasure.

We quickly become imbued with the general hopefulness of the place. Every one has the look of one making ready. You hear, all day long, when far enough from the waves, a vague, joyous hum of bustle pervading the town. The enterprising click of hammer or trowel falls constantly on the ear. The masons are at work upon the new villas, and our hotel is completing a fine addition for a café; the stores along the busy little main street are being put in order, the windows alluringly stocked, and bright awnings unrolled above them, fenders from the summer's heat. The hotels are fairly awake. Everything is rejoicing that the semi-hibernation is over.

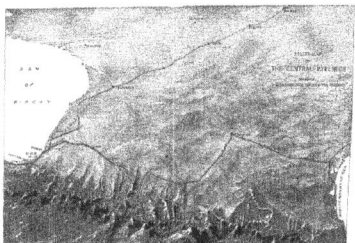

Biarritz, the town, is as delightful, if not as picturesque, as we had hoped. Perhaps it is too modern to be picturesque. In this part of the world at least, one rather requires the picturesque to be allied with the old. The nucleus of Biarritz is old, but that is out of sight in the modern overgrowth; Biarritz, as it is, is of this half century.

This is not, on the whole, to be regretted. Biarritz has no history, no past of associations, no landmarks to be guarded. Vandalism in the form of the modern rebuilder can here work more good than harm. Save for its location at the edge of the wild Basque country, and what it has seen, itself sheltered by obscurity, of the forays of that restless people, the place has little to tell. It is a watering-place, pure and simple, buoyed entirely by the prospering ebb and flow of modern fashion. Let us take it as of to-day, not of yesterday, content to seek its charms under that aspect alone, enjoying it for itself, not for its pedigree.

Biarritz is a prerogative instance of the magnetism of royalty,—of the social power of the court as an institution. It was a watering-place, in a small way, before Eugénie's advent; but there was not a tithe of its present size and popularity. In 1840, it numbered in all not more than fifty houses, a few of them lodgings or humble cafés, but the greater part staid little whitewashed summer-dwellings with green verandas and occasional roof-balconies; set down irregularly, without street or system, along the sunny slopes of the bluff. Murray's *Handbook* for 1848 gives it passing notice, and disrespectfully styles it the dullest place upon earth for one having no resources of friends upon the spot. But in the modern edition of forty years later, the same manual has come to describe the place in a very different strain; assigns it a population of nearly 6,000; details, with respect, its fashionable rank, its villas and increasing hotels, its graded streets and driveways; and among other things adds the simple remark that "about twenty-one thousand strangers now visit Biarritz every year." Evidently there has been some advance within the span.

It was the Empress of the French who distilled the life-elixir for the quiet little resort. As a maiden, she had spent long summers by its shore, and when she was become the first lady in the land, she turned still to Biarritz, and the midsummer tide of fashion followed after her. Across the downs, on the bluff, stands the *Villa Eugénie*, the handsel of Biarritz's prosperity; and here about us is the town that grew up to make her court.

Fair France lost as well as gained when the burning walls of the Tuileries crashed in. In these days of the plain French Republic,—of its sober, unor-

namental, business government,—the contrast is vivid with the glitter and "go" of Louis Napoleon's régime. And the nation feels it, and involuntarily grieves over it. The twenty years have far from sufficed to smother that certain inborn Gallic joy in monarchy,—autocratic rule, a brilliant court, leadership in fashion, and all the pomp and pageantry which the French love so well.

Little more than a century ago, stable governments seemed at last to be ruling the world; civilization had come to believe itself finally at peace; war, it was complacently said, had finished its work; the coming cycles would prove so far tamed as to have outgrown fightings and revolutions. Cultured modern history, like Nature, would refuse to proceed *per saltum*. Yet the hundred years since gone by have brought wars as fierce, "leaps" of government as tremendous, as any century in the past. It is this same fair France that has contributed more than her share of them, and the Fall of the Second Empire was one of the most dramatic. The world is not, after all, so securely merged from the darkness of the Dark Ages. Within that short century, in Paris itself, the very capital of cultured Europe, there has twice uprisen a human savagery immeasurably exceeding all the tales we are to tell of the fierce past of the Pyrenees.

It needs an effort to-day to picture the social power of France and Eugénie twenty years ago. The mantle has not fallen to England and Alexandra. Only a people like the French can endue fashion with absolutism.

So it was, that when the Empress came to Biarritz, "all the world" came also. From the building of her villa dates the true origin of Biarritz. From that time its growth was progressive and sound. When the empire finally fell, this creature of its making had already passed the danger-point, and so stood unshaken; Biarritz had become too popular, its clientèle too devoted, to part company. Even in the winter it has its increasing colony; in summer its vogue is beyond caprice. The sparkle of the royal occupation has gone, and the royal

villa is tenantless; but the place no longer needs a helping hand, for it is abundantly able to walk alone.

II.

In the afternoon we wander down to the sands. The tide is low. The long billows of the Bay of Biscay roll smugly in, hypocritical and placid, with nothing to betray the unenviable reputation they sustain *in mediis aquis*. The broad, smooth beach is not notably different in kind from other beaches; but we instantly see the peculiar charm of its location. The shore sweeps off in a long, lazy crescent, rounding up, a mile or two to the northward, with the light-house near Bayonne. Southward we cannot follow it from where we stand, for the near irregularities of cliff cut it off from sight. Back from the beach rises the bluff, curving northward with the crescent; at our left it comes boldly down toward the water, partitioning the beach and breaking up at the edge into strange, gaunt capes and peninsulas. Black masses of rock, large and small, are crouching out among the waves, tortured by storms into misshapen forms and anguished attitudes, patted and petted into fantastic humps and contortions. The strata dip at an angle of about twenty-five degrees, and the stone is friable and defenceless. Soothingly now the water is running over and around these rocks, or whitens their outlines with foam; granting their piteous torsos, in merciful caprice, a day's brief respite from the agony of its scourgings.

The afternoon sun shines brightly against the bathing pavilion, irradiating its red and yellow brick. Along the narrow; sheltered platform at its front, sit matronly French dowagers, holding their daughters, as it were, in leash, and talking of women and things, and affairs of state. Though early in the season, the beach is well sprinkled with people. A few attempt the bathing again, but the rest saunter here and there or enjoy beach-chairs at a stipulated rental. The elderly French gentleman, a dapper and interesting, specimen rarely paralleled at home, strolls about contentedly on the asphalt promenade back from the beach, smoking a cigar and fingering a light bamboo. Younger men, also well-dressed, pass in couples, or walk with a mother and daughter,—never with the daughter alone. Boatmen and candy-peddlers ramble in and out, a Basque fisherman or two linger about the scene, and dogs, a pony and a captive monkey, add an element of animal life.

Despite its sunny holiday temperament, Biarritz was one of certain Biscayan villages once denounced as "given up to the worship of the devil,"—thus denounced by Henry IV's blood-thirsty inquisitor, Pierre de Lancre, a veritable French Jeffreys, and the same who in 1609 put to death no less than eight hundred persons on the ground of sorcery. "He tells us that the devils and malignant spirits banished from Japan and the Indies took refuge here in the mountains of Labourd. Above all, he asserts that the young girls of Biarritz, always celebrated for their beauty, 'have in their left eye a mark impressed by the devil.'"

Happily we have no devil in this nineteenth century, and in the clear glance of these Biarritz peasants loitering on the sands, we find that his brand-marks have disappeared with him.

A few of the faces we meet are English; many are Spanish, and show that Biarritz draws its worshipers from the South as from the North. Indeed, a large proportion of its summer society wears the mantilla and wields the fan. Other marks, too, of Spanish dress are here, as where little girls in many-hued outfit romp along the sands, dragooned by dark-faced nurses in true Iberian costume. Three or four brilliant red parasols add amazingly to the general effect of the scene.

We repair to the stone parapet before the pavilion, and gravely paying our dues for chairs, sit and watch the pic-ture. There is no charge for sitting on the beach, but this is severely frowned upon at Biarritz. The dues are two sous per chair, and, with true Continental thrift, they are always rigorously collected. Whether one wanders into the open square of the Palais Royal at Paris, or listens to the music in the Place de Tourny at Bordeaux, or watches the waves at Biarritz, the old woman with her little black bag at once appears upon the scene. Some Frenchless friends in Paris, on one occasion, guilelessly seated in the gardens of the Palais Royal, took the collector simply for a pertinacious beggar-woman, and waved her airily off. She returned to the charge, of course, in indignant French, and grew angrier every moment as she found herself still loftily ignored. A warm fracas was in prospect, when a passing American fortunately cleared up the complication; the woman would have called in a gendarme unhesitatingly, to enforce her diminutive claim.

On the bluff, beyond the pavilion, Eugénie's villa, a square, rich building of English brick, surveys the scene its existence has brought about. Around us, on the beach, the nurses sit in the shade of the rocks and discourse on the respective failings of their charges. Children dig in the sand with pail and shovel, with the same zest as at home. Child-nature changes little with locality. So recently from the great unknown, it is not yet seamed and crusted by environment. I suppose that children fairly represent the prehistoric man. Impulse, appetite, passion,—all the gusts of the moment sway them. We quell our emotions so uniformly, as we grow on, that we finally hardly feel their struggles. The children have richer life than we, in some respects:

"Faith and wonder and the primal earth
Are born into the world with every child."

I make no doubt that Nimrod, or Achilles and Ajax, great children that they were, as ready to cry as to feast, to laugh as to fight, hunting mightily, sulking in the tent, or defying the lightning,—intense, sudden, human all through,—drank down their strong, muddy potion of existence with a smack far heartier than the reflective sips of life which civilization has now taught us to take. Childhood is wide and free and abounding and near to nature, and we can take thoughts from it, and ponder, perhaps dubiously, on the distance we since have traveled.

The children dig in the sand, and throw it over the nurses, just as they are doing at Old Orchard and Old Point. Here, with a maid, is a pair of children who freely show one attribute of childhood not so pleasing as others,—cruelty. They have a little monkey, fastened by collar and chain, and it is pitiful and yet ludicrous to see the close watch the animal keeps on his captors' movements. He has found a slack chain his best policy, and adapts his every motion anxiously and solicitously to the leaps of the boy. But the utmost vigilance avails him little. When the child is weary with running and sudden turns, which have called for marvelous dexterity of accommodation on the part of the monkey, the chain is hauled up, with the animal clinging worriedly to it, and he is flung far out into the fringe of waves, to pick his shivering way up again and again from the water. These children have a white rat, also, which they chase over the sand, and souse into puddles, and otherwise maltreat. It is useless to interfere parentally, and we hardly see our way to buying either rat or monkey, even to ensure them a peaceable old age. One wonders why children have this queer taint of cruelty. Unconscious cruelty it may be, but it seems none the less out of place in their fresh, unused nature. We outgrow some rude vices as well as rude virtues, in becoming older, and there is comfort in that.

III.

The bluff, coming out to the sea, cuts off, close at hand, the curve of the shore toward the south, and we climb by a sloping path. From the top, we look down upon, the beach we have left; back upon the downs cluster the numberless private villas which form a feature of Biarritz; to the left, over the near roofs and hotels of the town, we can see the first far-off pickets of the Pyrenees; while immediately in front now appear below us three or four rocky bays and coves, broken by the lines of the cliff and partly sheltered by the rocks out at sea. "Many of these rocks," writes an old-time visitor, in the pleasantly aging English of 1840, "are perforated with holes, so that, with a high sea and an incoming tide, and always, indeed, in some degree, when the tide flows, the water pours through these hollows and rents, presenting the singular appearance of many cascades. Some of the rocks lying close to the shore, and many of those which form the cliff, are worn into vast caverns. In these the waves make ceaseless music,—a hollow, dismal sound, like distant thunder,—and when a broad, swelling wave bounds into these caverns and breaks in some distant chamber, the shock, to one standing on the beach, is like a slight earthquake. But when a storm rises in the Bay of Biscay, and a northwest wind sweeps across the Atlantic, the scene is grand beyond the power of description. The whole space covered with rocks, which are scattered over the coast, is an expanse of foam, boiling whirlpools and cataracts, and the noise of the tremendous waves, rushing into these vast caverns and lashing their inner walls, is grander a thousand times than the most terrific thunder-storm that ever burst from the sky."

In these little coves now float idle pleasure-boats, bright with paint and listless awnings, and ready to be manned by their stout Basque rowers. Here, too, are the fishermen's cabins, snugly built in against the rocks, and garnished with baskets and poles, and with men repairing their nets. The irregular curves of the bluff, broken here into abrupt and dislocated masses, lend themselves readily to winding paths, and we ramble on, curving upward and downward, over short bridges and through little tunnels under the rocks, each turn giving a new view of the bay or the town.

Finally we round another promontory, cross a last bridge to a large rock-islet standing out from the mainland, and lo! the crescent of the coast is completed, and far to the south we see a low mountain ending the curve; it is Spain.

IV.

In the dreamy summer stillness, we sit with, content, looking at those distant hills, listening to the lapping of the waves, watching the sun sink lower toward the sea. The afternoon sunlight makes a glade across the waters,—seeming to one from a western seaboard like some strange disarrangement in the day.

The rounded mountains before us are indeed in Spain, a communicative fisherman tells us. At the foot of the outermost, eighteen miles away, is hidden the old Spanish town of Fuenterrabia. On its other side, in a hollow of the coast, lies San Sebastian. Nearer us, though well down along the sweep of the grey clay bluffs, is St. Jean de Luz, which, with the others, lies on our intended way.

We seem to see, conforming to the crescent of that foreign coast, the menacing crescent of the Armada, parting from Spanish shores, just three hundred years ago to a month, to crush Anglo-Saxon civilization. There before us lies the land of intolerance and bigotry which gave it being, the land of Philip the Second and his Inquisition. But for Drake and Howard and England's "wooden walls," events would have moved differently during the last three centuries,—in our country as in theirs.

V.

The last spark of the sun has disappeared in the water. We turn into the town in the fading light, passing another large bathing pavilion in a sheltered cove, and saunter homeward through an undulating street, the aorta of Biarritz. It is not a wide street, but it is busy and brisk, and it has a refurbished look like newly scoured metal. Neat dwelling-houses, guarded behind stone walls and well-kept hedges, display frequent signs of furnished apartments to let Small and large shops alternate sociably in the line; there is the *épicerie* or grocery-store, with raisins and olives and Albert biscuits in the window; next is a lace and worsted shop, where black Spanish nettings vie with gay crotchet-work,—"By Heaven, it is a splendid sight to see Their rival scarfs of mix'd embroidery," all made by hand, and bewilderingly low-priced. Now we come to a mirrored café, the Frenchman's hearth-side; it compels a détour into the middle of the street, since the sidewalk is quite pre-empted by its chairs and tiny tables. Here is another Spanish store, conspicuous for its painted tambourines with pendent webs of red and yellow worsted, and for its spreading fans, color-dashed with exciting pictures of bull-fights and spangled matadors. A hotel appears next, across the way, standing back from the street, with: a small, triangular park between; and then comes a pretentious bric-à-brac bazaar, and another café, and a confectioner's, and a tobacco-store,—each presided over by a buxom French matron, affable and vigilant, and clearly the animating spirit of the establishment.

Tiny carriages of a peculiar species, with donkeys and boy drivers, line the streets. The carriage holds one,—say an infirm dowager seeking the afternoon breeze,—and if the driver's attendance is desired, he is able to run beside it for miles. It is light and noiseless, comfortably cushioned, always within call, and governed by a beneficently trifling tariff. These *vinaigrettes*, as they are called, would be appreciated at home, if habit took kindly to novelties. How greatly they might simplify problems of calling and shopping! Our conveyances are all cumbrous. We must have the huge barouche, the coach, the close-shut coupé. Even the phaeton yields to the high T-cart. But convention is autocratic, and would frown on these vinaigrettes as it frowns on many useful ideas. Another unfortunate victim of its taboo is the sedan-chair, which would be lustily stared at to-day, yet the utility of which might be made positively inestimable. One who reads of the Chinese palanquins, or sees the carrying-chairs of Switzerland, convenient and always in demand, or who watches these agile little vinaigrettes darting along the ways, wonders that similar devices do not force their way, if need be, into universal favor.

Another mode of conveyance, once peculiarly popular with Biarritz, might be more difficult of exportation. This was the *promenade en cacolet*. The town of Bayonne is but five miles distant, by a delightful road, and formerly, particularly before the railroad came in, to ridicule old ways, every one went to Bayonne *en cacolet*. It is no longer so, and the world has lost a unique custom. The contrivance was very simple: the motive power was a donkey or a horse, and the conveyance consisted of a wooden frame or yoke fitting across the animal's back, with a seat projecting from each side. One seat was for the driver, usually a lively Basque peasant-woman; the other was for the passenger. There was a small arm-piece, at the outside of each seat, and generally there was a cushion. This was once a favorite means of travel between Bayonne and Biarritz. It was expeditious, enlivening,—and highly insecure; that was one of its charms. Throughout the ride there was a ludicrous titillation of insecurity; but it was greatest at the start and at the finish. For, the seats being evenly balanced, to mount was in itself high art. Driver and passenger needed to spring at precisely the same instant, or the result was dust and ashes. Trial after trial was needed by the neophyte; he must be, as an eye-witness of long ago aptly describes it, "as watchful of the mutual signal as a file of soldiers who wait the command 'make ready,—present,—fire!' A second's delay,—a second's precipitation,—proves fatal; the seat is attained, and at the same moment up goes the opposite empty seat, and down goes the equestrian between the horse's feet. In descending, it is still worse; because there is more hurry, more impatience, on arriving at the end of a journey; and an injudicious descent does not visit its effects upon one but upon both travelers; for unless the person who descends be extremely quick in his motions, his seat flies up before he has quite left it, and oversets him, and the opposite weight, of course, goes plump to the ground,—with as fatal effects as cutting the hammock-strings of a middy's berth."

Perilous balancing feats and a high degree of skill were evidently demanded of him who would journey *en cacolet*. Requiring thus a special training, so to speak, as well as a nice equivalence in weight between passenger and driver difficult to always realize, its use is not likely to supersede that of wheeled vehicles. To take a ride *en cacolet*, one might have a long hunt before finding a driver who should be his proper counterpoise; and it would be often inconvenient, not to say impracticable, thus to have to order one's driver according to measure.

It is the evening dining-hour as we find ourselves at last in the open courtyard of our hotel and seek the welcoming light of its *salle*. The hotels of Biarritz are handsome, even to elegance,—elegance which seems wasted on the few people now in them. But numbers do not seem to affect the anxious concern of Continental hotel-keepers. The same elaborate and formal table-d'hôte is served for our small company and a few others, as will, later on, be prepared for a houseful of guests. The waiters don the same ducal costume and with it the same grave decorum; and our attendant Ganymede, bending respectfully to present his laden salver, watches my selection of a portion of the pullet with as anxious solicitude as could be shown by the mother hen herself. The solemnity of a table-d'hôte, and the silencing effect it has on the most talka-tive, is invariable, as it is inexplicable, and accents sharply the contrast with the breezy clatter of the American summer hotel dining-hall. This is not to say that either is, in all ways, to be preferred. Each in its own setting. There is a comforting stir and whir about the great, bare, sociable dining-hall at Crawford's or at the Grand Union, which causes a European table-d'hôte utterly to pale and dwindle. And there is a satisfying quiet, a self-respecting, ritualistic calm, in the frescoed salle-a-manger of the Schweizerhof, or of the Grand Hotel at Biarritz, which makes its American rival seem impetuous and unrestful, and even a trifle garish. 'Tis hard to choose. Man and mood both vary. There is no parallel. The two modes of dining are as wide apart as the countries and their characteristics, and each is, in the best sense, distinctly typical.

VI

There is music during the evening in the little park we passed, and the best of Biarritz assembles to enjoy the programme. We charter chairs with the rest. Tables go with the chairs without extra charge, waiters follow up the tables, and soon all the world is sipping its coffee or cordials, and listening to Zampa. Outside, around the fence enclosing the little park, revolves an endless procession of the poorer people,—thrifty folk who are here as earners, not spenders, and would not dream of melting their two sous into a chair. Round the small enclosure they go, by couples or threes, like asteroids round the sun, staring with interest at the more aristocratic assemblage within,—just as the family circle stares at the boxes. And the music sings on pleasantly for all, this mild summer evening in Biarritz.

CHAPTER III.

BAYONNE, THE INVINCIBLE.

"I am here on purpose to visit the sixteenth century; one makes a journey for the sake of changing not place but ideas. "

In the morning, a dashing equipage rolls up to the doorway of the Grand Hotel. A "break" is its Gallicized English name. It has four white horses, with bells on the harness, and the driver is richly bedight in a scarlet-faced coat, blazing with buttons and silver lace; a black glazed hat, and very white duck trousers. We ascend, the ladder is removed, the porter bows, his thanks, the whip signals, and we roll out of the court-yard for a six-mile drive northward to Bayonne.

We take the sea-road in going, following the bluff as it trends northward, and having dazzling views of blue sky and blue water. There is a fresh, sweet, morning breeze, which exhilarates. Truly here is the joy of travel! Kilometre-stones pass, one after another, to the rear. Still the road presses on, winding over the downs, or between long rows of pines and poplars standing even and equidistant for mile after mile. The light-house at the end of the crescent beach comes nearer. Few teams are met, and fewer travelers; for the main highway to Bayonne, which lies inland and by which we are to return, is shorter than this, and draws to itself the most of the traffic.

At length, the light-house is neared, and to the right Bayonne is seen, not far off. The break turns to the right along the river Adour, which here runs to the sea, and, skirting the long stone jetties, we roll toward town by the *Allées Marines*, a wide promenade along the river, cross the bridge, rattle through the streets, and draw up before the hotel in the open square with a jingle and whip-cracking and general hullaballoo which fills the street urchins with awe and gives unmixed joy to our jolly driver.

II.

Bayonne has been a centre.

A few cities are suns, the rest planets. This, with regard to their importance, not their size.

If Bordeaux is the sun of southwestern French commerce, Bayonne has at least been the most important planet, with the towns and villages of a wide district for its satellites.

Here we catch the first breath of the bracing mediæval air we shall breathe in the Pyrenees. Bayonne has still a trace of the free, out-of-door spirit of its lawless prime. Miniature epics, more than one, have clustered around it. The rallying-cry, "Men of Bayonne!" has always appealed to the intensest local pride to be found perhaps in France, and the boast of the city still is that it has never been conquered. Looking back to the sharp times when every near warfare centred about Bayonne,—when feudal enmities were constantly outcropping on quick pretexts,—when the issue always gathered itself into hand-to-hand encounter, and was determined by personal prowess,—the boast is not meaningless.

The Basques, who are close neighbors to Bayonne, make the same boast. As Basques and Bayonnais were always fighting, their respective boasts seem to be continuing the conflict. But these old feuds, desperately bitter, were after all local and guerilla-like, and the advantages ephemeral. At few times did either people clash arms with the other in a general war. Thus neither conquered the other, and in peace their boasts joined hands against all comers.

III.

Bestriding both the river Nive and the swift Adour, Bayonne seems a healthy and healthful city, viewed in this June sunshine. But there is little of the new about it. The horses are taken from the break, we leave at the hotel a requisition for lunch, and move forth for a survey. The chief streets are wide and airy, but a turn places one instantly in an older France. We ramble with curiosity in and out among the streets and shops, finding no one preeminent attraction, but an infinite number of minor ones which maintain the equation. In fact there is little for the guide-book sight-seer in Bayonne. The cathedral leaves only a dim impression of being in no wise remarkable. The citadel affords, it is said, a wide-ranging view, but we prefer the arcades and the people to the heat of the climb. The shops along the square are small but characteristic; they are evidently for the Bayonnais themselves rather than for strangers; this gives them their only charm for strangers. But taken in its entirety and not in single effects, the town is wholly pleasing. These dark, ancient arcades, its old houses, its rough-cobbled pavements, its general appearance of fustiness, give it a charmingly individual air.

They contrast it, however, completely with Biarritz. Bayonne is a staid and serious city, Biarritz a youthful-hearted resort. Bayonne is reminiscent of the past; Biarritz is alive with its present. The genie of modern improvement has not yet come, to rebuild Bayonne. Neither fashion nor commerce has sufficiently rubbed the lamp. It holds unlessened its long-time population of about thirty thousand souls; it still drives its comfortable, trade as the second port of southwestern France; it is known as enjoying a mild commercial specialty or two, as in the line of textiles, particularly wools and woolen fabrics; and it displays an artless pride in its reputation for excellent chocolate. It even pets, a little suburb of winter visitors, and it has caught some quickening rays from the summer prosperity of its neighbor. But it will never feel the bounding impulse of rejuvenescence that has come to Biarritz. Bayonne has no potentialities. It will continue in its afternoon of peace, of easy, quiet thrift, contentedly aside from the main current of events, recounting its traditions, prodigiously and harmlessly proud of its local prestige; like a tribal chieftain of the homage of his clan.

Basques abound in the streets, and the varied costumes to be seen show the influence of that strange race. There are Spaniards here, too, and Jews in plenty, mingling with the native French element. The men wear the *berret*, a wool cap, like that of the Scotch lowlander, but smaller. It is of dark blue or brown, and in universal use from Bordeaux southward. When capping the Basque, particularly, with his rusty velvet sack, crimson sash, dark knee-breeches and stockings, and the sandals or wooden sabots worn on the feet, its effect is vividly picturesque. The poorer women, as elsewhere on the Continent, become hard-featured and muscular with age; saving a few beggars, they all seem to be busy,—carrying burdens, washing linen, watching their huckster-stalls or the dark little shops under the arcades. Here, however, the men themselves are not idle. One seldomer sees in southern France a sight frequent in Italy and many other parts of Europe,—that of a woman toilsomely dragging a hand-cart or shouldering a burden while her spouse walks idly by and smokes a thankful pipe.

Diminutive donkeys, hardy and hoarse, are in great use, and we hear in the streets their plaintive and sonorous denunciations of men and manners. The donkey here seems to take the place of the dog, which in Holland and Scandinavia is taught the ways of constant and praiseworthy usefulness. There, with a voluble old woman for yoke-fellow, he draws the small market-carts about the streets and grows lusty-limbed in the service. Here, the donkey does duty for both, dog and old woman, and must develop both muscle and tongue to offset their respective specialties.

IV.

An afternoon of peace, such towns as Bayonne have earned and gained. This one has added few notable pages to universal history, but its own personal biography would be an exciting one. It is worn with adventure, and old before its time. The quarrelings of its hot youth, the tension of strife and insecurity, the life of alarms it has lived, have aged it. They have aged many another city of Europe, and endeared the blessing of repose.

They were different days, those of the past of Bayonne. These streets are narrow, the houses stoutly walled, because they were built for siege as well as shelter. The doorways are low-browed, the stone-lined rooms little lighter than caves, because every man's hand might rise against his neighbor, and every man's hovel become his castle. Humanity was a hopeless discord; individual security lay only in individual strength. It is hard to conceive clearly the fierce life of the Darker Ages. The rough jostling, the discomfort and pitilessness, the utter animality of it all,—it is hard to conceive it even inadequately. The curtest historical sweep from then to now, shows how far the world has come. The savage unrest of slum and faubourg to-day shows too how far the world has yet to go. Not till civilization becomes more than a veneer, will it lose its liability to crack.

The picture is not wholly dark. There were many of the humanities. There was culture and thought and refinement, much of it of a high type. Light and shade,—both were strongly limned. But in the mass, it was barbarism. For the lower classes, occupation, brawling; mental thermometer at zero; cruelty and greed the ethical code. "You should feel here," declares Taine, "what men felt six hundred years ago, when they swarmed forth from their hovels, from their unpaved, six-feet-wide streets, sinks of uncleanness, and reeking with fever and leprosy; when their unclad bodies, undermined by famine, sent a thin blood to their brutish brains; when wars, atrocious laws, and legends of sorcery filled their dreams with vivid and melancholy images." Hear him tell over one of the trenchant tales from the annals of Bayonne:

V.

"Pé de Puyane was a brave man and a skillful sailor, who, in his day, was Mayor of Bayonne and admiral; but he was harsh with his men, like all who have managed vessels, and would any day rather fell a man than take off his cap. He had long waged war against the seamen of Normandy, and on one occasion he hung seventy of them to his yards, cheek by jowl with some dogs. He hoisted on his galleys red flags, signifying death and no quarter, and led to the battle of Écluse the great Genoese ship Christophle, and managed his hands so well that no Frenchman escaped; for they were all drowned or killed, and the two admirals, Quieret and Bahuchet, having surrendered themselves, Bahuchet had a cord tightened around his neck, while Quieret had his throat cut. That was good management; for the more one kills of his enemies, the less he has of them. For this reason, the people of Bayonne, on his return, entertained him with such a noise, such a clatter of horns, of cornets, of drums and all sorts of instruments, that it would have been impossible on that day to hear even the thunder of God.

"It happened that the Basques would no longer pay the tax upon cider, which was brewed at Bayonne for sale in their country, Pé de Puyane said that the merchants, of the city should carry them no more, and that if any one carried them any, he should have his hand cut off. Pierre Cambo, indeed, a poor man, having carted two hogsheads of it by night, was led out upon the market-place, before Notre Dame de Saint-Léon, which was then building, and had his hand amputated, and the veins afterwards stopped with red-hot irons; after that, he was driven in a tumbrel throughout the city, which was an excellent example; for the smaller folk should-always do: the bidding of men in high position.

"Afterwards, Pé de Puyane having assembled the hundred peers in the townhouse, showed them that the Basques, being traitors, rebels toward the seigniory of Bayonne, should no longer keep the franchises which had been granted them; that the seigniory of Bayonne, possessing the sovereignty of the sea, might with justice impose a tax in all the places to which the sea rose, as if they were in its port, and that accordingly the Basques should henceforth pay for passing to Villefranche, to the bridge of the Nive, the limit of high tide. All cried out that that was but just, and Pé de Puyane declared the toll to the Basques; but they all fell to laughing, saying they were not dogs of sailors like the mayor's subjects. Then having come in force, they beat the bridgemen, and left three of them for dead.

"Pé said nothing, for he was no great

talker; but he clinched his teeth, and looked so terribly around him that none dared ask him what he would do nor urge him on nor indeed breathe a word. From the first Saturday in April to the middle of August, several men were beaten, as well Bayonnais as Basques, but still war was not declared, and when they talked of it to the mayor, he turned his back.

"The twenty-fourth day of August, many noble men among the Basques, and several young people, good leapers and dancers, came to the castle of Miot for the festival of Saint Bartholomew. They feasted and showed off, the whole day, and the young people who jumped the pole, with their red sashes and white breeches, appeared adroit and handsome. That night came a man who talked low to the mayor, and he, who ordinarily wore a grave and judicial air, suddenly had eyes as bright as those of a youth who sees the coming of his bride. He went down his staircase with four bounds, led out a band of old sailors who were come one by one, covertly, into the lower hall, and set out by dark night with several of the wardens, having closed the gates of the city for fear that some traitor, such as there are everywhere, should go before them.

"Having arrived at the castle, they found the draw-bridge down and the postern open, so confident and unsuspecting were the Basques, and entered, cutlasses drawn and pikes forward, into the great hall. There were killed seven young men, who had barricaded themselves behind tables and would there make sport with their dirks, but the good halberds, well pointed and sharp as they were, soon silenced them. The others, having closed the gates, from within, thought that they would have power to defend themselves or time to flee; but the Bayonne marines, with their great axes, hewed down the planks, and split the first brains which happened to be near. The mayor, seeing that the Basques were tightly girt with their red sashes, went about saying, (for he was unusually facetious on days of battle,) 'Lard these fine gallants for me! Forward the spit into their flesh justi-

coats!' And, in fact, the spits went forward so that all were perforated and opened, some through and through, so that you might have seen daylight through them, and that the hall, half an hour after, was full of pale and red bodies, several bent over benches, others in a pile in the corners, some with their noses glued to the table like drunkards, so that a Bayonnais, looking at them, said, 'This is the veal market!' Many, pricked from behind, had leaped through the windows, and were found next morning, with cleft head or broken spine, in the ditches.

"There remained only five men alive, noblemen, two named D'Urtubie, two De Saint-Pé, and one De Lahet, whom the mayor had set aside as a precious commodity. Then, having sent some one to open the gates of Bayonne and command the people to come, he ordered them to set fire to the castle. It was a fine sight, for the castle burned from midnight until morning. As each turret, wall or floor fell, the people, delighted, raised a great shout. There were volleys of sparks in the smoke and flames, that stopped short, then began again suddenly, as at public rejoicings, so that the warden, an honorable advocate and a great literary man, uttered this saying: 'Fine festival for Bayonne folk; for the Basques, great barbecue of hogs!'

"The castle being burned, the mayor said to the five noblemen that he wished to deal with them with all friendliness, and that they should themselves be judges if the tide came as far as the bridge. Then he had them fastened two by two to the arches, until the tide should rise, assuring them that they were in a good place for seeing. The people were all on the bridge and along the banks, watching the swelling of the flood. Little by little it mounted to their breasts, then to their necks, and they threw back their heads so as to lift their mouths a little higher. The people laughed aloud, calling out to them that the time for drinking had come, as with the monks at matins, and that they would have enough for the rest of their days. Then the water entered the mouth

and nose of the three who were lowest; their throats gurgled as when bottles are filled, and the people applauded, saying that the drunkards swallowed too fast and were going to strangle themselves out of pure greediness.

"There remained only the two men D'Urtubie, bound to the principal arch, father and son, the son a little lower down. When the father saw his child choking, he stretched out his arms with such force that a cord broke; but that was all, and the hemp cut into his flesh without his being able to get any further. Those above, seeing that the youth's eyes were rolling, while the veins on his forehead were purple and swollen, and that the water bubbled around him with his hiccough, called him baby, and asked why he had sucked so hard, and if nurse was not coming soon to put him to bed. At this, the father cried out like a wolf, spat into the air at them, and called them butchers and cowards. That offended them so, that they began throwing stones at him, with such sure aim that his white head was soon reddened and his right eye gushed out; it was small loss to him, for shortly after the mounting wave shut up the other.

"When the water was gone down, the mayor commanded that the five bodies, which hung with necks twisted and limp, should be left a testimony to the Basques that the water of Bayonne did come up to the bridge and that the toll was justly due from them. He then returned home amidst the acclamations of his people, who were delighted that they had so good a mayor, a sensible man, a great lover of justice, quick in wise enterprises, and who rendered to every man his due."

VI.

One asks where were the preceding ages of civilization. Where was the influence of Babylonia and Egypt, of Athens and of Rome? Here in mid-Europe, nearly two thousand years after Socrates, and in the second millenary of the white light of Christianity, men were like wolves, nay worse, rending their prey or each other not under the lashing of hunger but from very ferocity.

By way of contrast, take a fête given in Bayonne in happier years. An account of it, garnered from old records, I translate from the French of Lagrèze.

Elizabeth, sister of Charles IX and wife of Philip of Spain, was returning from the Baths of Cauterets and passing through the city; the fête was in her honor. Charles was there, the King of France, with the queen-mother, Catherine de Medici; Marguerite of Valois, and her future husband, the young Henry of Navarre.

"The place for the fête had been well chosen: it was an isle of the Adour. In the centre, a border of ancient oaks encircling a grassy glade framed it round into a kind of arboreal parlor. Under the shade of these great trees, in the multitude of their leafy nooks, were disposed the tables. That of royalty rose in the midst, elevated above all the rest; it was reached by four grassy steps.

"Decorated barges transported the guests to the enchanted isle; at their approach, in honor of the arrival, strains of soft music fell upon the ear. The musicians represented Neptune, Arion, six tritons, three sirens, and numberless minor marine deities; the sirens chanted sweet songs of romance and chivalry, seeking to approve the fabled charm of siren voices.

"Rivulets of water, skillfully led in along tiny grooves, serpentined among the parterres, half hidden in rare and brilliant flowers. Dainty shepherdesses in waiting line stretched hand in hand to the water's edge, and formed a species of avenue leading to the table of honor.

"In advance of the retinue went Orpheus and Linus, accompanied by three nymphs, reciting verses to their Majesties,—who had, however, at this moment, more eyes than ears, and could not cease admiring the bevy of shepherdesses in their picturesque costumes, brightly colored and so varied. These shepherdesses, forming afterward into separate groups, each group the graceful rival of the next, wore the costumes of the different provinces and danced to music the respective dances there in usage: those of Poitiers to the music of

the bagpipe, those of Provence to the kettle-drums, the Champenoises to the small hautboys, the violins and the tambourines, and so for the rest.

"The aged trees which covered with shade the banqueting tables formed a vast octagonal hall, in the centre of which rose in all its majesty a gigantic oak-tree. At its base vaulted the jet of a fountain, the limpid waters springing from a basin of glittering shells.

"The table of honor was taken by the king; his mother, Catherine de Medici; the Duke of Anjou, who was afterward to become Henry III; the Queen of Spain; Henry of Navarre, (afterward Henry IV,) and Margot, his future wife.

"The repast was served with promptness. Six proficient bagpipe-players went before five shepherds and ten shepherdesses, who advanced three by three, each bearing a salver. Six stewards guided them by crooks ornamented by flowers. Following this, eight shepherds and sixteen shepherdesses made the service at the other tables; one and two advanced at a time, depositing their salvers and retiring to make way for others.

"At the latter part of the repast, appeared six violin-players, resplendent in tinseled garb; also nine nymphs of a marvelous beauty; a swarm of musicians accompanied them, disguised as satyrs.

"Toward nightfall, to the astonishment of all, suddenly shone out a luminous rock lit up with fantastic glow; out of which came forth as by magic countless naiads, their soft robes glistening with jewels; they dart out upon the sward and join in a fair and lissome dance."

But one thing was wanting to crown this princely picnic,—a storm. It came. Says the queen Margot, who was pleased to relate herself the details of this fête: "Envious Fortune, unable to suffer the glory of this fair dance, hurled upon us a strange rain and tempest; and the confusion of the sudden evening retreat by boat across the river brought out next day as many mirthful anecdotes as the lavish festival itself had brought gratifications."

Such was a *fête champêtre* in the sixteenth century,—filled in with all the luxuriant pomp and splendor which the French love so dearly.

Yet, only seven years after this scene of flowers and song, France was in blood, and the age had darkened once more; the evil-minded De Medicis, queen-mother and king, had given the signal for the Massacre of St. Bartholomew.

VII.

It was Bayonne, too, whose governor, when ordered in advance by the king to arrange for massacring the Huguenots in his city on that epoch-making night, dared to send back a prompt and spirited refusal. "Your Majesty," he reported, "I have examined those under my command touching your mandate; all are good citizens and brave soldiers, but I am unable to find for you among them a single executioner!"

The Queen of Spain, widow of Charles II, resided here from 1706 until 1738. Many stories are told of her good-heartedness and her lavish fondness for display. The Bayonnais were children still, and loved her for it. She, too, gave a festival and banquet,—in honor of some Spanish successes; "it lasted even till the next day among the people, and on board the vessels in the river; and the windows of every house were illuminated. After the repast was finished," adds the grave record, "much to the satisfaction of all, a *panperruque* was danced through the town. M. de Gibaudière led the dance, holding the hand of the Mayor of Bayonne; the Marquis de Poyanne bringing up the rear; so that this dance rejoiced all the people, who on their side gave many demonstrations of joy."

The world has grown stiffer since, and Mayors and Marquises are no longer wont to caper about the streets of great cities in the sportive *abandon* of a festival dance; in those days it seems not to have abated a jot of their serious dignity.

Bayonne is the key to all roads south and east. It has a superb citadel. It has been a valuable military position, has withstood seventeen sieges in its day, and is still an important strategic point. Here were exciting times during the Peninsular war, when Wellington on his northward march from Spain found Bayonne in his way and undertook to capture it. More a fancy than a fact, however, is probably the tradition that the bayonet was invented in this locality and took its name from the city. The story of the Basque regiment running short of ammunition and being prompted by the exigency to insert their long-handled knives into the musket-muzzles, has since had grave doubts cast upon its veraciousness. This is most unfortunate, for it was a story which travelers delighted to honor.

VIII.

It is mid-afternoon as our breack clatters out again over the paved roadway of the bridge and we turn westward along the river for the return to Biarritz. A few vessels stand idly moored to the quays. The *Allées Marines* are quiet and still; later they will be thronged. They are the favorite promenade of Bayonne, which thus holds here a species of daily "town-meeting" as the dusk comes on. At present we see merely a few old women bearing panniers toward the city, and rope-makers at work upon great streamers of hemp which stretch from tree to tree. Soon we turn off to the southward, and are on the main highway to Biarritz.

This highway sees a considerable traffic. Bayonne furnishes carts, Biarritz carriages. Omnibuses ply to and fro; market-barrows are drawn frequently past; burden-bearers and peasants are met or overtaken trudging contentedly on. The latter cheat both the omnibus and themselves, for the fare is but a trifle, and the road hot and sandy. It is abundantly shaded by trees, but we agree that it is far better enjoyed *en breach* than on foot.

This is the road once famous for the *cacolet*. It must have been a pleasing and peculiar sight, in the years ago, to see the jolly Duchess of Berri and her fashionable companions sociably hobnobbing with their peasant drivers *en cacolet* in the pleasant summer afternoons.

CHAPTER IV.

SAINT JOHN OF LIGHT.

*"Guibelerat so'guin eta
Hasperrenak ardura?"*
"As we pursue our mountain track,
Shall we not sigh as we look back?"
—Basque Song.

The days pass happily by, at Biarritz. One quickly feels the charm of the place; it has its own delightfulness, apart from the season and its amusements. In the season, however, the amusements are not once allowed to flag. By half-past ten, fashion is astir and gathers toward the beach for the bathing hour; then parts to walk and drive, and afterward to lunch. It takes its siesta as does the nation its neighbor; meets once more for the afternoon hour on the sands, and at six drifts to the Casino, where children are soon dancing, little glasses clinking, and mild gambling games in full swing. The thought of dinner deepens with the dusk, but in the evening the tide sets again to the Casino, and a concert or a ball rounds up the day.

The scope of diversions is much the same as on the opposite edge of the Atlantic,—with due allowance for national types; but here there is perhaps more color to the scene. European watering-places are naturally cosmopolitan. Here at Biarritz, English society mingles with the French, and both are strongly reinforced from Spain. Only thirteen hours from Paris, or twenty-two, actual travel, from London, it is but one from the Spanish frontier and eighteen from Madrid. Memories of Orleans, Pavia and the Armada are canceled in the common pursuit of pleasure.
"Three hosts combine to offer sacrifice;
Three tongues prefer strange orisons on high;
Three gaudy standards flout the pale blue skies;
The shouts are, France, Spain, Albion, Victory!"
There is besides a goodly sprinkling from other countries. A Russian nobleman and his family are to arrive at our

hotel to-morrow. The spot is not difficult of access for Italians. The Austrians have long appreciated it. And do we not constitute at least a small contingent from across the ocean?

Not only visitors make up the particolored effect. There are all grades in Biarritz,—visitors and home-stayers, rich and poor,—
"From point and saucy ermine, down
To the plain coif and rustic gown."
The natives have their peculiar air and customs, and the Basques are always picturesque. Spanish guitar-players vie with Neapolitan harpists, and both with the waves and the hum of talk. The lottery spirit shoots up here from its hotbed in Spain. Small boys wander about the beach with long, cylindrical tin boxes painted a bright red and carried by a strap from the shoulder. The rim of the lid is marked off into numbered compartments, and in its centre is an upright teetotum with a bone projection; while the cylinder itself is filled with cones of crisp, flaky sweet-wafers, stacked one into another like cornucopias. The charge is one sou for a spin, and the figure opposite which the projecting bone-piece stops indicates the number of cones due the spinner. The figures vary from 2 to 30, and there are no blanks. Every one appears to patronize the contrivance, and you constantly hear the click of the teetotum along the beach. Though there are but two 30's in the circumference, each who spins fondly hopes to gain one, and thus the same spirit which supports Monte Carlo in splendor gives these boys a thriving trade.

II.

We spend an idle morning on the projecting point of bluff overlooking the coves and the fishermen's cabins. This promontory uplifts a signal-station, the *Atalaye*. Down at the left and rear, cutting inland, is the *Port Vieux*, where the second bathing pavilion stands; and, sending up their cries and shoutings to the heights, we
"see the children sport along the shore,
And hear the mighty waters rolling evermore."

The day is breezy and not too warm. We feel few ambitions. Has the dreamy spirit of the South come upon us so soon?

It will be a perfect spot for a picnic lunch.

We will imitate the *fête champêtre* of Charles and Catherine held on the isle of the Adour. The ladies give their sanction, and three of us are promptly appointed commissaries. We take the path down to the street, and find a promising little grocery-store. The madame bows a welcome.

"Can one obtain here of the bread?" we ask.

"Ah, no," deprecatingly, "that is only with the baker."

"A little of cheese, then? and some Albert biscuits? And a bottle or two of lemonade, and one of light wine?"

"But yes, without doubt; monsieur shall have these instantly;" and a bright-faced little girl proceeds to collect the supplies.

"Might one carry away the bottles, and afterward return them?" we venture.

Here the madame begins to appear suspicious. It is evidently an irregular purchase at best, and this request seems to make her a trifle frosty.

"A deposit should perhaps be necessary," we suggest; "how much is desired?"

Madame gives the subject a moment's thought. "Monsieur would have to leave at least four sous on each bottle," she finally declares.

"And could madame also lend us some small drinking-glasses, it may be, and a little corkscrew?"

The old lady is visibly hardening. She is clearly averse to mysteries. We may be contrabandists, or political exiles, or any variety of refugee foreigners. She hesitates about the drinking-glasses; is not sure she *has* a corkscrew. But another deposit is soothingly arranged for and paid, and the articles are found.

"And now could we ask to borrow a basket?—also on deposit."

But here the madame's obligingness quite deserts her. The refusal is flat. She has no basket which can possibly be spared.

It is, we see, plainly time that we should explain our mysterious selections. Confidingly we entrust her with the secret, and lay bare our unconventional plan. At the first she listens unmoved, but the idea of "pique-nique" is soon borne in upon her, and lets in a ray of light. The frost thaws a trifle. "We are with friends," we say; "they are on the bluffs; they have desired to make a luncheon for once without the fork,— to eat their little breads in the open air, upon the rocks." Our listener nods, half doubtfully. Then we play our highest trump: "We are but on a visit to Biarritz; we have come from far away; we are Americans."

Instantly the barriers are down; madame is our firmest ally. "Run, Élise, seek the large pannier for our friends! Is it that you are of the fair America?— *la belle Amérique.* Ah, but monsieur, why have you not said thus before? You should most charmingly have been supplied; are they not indeed always the friends of our country,—the Americans! You shall bring here the breads you buy at the bakery; we will add knives and plates and some fruit, and Élise shall herself carry for you the full basket to the place of the pique-nique."

Verily the Stars and Stripes are words to conjure with! The picnic is a complete success. The De Medici fête is more than surpassed; even an attendant nymph, in the person of the rustic Élise, is not wanting; the historical parallel is perfect.

In fact, the parallel finally carries itself too far. So small an affair even as this, it appears, cannot escape the hostility of "envious Fortune,"—the same who untimely cut off its lamented rival. A large, black cloud, coming up over us like a vengeful harpy, forebodes the invariable downpour, and grimly compels us to shorten the feast.

On Sunday, we attend the English service; Britain is sufficiently well represented at Biarritz to support one during both summer and winter. The day is restful and calm, and we stroll out afterward along the beach and over to the deserted villa of the Empress, returning by the path on the bluff. The sound of trowels and hammers is in part stilled about the town, and the afternoon takes on a comfortingly peaceful tone in consequence. The English-speaking contingent keeps the day as quietly as may be; the Continental majority of course does not. In a few weeks, posters will adorn the Saturday bulletins, announcing the next day's bull-fight in San Sebastian, over the border; and if Sunday is quiet at Biarritz in the season, it is simply because all the world spends the day at San Sebastian.

III.

But Spain and the Pyrenees lie before us, and we cannot tarry longer at Biarritz. We shall long feel the warm life of the fresh June days by the sea. The breack rolls again into the court-yard; we pay our devoirs to mine host and our dues to his minions, and once more we start, this time toward the south.

We are to dip into Spain for a day, and have chosen to go by road as far on the way toward the frontier as St. Jean de Luz, before taking the train. St. Jean lies on the crescent of the shore only eight miles away, and the road, like the sea-road to Bayonne, follows the curve of the higher land, and shows beach and hill and sea in turn as it trends over the downs. It is another clear, taintless morning. The sun is already high; but, though having the sky wholly to himself, he is forbearing in his power. Palisades of poplars lend us their shadows; clumps of protecting firs stand aside for the road, each with a great gash down its side and a cup fastened below to catch the bleeding pitch. Now we are facing the Pyrenees; a little to the left they rise before us, still miles away. These are not the high Pyrenees; the monarchs stand in the centre of their realm, and are hardly to be seen, even distantly, until we shall in a day or two turn inland and approach them. The mountain wall is broken and lower near the sea, both east and west; yet even here it rises commandingly, filling the horizon with its hazy hills.

The road is the counterpart of that to Bayonne. We fly smoothly on, above its hard, thin crackle of sand. We meet peasants afoot, and burdened horses, on their morning way to Biarritz or Bayonne. The men ornament their loose, blue linen frocks and brown trousers with the bright scarlet sash so popular in this region. Heavy oxen draw their creaking loads toward the same centres,—their bowed heads yoked by the horns, which are cushioned with a woolly sheepskin mat and tasseled with red netting. They pull strongly, for the loads are not light, and the clumsy wheels are disks of solid wood. Little donkeys trot amiably by, with huge double panniers that recall the *cacolet*. A file of marching soldiers is overtaken; small villages are passed, each one agog with the stir of our transit; while now and then we meet a dog-cart and cob or a stylish span, antennae of the coming season of fashion.

To the right is the accurate level of the sea-horizon; about us are the heath and furze and the sand-dunes; and far along to the south we can trace the arc of the beach, until it ends in the projecting hills of Spain.

St. Jean is reached almost too soon, for the drive has been exhilarating. We enter by a long, narrow street, which is found to be alive with people. A small procession is in motion, enlivened by a band. Every one seems in holiday dress. Our driver has before shown his easy conviction that streets were intended first for breacks, secondly for citizens; and now he urges his horses down this narrow way without a pause in their gallop. The whip signals, the bells on the harness jingle furiously, the wheels clatter along the cobbles; and, almost before we have time to order a slackening, procession and by-standers, like a flock of sheep, go in disorder to the wall, and our breack sweeps by into the central square.

It is the festival, we find, of the village's patron saint, St. John the Baptist. The twenty-fifth of June renews his yearly compact of protection. In the afternoon, there will be the full procession, led by the priests, and with a canopied effigy of the saint or of the Virgin borne in solemnity behind them. Services in the cathedral will follow, and probably an evening of illumination. We enter the cathedral. Its floor has been newly strewn with sweet hay, and near the altar, is the sacred image itself, adorned for the procession, dressed in linen and velvet and gilt lace, and with a chaplet of beads in its wooden hand. The canopy-frame, ready prepared, is close by, with its projecting handle-bars, its four upright poles and its roof of white satin embroidered with gold.

The cathedral itself is somewhat more interesting than we expected to see; it is a Basque rather than a French church, has a very high chancel and altar and no transepts, and the altar is marked by a striking profusion of color and of gilding, which does not degenerate into the tawdry and which lights up vividly under the entering noon light. The chapels at the sides are similarly decorated. Dark oaken balconies, elaborately carved, run in three tiers along the upper part of the nave. The seats in these are reserved for the men, the women being relegated to small black cushions placed on the chairless floor.

St. Jean's one great event was the marriage of Louis XIV with the Infanta of Spain, which took place in this same church. "A raised platform extended from the residence of Anne of Austria to the entrance of the church, which was richly carpeted. The young queen was robed in a royal mantle of violet-colored velvet, powdered with *fleurs-de-lis*, over a white dress, and wore a crown upon her head. Her train was carried by Mesdemoiselles d'Alençon and de Valois and the Princess of Carignan. After the ceremony, the queen complained of fatigue, and retired for a few hours to her chamber where she dined alone. In the evening, she received the court, dressed in the French style; and gold and silver tokens commemorative of the royal marriage were profusely showered from the windows of her apart-

ment."

Without, as we turn for an idle stroll, we find a fair-sized town, with provincial streets like much of Bayonne. Often the stories of the houses jut out, one over the other. These projections give a relish of local color to the crooking ways, intensified by the round-tiled roofs and by occasional red or blood-colored beams and doorposts. Although we are still on the French side of the frontier, Spanish influence is already marked, while that of the Basques predominates over both. St. Jean is also a summer resort, in a modest way, chiefly for quiet Spanish families; and from the heavy stone sea-wall built along the beach we see many of their villas. In days before the railroad went beyond, the port exchanged regular and almost daily steamers with San Sebastian and Santander, thus connecting with the Spanish rail, and giving a rather important traffic advantage. It fostered, besides, extensive cod-fishing and even whaling enterprises. Its harbor has suffered since; the rails too have gone through to Spain, and St. Jean is left mildly and interestingly mournful, in its lessened power, its decayed gentility.

IV.

In St. Jean de Luz, we are fairly in the country of the Basques. One sees so many of that singular people in the streets, and along the Biscayan shore generally, that inquiries about them are almost forced upon the attention. The Basques are still the curiously ill-explained race they have always been; the learned still disagree over their origin, and the world at large scarcely knows of them more than the name. They are scattered all through this lower sea-corner of France, shading off near Bayonne; and are in yet greater numbers in the adjoining upper edges of Spain. It seems strange that the beginnings of this isolated race should to-day be almost no better settled than in the time of Humboldt or Ramond. Yet they contrive still to embroil the philologists and historians. Here the race has lived, certainly since the days of the Romans, probably since long before, out of kin with all the world, and the world's periods have passed on and left them. No one knows their birth-mark; they have forgotten it themselves. Of theories, numberless and hopelessly in discord, each still offers its weighty arguments, and each destroys the certainty of any.

This appears incredible. What mystery is insoluble in the sharp light of modern research? Yet until the defenders of the view that the Basques came from Atlantis can make truce with the advocates of their Phoenician origin,—until the well-attested theory of their affinity with certain South American races can overthrow the better-attested theory that they are the remains of the ancient Iberians,—until Moor and Finn, Tartar and Coptic, can amicably blend their claims to relationship, the Basques must remain as they are,—foundlings; or rather, a race whose length of pedigree has swallowed up its beginnings.

It is these unattached sea and mountain races who are always hardest to conquer. Hence the boast of the Basques. Even the Romans, though they could defeat, could not subdue them. The strong Roman fortress of Lapurdum (now Bayonne) did not succeed in even terrifying them, though they were worsted several times by its legions. Down through all the early part of the long Christian era, the forefathers of these frank-faced fishers and mountaineers we see here in the streets of St. Jean kept their hills stubbornly to themselves. Later, as much perhaps from policy as necessity, the race came gradually to fall in with the general governments crystallizing about them. The Spanish Basques came first into the traces, though not until the thirteenth century; they were then finally incorporated into the Castilian monarchy. But they claimed and held marked rights in compensation. While special privileges—*fueros*—were accorded to certain other provinces as well as to them, theirs were the widest and endured the longest. They had five special exemptions: they were not subject to military conscription; nor to certain imposts and taxes, (paying a gross composition in

their place;) nor in general to trial outside their province; nor to the quartering of troops; nor to any regulations of their internal affairs beyond that of the *corregidor*, a representative magistrate appointed by the king. These *fueros* lasted in substance even up to 1876, when Alfonso's government finally repealed them. While thus the Spanish Basques have, even under allegiance, held stoutly to the right of virtual self-government, their brethren north of the Pyrenees long preserved a still fuller autonomy, only coming into the national fold of France under the impetus of the Revolution.

Thus the Basques have a stiff record of independence; it keeps them in no little esteem, both with themselves and with their neighbors. Trains, travel, traffic, eat into their solidarity, and may in time disintegrate it; but a Basque has not yet lost a particle of his pride of clan; it is inborn and ineradicable; he would be no other than he is; "*je ne suis pas un homme*" he boasts, "*je suis un Basque*." You note instinctively his straighter bearing among the neighboring French peasantry; you can often single out a Basque by his air. This hardens into a peculiar result: since they are all of the same high lineage, all are aristocrats; every Basque is *ex officio* a nobleman; this is seriously meant and seriously believed. There are no degrees of caste, the highest is the only; the entire race is blood-proud, ancestor-proud. A Basque family might not improbably have been the originators of that celebrated family tree which remarked, in a marginal note only midway back, that "about this time the Creation took place."

They are not stilted in their pride, however; your true Basque cares much for his descent and little for its dignities. "Where the McGregor sits," he would affirm, "there is the head of the table," and so he cares nothing about the nominal headship. He lives a free, busy life in the hill-country or near the sea, stalwart, swarthy, a lover of the open air, apt at work and sufficiently enterprising, self-respecting, "proud as Lucifer and combustible as his matches," in no

case pinchingly poor, but rarely rich, and never in awe of his own coat-of-arms.

Writers uniformly take a wicked pleasure in maligning the Basque language. Its spelling and syntax, its words and sentences, its methods of construction, are openly derided. Unusual word-forms and distended proper names are singled out and held up to jeers and contumely. A Spanish proverb asserts that as to pronunciation the Basques write "Solomon" and pronounce it "Nebuchadnezzar." The devil, it is alleged, studied for seven years to learn the Basque tongue; at the end of that time he had mastered only three words and abandoned the task in disgust. "And the result is," adds a vivacious writer, "that he is unable to tempt a Basque, because he cannot speak to him, and that consequently every Basque goes straight to heaven. Unfortunately, now that the population is beginning to talk French, (which the devil knows terribly well,) this privilege is disappearing."

Overhearing disjointed Basque phrases on the Biarritz beach or here in the streets and cafés of St. Jean, one will not blame the devil's discouragement. There is scarcely one familiar Aryan syllable. For centuries their speech was not even a written one; there is said to be no book in Basque older than two hundred years. But, its strangeness and isolation once allowed for, there is in reality much to defend in the Basque language. As spoken, it is far from being harsh, and falls pleasantly, often softly, on the ear; the sounds are clear, the articulations rarely, hurried as with the French. The words, other than a few proper names, do not exceed a sober and reasonable length, and as to spelling, every letter has its assigned use and duty; there are no phonetic drones. The original root-forms are short and always recognizable; the full words grow from these by an orderly if intricate system of inflections and the forming of derivatives.

The inflections are, it must be admitted, intricate. Each noun boasts two separate forms, and each of its declension-cases keeps a group of sub-cases within reach for special emergencies. There are only two regularly ordained verbs,—"to be" and "to have"; but they don don different canonicals for each different ceremony, and their varying garbs seem fairly without limit. In the Grammaire Basque of M. Gèze, published in Bayonne, I count no less than one hundred and eight pages of closely-set tables needed to paint the opalescent hues of these multiform auxiliaries,—and this only in one dialect, out of six in all. M. Chaho, an essayist of weight and himself a Basque, informs us artlessly and seriously that one counts a thousand and forty-five forms for their combined present indicatives, and a trifle over ten thousand forms for the two fully expanded verbs; and yet the language, he hastens to add, is so magically simple that even a Basque child never makes an error!

As to its appearance in print, the reader may judge for himself, for here is one of their favorite love-songs. These light songs abound, many being surprisingly delicate and dainty.

BASQUE SONG
"*Chorittoua, nourat houa,*
Bi hegalez airian?
Españalat jouaiteco,
Elhurra duc bortean.
Algarreki jouanen guiuc
Elhurra hourtzen denian.
"*San Josefen ermita*
Desertion gora da.
Españalat jouaiteco,
Han da goure pausada.
Guibelerat so'guin eta
Hasperrenak ardura?
"*Hasperrena, habiloua*
Maitiaren borthala.
Bihotzian sar hakio
Houra eni beçala;
Eta guero erran izoc
Nic igorten haidala."
A graceful English version of the above is in existence, and will fitly complement its original:
"Borne on thy wings amidst the air,
Sweet bird, where wilt thou go?
For if thou wouldst to Spain repair,
The ports are filled with snow.
Wait, and we will fly together,
When the Spring brings sunny weather.

"St. Joseph's hermitage is lone,
Amidst the desert bare,
And when we on our way are gone,
Awhile we'll rest us there;
As we pursue our mountain track,
Shall we not sigh as we look back?
"Go to my love, O gentle sigh,
And near her chamber hover nigh;
Glide to her heart, make that thy shrine,
As she is fondly kept in mine.
Then thou mayst tell her it is I
Who sent thee to her, gentle sigh!"
—COSTELLO.

In regard to length of words, there exist undoubtedly some surprising examples, but they are merely compound expressions and quite in analogy with those of better known and less abused tongues. The German, for one, indulges in such with notorious yet unrebuked frequency. One is naturally startled at encountering in Basque such imbrications as *Izarysaroyarenlarrearenbarena*, or *Ardanzesaroyareniturricoburua*, which are actual names of places in Spanish Basque-land; but they are mercifully rare, and when analyzed prove to be rational and even poetic formations, laden with a full equivalent of import,— the first of the above two signifying "the centre of the field of the mountain of the star," and the second, "the summit of the fountain of the mountain of the vine."

These be scarcely fair samples, however. Commoner words and some of their more musical phrases are instanced in the following, taken in the dialect of this region of St. Jean:

Haran,	Valley.	*Lo,*	Sl
Etchelde,	Farm.	*Etche,*	H
Ogi,	Bread.	*Etchetar,*	H
Egur,	Wood.	*Nerhaba,*	Cl
Maraza,	Hatchet.	*Nescatcha,*	M
Nekarsale,	Workman.	*Zorioneko,*	H
Aita,	My father.	*Ama,*	M
			er.
Neure maiteak,	My loved ones.		

Home words, such as these latter, give a glimpse of this people's home life. For they are devoted to their household as to their tribe, and uniformly show a certain homely honesty and simplicity underneath all their free ways. Love of

smuggling does not impugn this honesty,—in their own view, at all events; for the Basque, man and woman, is a born smuggler, and believing it right is not ashamed. Indeed, they make common cause of it; for years, if a revenue officer detected and shot a Basque in the act, he had to fly the land at once, for the entire neighborhood united in seeking hot and deadly vengeance.

The race is notably fond of dancing and drama, and the villages hold frequent open-air theatricals, generally upon religious themes, which they always handle with great seriousness. They have at intervals unique contests in improvisation, rivaling Wolfram and Tannhaüser, or the Meistersingers, in this special talent. They are fruitful, too, in proverb lore, as would be expected in an old race. Their wise saws are sharp, often rasping:
"Hard bread makes sharp teeth." (*Ogi gogorrari haguin sorroza.*)
"One eye suffices the seller; the buyer has need of a hundred."
"Marriage-day is the next day after happiness."
"Avarice, having killed a man, took refuge in the Church; it has never gone out since."
Husbandmen, herdsmen, fishermen,— such are the majority. The farms are small, averaging four or five acres, and descend by primogeniture; flax, hemp, corn, are their staples. Basques were the first whalers, so it is declared, and St. Jean used to be a noted port for their vessels; the whales have since sought more northern banks, and St. Jean is reduced to the humbler quest of sardines and anchovies. There are iron-mines and marble-quarries, besides, to engage many; hunting and logging are favored pursuits; Basque sailors are to be found in all waters, while great numbers of the younger men are now yearly emigrating to the South American coasts, to make a better living,—and to avoid conscription.

Those of the race we see in our transit impress one, on the whole, favorably. The men have, in the main, the lithe, firm port attributed to them, though there are Basque "trash," as there are

Georgia "crackers," and average-lesseners everywhere. The women are often noticeably attractive; the younger ones have a ruddy face and full, clear eye, but the skin shrivels and wears with middle age, as does that of their French peasant sisters. The Basques about Biarritz and St. Jean appear to associate with the French element in entire amity; the race strives still to keep distinct, but habits and idioms and manners imperceptibly mingle; they speak French or patois quite as much as their own tongue, and in divers ways hint at the working of amalgamation and assimilation.

Mention of this bizarre tribe is perhaps not untimely; the leveling process progresses fast, over Basque-land as in all the world; steam and lightning are the genii of the age, but they destroy while they build. As a significant straw, the French government enforces here, in the public schools, the teaching and speaking of French to supersede the Basque. Similarly, Spanish is required in the schools over the border. In some of these, a child detected in a lapse into Basque must wear a certain ring, which he is allowed to pass on to the first companion he catches likewise tripping. The latter may pass it on in turn. At the end of the week comes the reckoning-day, and the unhappy individual then found with the ring is, punished for the collective sinners of the week. Few more ingenious, even if demoralizing, expedients could be devised to put the native tongue and sentiments under ban.

"It has been truthfully observed," says one, "that, in ancient times, the Basques kept themselves outside of the Roman world; in the middle age they remained outside of feudal society; while to-day they would fain keep out of the modern world. The spectacle of this little confederacy, steadily maintaining its isolation for so many centuries, is most interesting, and, in some aspects, affecting; but the very stubbornness and the prolonged success of its resistance to all attempts to draw it into the current of modern life and thought only enhances the significance of its ultimate failure, and furnishes an expressive commentary upon the futility of a people's most

determined efforts to hold itself aloof from the brotherhood of nations. Contact is God's manifest decree. The five Basques at Bayonne bridge, helpless against the incoming tide, present a truthful prophecy of the destiny of the whole race before the advancing and mounting wave of modern civilization."

V.

In this region, too, lies the famous pass of Ibañeta or Roncesvalles. It may be readily visited in a two days' excursion from St. Jean or from Biarritz. There is a carriage-road to Valcarlos, a small village on the way; beyond, a mule-path winds on up through the pass and down to the convent on the other side.

This convent was founded to commemorate the one greatest tradition of the pass,—the destruction of Charlemagne's rear-guard by the Basques in ambush and the death of the hero Roland.
"Oh for a blast of that dread horn
On Fontarabian echoes borne
That to King Charles did come;
When Rowland brave and Olivier
And every paladin and peer
On Roncesvalles died!"
Of the few writers who have visited this region, all make airy mention of the battle of Roncesvalles; scarcely one, however, condescends to details. Yet it gave rise to a great epic poem,—the greatest epic of France, the delight of all her ancient minstrels. One often hears named the *Song of Roland*; one seldom hears more than the name. By many the charm of its story is all unknown.

"In truth and fact," observes a recent anonymous writer, "the chain can claim one single real legend. That one, however, is so great, so grand, so dominating,—it is so immense, so universal, so world-wide,—that it suffices all alone; it creates a doctrine by itself, it needs no aid, no support, no companions,—it is the mighty tale of Roland. The mountain is full of Roland. His hands, his feet, his horse, his sword, his voice, have left their puissant mark on almost every crest, in almost every glen. Above Gavarnie, amidst the eternal snow, gapes the slashed fissure hewn by Durandal, his sword; ten miles off in a

gorge you see the indents of the hoofs of Bayard on a rock which served as his half-way touching-point when he sprang in two flying bounds from the Breach to the Peak of the Chevalier near St. Sauveur. At the Pass of Roland, above Cambo, the rock remains split open where the hero stamped and claimed a passage. The ponds of Vivier Lion, near Lourdes, were dug by the pressure of his foot and knee when Vaillantif, a charger which carried him in his last fight, but who was then unbroken, had the audacity to throw him. At St. Savin, where the monks had lodged him, he paid his bill by slaying the irreverent giants, Passamont and Alabaster, whose neighborhood, was unpleasant to the convent. And so on, all about. His tremendous figure is everywhere, all full of the superbest violence and of the most wondrous acrobatry. But it is at Roncesvalles that his great name is greatest. There, where he died, his memory lives in an unfading halo. In Spain, beneath the Peak of Altabiscar amongst the beech groves, on the 15th of August, 778, perished the astounding paladin. The *Song of Roland* tells how he fell, not quite exactly but very amazingly; the story is so intensely interesting that the reader is carried away by it and finds himself for a moment almost able to believe it. It does not matter that the defeat is attributed to the Saracens, not one of whom was present, (the whole thing having been got up and carried out by the Basques alone;) that error was indispensable to the tale, and gives it much of its strange charm."

There is an excellent reason why the poem might fail in sharp historical accuracy; it was not formally composed until between three and four hundred years after the battle. The event itself happened in 778; the first known MS. was made, by a scribe, about 1150. All during the long interval, ballad-singers and minstrels had been extolling France and Roland; the love of the heroic was as strong as before Homer; the hero's name had grown: with his fame into titanic proportions; the actual author, (conjectured to have been one Turoldus or Theurolde, a monk,) had but to take the poetic material ready at his hand and fashion it into the epic. Time had dimmed and enlarged the details; the *Song of Roland* deals in mass and massive heroes; in this it is like a book from the Iliad.

It is not a long poem; there are only about 3,500 lines in all, but the Old French in which it is written makes it difficult reading, at least to one not a Frenchman. The briefest citation will show this:

"Carles li Reis, nostre Emperere magnes,
Sela anz tuz pleins ad estet en Espaigne;
Tresqu'en la mer, cunquist la tere altaigne.
N'i ad castel ki devant lui remagnet."
("Charles le Roi, notre grand Empereur,
Sept ans entiers est resté en Espagne;
Jusqu' à la mer, il a conquis la haute terre.
Pas de château qui tienne devant lui."
—GAUTIER.)

However, it has been transmuted into modern French, and latterly twice translated into English verse; and the English translations appear to have preserved remarkably both the power and sweetness of the original.

The poem centres almost wholly upon this deadly battle in the Pyrenees,— the last battle of Roland its hero. Charlemagne and the Franks had invaded Spain, and spent seven years warring with the Moors and conquering their cities. On their return, as the poem narrates it, the Moors, instigated by a traitor in Charlemagne's army, plotted an ambush in this pass of Roncesvalles. The army began its march. The main body defiled through in safety, and turned westward to await the rear-guard nearer the coast. But when that division, the flower of the Frankish forces,— commanded by Roland, his bosom friend Oliver, the warrior-archbishop Turpin, and the others of the twelve great paladins,—reached the pass, hostiles began to appear,—in front, above, behind. More and more they thickened around it,—fierce Basques or swarthy Moslems, "a hundred thousand heathen men;" and the three leaders soon realized their betrayal. Oliver exclaimed:

"'Ganelon wrought this perfidy!
It was he who doomed us to hold the rear.'
'Hush,' said Roland, 'O Olivier,
No word be said of my step-sire here,'"
—a touch of magnanimity strange for that brutal age, yet only one of many in the poem. Roland rather exulted than shrank at the prospect of a battle, by whatever means brought about. Oliver was the cooler of the two, and he promptly urged Roland to sound his great horn, which might be heard for thirty leagues, and so summon Charlemagne to the rescue. He saw that the danger was real, for the odds were overwhelmingly against them. But Roland impetuously refused. Thrice, though not in cowardice, Oliver pleaded with him:

"'Roland, Roland, yet wind one blast!
Karl will hear ere the gorge be past,
And the Franks return on their path full fast.'
'I will not sound on mine ivory horn!
It shall never be spoken of me in scorn
That for heathen felons one blast I blew.
I may not dishonor my lineage true.
* * *
"'Death were better than fame laid low.
Our Emperor loveth a downright blow!'"
The Moors at last swarmed to the attack. They were no cravens, the Moors; the fight grew rapidly desperate. The Franks performed wonders; they tingled with the Archbishop's glorious assoilment:
"In God's high name the host he blest,
And for penance he gave them—to smite their best!"
The twelve paladins slew twelve renowned Paynims; the mailed phalanx hewed its way into the infidels, laying them low by thousands. But thousands more were behind,—the reserve was inexhaustible; the "hundred thousand" were cut to pieces, when the Moorish king, hastily summoned, came up with a fresh army of myriads more. It was too much; little by little the Franks were beaten down, not back, and melted unyielding away. The peers fell one by one, upon heaps of the Moslem dead; the day wore on; of the twenty thousand Frankish warriors, but sixty men at length remained. Too late Roland would wind his horn; it was Oliver's turn to disdain the now useless expedient. Roland sounded nevertheless:
"The mountain peaks soared high around;
Thirty leagues was borne the sound.
Karl hath heard it and all his band;
'Our men have battle,' he said, 'on hand!'
Ganelon rose in front and cried;
'If another spake, I would say he lied!'"
Again the desperate sound was faintly heard:
"'It is Roland's horn,' said the Emperor,
'And save in battle he had not blown!'
'Battle,' said Ganelon, 'is there none.
Old you have grown,—all white and hoar!
* * *
"'He would sound all day for a single hare.'"
The third time, Roland blew; his nostrils and mouth are filled with blood, his temples crack with the stress:
"Said Karl: 'That horn is full of breath!'
Said Naimes: ''Tis Roland who travaileth,'"
—and the Emperor instantly gave the command to turn and rush to the rescue.

But the battle had gone too far. Again and again the little band of Franks clove its way into the enemy; the latter wavered, retreated, fell by hundreds, and came back in thousands. Roland's tears fell fast over his dead companions:
"'Land of France, thou art soothly fair!
To-day thou liest bereaved and bare.
It was all for me your lives ye gave,
And I was helpless to shield or save.'"
The last Frankish man-at-arms at length fell; only the three foremost paladins remained of all the host. But the Saracens dared no longer to approach them; they hurled their lances from afar. Spent and faint and bleeding, the three still stood out, but the death-wound of Oliver finally came; his vision swam, he swayed blindly on his horse. There is no more touching and beautiful incident in the whole range of song than this of his death:
"His eyes from bleeding are dimmed and dark,
Nor mortal near or far can mark;

And when his comrade beside him pressed,
Fiercely he smote on his golden crest;
Down to the nasal the helm he shred,—
But passed no further nor pierced his head.
Roland marveled at such a blow,
And thus bespake him, soft and low:
'Hast thou done it, my comrade, wittingly?
Roland, who loves thee so dear, am I;
Thou hast no quarrel with me to seek?'
Oliver answered: 'I hear thee speak,
But I see thee not. God seeth thee.
Have I struck thee, brother? Forgive it me.'
'I am not hurt, O Olivier,
And in sight of God I forgive thee here.
'
Then each to each his head hath laid,
And in love like this was their parting made."

And now but Roland and the Archbishop were left,—the former on foot, his charger dead. Wounded and gasping, they rushed forward upon the enemy; the sword-arm of the Moorish king was cut from his side, his son fell dead before him. The Moors quailed; their lances fell in storms upon the heroes. Suddenly a long, far sound was heard; it was of the trumpets of Charlemagne's returning army rushing to the rescue but still miles and hours away. The Saracens turned at the very sound; a final lance-shower, and they fled; the two held the pass of Roncesvalles, unconquered,—but dying.

For it was too late.

The Archbishop had sunk to the ground, gasping,—lifeless. Roland, stricken himself, placed his companion gently on the grass:
"He took the fair white hands outspread,
Crossed and clasped them upon his breast."
Then with his remaining strength, he sought one by one for the corpses of the other ten paladins; one by one he brought them to the feet of the dead prelate and laid them before the august body,—Oliver's corpse last and dearest of all. There he might leave them, the solemn assembly of the peers. It was his last task. His wound too was mortal; his

time had come to join them.

"In vigor and pathos," justly observes the review before mentioned, "this poem rises to the end. There are few things in poetry more simply grand than the death of Roland. He moves feebly back to the adjoining limit-line of Spain,— the land which his well-loved master has conquered,—and a bow-shot beyond it, and then drops to the ground:"
"That death was on him he knew full well;
Down from his head to his heart it fell.
On the grass beneath a pine tree's shade,
With face to earth, his form he laid;
Beneath him placed he his horn and sword,
And turned his face to the heathen horde
Thus hath he done the sooth to show
That Karl and his warriors all may know
That the gentle Count a conqueror died.
'Mea culpa,' full oft he cried,
And for all his sins, unto God above
In sign of penance he raised his glove.
* * *
"He did his right-hand glove uplift;
Saint Gabriel took from his hand the gift.
—Then drooped his head upon his breast,
And with clasped hands he went to rest.
"
There is indeed little in epic poetry to surpass the high simplicity of this loving portrayal of a hero's death.

It is the climax of the poem. The Emperor's army burst upon the scene, frantic with anxiety; but no eye was open to give them greeting. Roland was dead with his slaughtered rear-guard, and lying with his face to the foe. For three days the sun stayed its motion, at Charlemagne's frenzied petition, and the Moors were chased and cut to pieces, Saragossa taken,—a full and furious vengeance exacted. The whole army mourned for their companions; holy rites attended their stately burial; Ganelon was tried, condemned, torn to pieces by wild horses. But the joy of the Franks, their hero, their idol, was gone forever from them; retribution, even the bitterest, could count for little against the passing of that peerless spirit.

A pathetic meeting was afterward the old Emperor's with Alva, the affianced of Roland:
"'Where is my Roland, sire,' she cried,
'Who vowed to take me for his bride?'"
Brokenly at length he told her of the news. A moment she gazed at him unseeing:
"'God and his angels forbid, that I
Should live on earth if Roland die!'
Pale grew her cheek,—she sank amain
Down at the feet of Charlemagne."
So let us leave this tender poem, tender unwontedly among its times; an epic which sincerely merits a vogue more near to its value.

CHAPTER V.

THE CITY OF THE ARROW-PIERCED SAINT;

We glide smoothly away from St. Jean de Luz and its legends, by the unlegendary railroad. The track curves southward, with frequent views of the coast, and it will be but a few minutes before we shall be in Spain. We instinctively feel for the reassuring rustle of our passports, duly viséd at Bordeaux. The low mountain that overhangs Fuenterrabia, one of the nearest Spanish towns, comes closer, and soon the train whistles shrilly into the long station at Hendaye, the last French village, in great repute for its delicious cordial. It is on the edge of the Bidassoa, a placid, shallow river which here lazily acts as the international boundary. Irun, the first town of the peninsula, is across the bridge, and after a short delay the train crosses,—and we instantly feel a hundred miles nearer to the Escorial, a hundred years nearer to Philip and the auto-da-fé.

The change of nationality at these frontier towns is always distinct and surprising, and more so than elsewhere here in Irun. Within three minutes we have in every sense passed from France into Spain. Language not only, but the type of face and dress, have altered in a flash. We are not conscious, however, of any increased governmental surveillance; passports are not asked for at all, and the customs-official gives but a light inspection to trunk and satchels.

But he is in considerable perplexity over the camera. This he is scrutinizing very suspiciously. We assume that a true Greek compound should pass current everywhere, if given a proper local termination, and so confidently hazard, "*photo-grafia.*"

I still believe that the word was skilfully and philologically evolved, but it seems to fail of its effect. We repeat it, with appropriate gestures; the official looks puzzled but not enlightened. He inspects the lens, the bellows, the slides. We fear for the negatives and the unexposed plates. Prompt action is needed, for already his hand is approaching them; and boldly withdrawing the closed plate-holders from the camera we defiantly pocket them before his eyes.

A short, clicking sound caused by the act of withdrawal gives the inspector an idea. He looks up hopefully.

"*Telegrafo*?" he asks.

We nod with vigor and even more hopefully, and are inspired to add:

"*Si, señor, telegrafo! Americano; caramba!*"

This has the desired effect. The mystery is explained. The government's hand is stayed, its doubt vanishes; the precious scroll of chalk is made, and the plates are saved to darkness and to good works.

It is necessary to change cars at Irun. Trains cannot possibly go through, owing to a difference in gauge,—a difference purposely devised by moody Spain, in order to impede hostile invasion. There is also a wait of an hour. The Spaniard does not assent to the equation between time and money. The lunch at the buffet in the station is ceremonious and calm; the successive courses are gravely served at its naperied tables with the same deliberation, the same care and attention to detail, as at a hotel. It is but a short journey to San Sebastian, and in half an hour after leaving Irun we are at our destination.

II.

San Sebastian is both a city unto itself, and a summer resort unto others. As to the latter, it is among the most popular watering-places in Spain, and is styled "the Brighton of Madrid." As to the former, it is a home for twenty thousand human beings of its own; it earns a sufficing competence, chiefly in exchanges with its surrounding province; and it has a monopoly of centralization over a wide region, for no other important Spanish city lies nearer than Pampeluna or Burgos. Burgos is not actually so very remote,—only a short hundred and fifty miles beyond; and we had spoken of a visit to its renowned cathedral. But we had not reckoned with Spanish railway speed; it was found that the time required solely to go and come would be nearly fifteen hours! Unvisited, we saw, must remain the cathedral within which the hot-headed Protestant missionary blew out the sacred light that had burned for three hundred years. Owing to the Hispanian misconception of horological values, Burgos is practically, if not actually, exceedingly remote from San Sebastian.

The latter, however, is so fortunately close to the edge of France that those who come as near as Biarritz or Pau should assuredly make this brief dip over the border.

San Sebastian is strictly new; its predecessors have been burned five times, one upon the other, the last being brought to ashes by the soldiers of Wellington; and it is liable to be burned again whenever France and Spain begin to fight again across it. It is an excellent model for that worthy fowl, the phoenix, for it has risen with undismayed cheerfulness from each holocaust. The present representative is in three segments. The city itself is composed of two, and the citadel makes a fairly important third. From a military point of view, the citadel was once counted first, and the city itself made an unimportant third,—with no second. But modern gunnery has changed that estimate.

Of the two parts of the city proper, one is national, the other international; they do not unite, but adjoin, welded by a central promenade, the *Alameda*. Each is distinct, and has little to do with the life of the other. The native population centres wholly in the west half; we drift first over to this, in our afternoon walk, and scan its appearance and people with inquisitive though decorous interest. This section, comprising much of what was the old town, has evidently aimed to reproduce it; it has been rebuilt with persistent regard to the former municipal type, and shows to-day a curious combination of bright, new and well constructed tenements, built on a dark, old and ill instructed plan. The streets are left narrow,—very narrow. The black doorways and halls, as we peer in, in passing, are cramped and forbidding; the projecting balconies approach each other overhead, and the oblong yellow buildings themselves rise to overshadowing height. Like soldiers on dress parade they stand, relentlessly regular and uniform, block after block, and their walled lanes, straight and similar and uncharacteristic, cross and weave themselves into a stiff, right-angled check, exasperating and profitless, unrelieved by a hint at variation of outline, by a picturesque eave or gable, or a single artistic "bit;"

The cathedral does indeed possess some interest, particularly its carved front of light-colored stone; and here and there about it are a few old houses, unsutteed relics, that have not bowed to the new régime. The shops in this part of the town are less individual than one would expect, though we find them not devoid of a certain variety. The specialty of the place is the enameling of gold and silver upon iron. Jewelry and small articles are made of this ware in elaborate designs and with great daintiness and skill. Outside of this, San Sebastian does not seem to have invented any new wants for humanity, and its shops do not seek to supply any but the old.

The other half of the town I have called international. This is the section of the hotels, of wide streets and flagged walks, of massy squares of business buildings, of villas and a park and the bathing circle. The sea swings around the projecting cape of the citadel into a deeply notched bay, small and still, and on its edge which meets the town you find pavilions and beach-chairs and their usual accompaniment of idling humanity. The Casino stands boldly up, a little to the right, and in front of it, on the Alameda, the band will play in the coming summer evenings for all the élite of Madrid.

The fine Hôtel de Londres is large and well kept, and, like all Spanish hotels, charges on the good American plan of so much per day. One gratefully appreciates this, after juggling every few days with disheartening lists of accumulated coffees and eggs and dinners and rooms and mineral waters and service and *bougies*, and the others. The infinitude of microscopic book-keeping made necessary by the Continental system is a thought to shudder at. For the rest, the hotel is only unsatisfying because it seems in nowise distinctively Spanish. We almost wish we had chosen a certain other hostelry equally well spoken of, which, instead of Hotel, had alluringly styled itself a *Fonda*. Probably we might have found as little there as here that was pure Castilian. Save in language and location, San Sebastian is not of Spain, Spanish. And as with Biarritz, it is not to be sought for its reminiscences of old age. It is trim and "kempt" and modern, and lives strictly in the present. We soon come to realize this, cease longing for the unattainable, and enjoy the place for what it is. Perhaps we shall recoup the vanished *patina* to-morrow, when we visit an older and far different town,—Fuenterrabia.

III.

The Sebastian season is coëxtensive with the summer season at Biarritz; perhaps rather tardier in its beginnings. Consequently we are still somewhat in advance of the tide. This is distinctly a disadvantage, as it was in part at Biarritz. There are places whose very reason for existence is society. Only in this costume are they rightly themselves; only in full dress, so to say, should they

be called upon. In a true "sentimental journey," art and nature and history should take but equal turn with the life of the present. The ideal traveler courts solitude in a ruin and society in a resort. The spirit of each is differently divined.

And San Sebastian out of season is a casket without its jewels,—modern-made casket at that, costly but uncharacteristic, and with nothing of an heirloom's charm; a casket neither encased in time's antique leather nor encrusted with true Spanish enamel.

However, we are not wholly out of the season. We are in the van of it, but day breaks before the sun rises. San Sebastian is partially awake already and rubbing its eyes. The season's contingent is arriving in daily portions. The Queen Regent is coming soon, to spend the summer; this draws an additional number in advance, thus influenced to summer here themselves. The beach is already mildly popular, and the cabmen mildly independent. We drive out from the town around the bend of the little bay, and see opening villas and other marks of awakening life. But we sigh for music on the quiet plaza; hope in vain for a concert or ball in the Casino; and, above all, mourn and refuse to be comforted, for there is no bull-fight. After Wellington, whose way to Waterloo left here its fiery track, we exclaim: "O for August or Madrid!" In Madrid, they are holding bull-fights even now in June; in August, they will be holding them here.

IV.

As to the citadel, sight-seers are not so-licitously catered to by the authorities. I stroll up there in the afternoon. The citadel hill is known as the Monte Orgullo. The spirals of the road lead out to and around the edge of the promontory to its ocean side, and curve steadily upward during a rise of four hundred feet. There are pleasant views of the sea,—the Spanish main in literal fact,—and of the hills across the little notch of water that turns in at the left toward the town. I near the summit, pass under an untended gateway, work upward still by a narrow lane shut in with high stone

walls, and finally reach the foot of a long flight of stone steps and see the citadel looming above. It is Spain, and my passport is at the hotel. They are said to be very suspicious in Spain; to act first and investigate afterward. My whole vocabulary has already been employed at the custom-house, and consists of "*Americano*," "*caramba*," and "*Si, Señor*." It won the day at Irun. Will it win the day here?

Boldly I begin ascending the steps. They are many and wide, confined by the same high walls, and commanded from above by the battlements of the fort. There is commotion on the parapet at the unmuffled sound of the foreigner's foot-fall, and armed figures at once appear at the edge.

I pause half-way, and look expectantly upward.

"*Caramba*?" I inquire.

A soldier shakes, his head.

"*Americano*," I insinuate, sweetly.

Another shake, more decided.

I grieve for a somewhat fuller technical familiarity with the Spanish military idiom. Undismayed, however, I resort to the sign language, and make gestures to signify that I want to ascend.

Either the proposal is rejected or it is not comprehended, and I act it out again, with a cajoling "*Si, Señor*." Then, to make the idea clearer, I move on up the steps.

But now there is a vigorous negative. More armed figures, appear at the parapet, and, while I pause again, one of them explains his position in a few well-chosen and emphatic phrases, and illustrates his views by a pointed gesture toward his gun. The illustration at least is definite and unmistakable.

International complications are never to be recklessly brought on. But shall the assailing traveler quail before a gesture? My store of Spanish passwords is exhausted, but there is one solvent yet remaining,—the universal countersign. With undiminished cheerfulness, I select from my pocket a stamped silver disk of well-known design, hold it significantly a moment in full view, and then confidently proceed up the staircase.

The armed figures vanish from view. There is a foreboding silence as I near the heavy entrance-way at the top. But before I can pound for admittance, the great door swings deferentially open, a guard within salutes still more deferentially, I advance, friend, and proffer the countersign,—and the Monte Orgullo is won!

The view from this hill of Mars well merits the climb and any attendant risk to the home State Department. The air is warm and still. In front, the sea stretches to the horizon, smooth as the fair Glimmerglass loved by Deerslayer. To the right flows a clear, quiet river, the Urumea, to meet it,—a river on whose nearer bank below us lies buried many a brave English soldier, their graves marked by white headstones; and from the farther shore of which once flew leaden rain and iron hail from conquering English guns. Behind us lies the city, asleep in the warm afternoon haze, and in the distance are the forms of purplish Pyrenees hills; while farther around opens the bright little bay,—the *Concha* or Shell, happily so called,— with villas fringing it's curve, and an islet-pearl in its centre. A wistful touch of peace and sunshine is over all the scene, as one views it, in the irony of fact, from this storm-centre of war.

There are barracks within the walls, and monster guns and other usual martial furnishings, and the fortifications themselves have, to some extent, been put in touch with modern requirements. The garrison's life is not hard, and they live contentedly through drill and evolution, ration and routine, and stroll down to the Alameda and Casino in hours of leave. But theirs is a post of honor and danger, nevertheless. San Sebastian lies foremost in the route of possible invasion. It could not be ignored nor left untaken. And the very isolation of this fortress, once its strength, is now its weakness. It might serve to delay an onrushing army for a saving moment,— a dog thrown out to check the wolves. It could accomplish little more against the terrific artillery of to-day; and,—as with the dog,—the interval would prove a period of marked unrest to the fated garrison.

However, war is now at last, if never hitherto, extinct for all time, so trusts the world at peace. And barrack-life is dreamy and easy, and the stroll down to the Alameda very pleasant, these fair days of summer.

But the white headstones on the river slope come out into view again, for a time, as I wander back down the spiral road toward the town and think on these things; a cloud drifts across the sun and dims their brightness; then the light pours down as before.

V.

Wellington fought his way over this region in 1813, and took San Sebastian,— took it by storm and thunder-storm,— took it in fire and hail, at fearful cost, and over the dead bodies of a quarter of his stormers. The place blocked his northward way to meet the Man of Destiny. Destiny decreed its fall. For seven weeks, the siege, octopus-like, wound its long tentacles about its victim, sucking away the life. On the last day of summer, the assault was let loose. The attack seemed irresistible; the defence impregnable. All that furious morning, column after column of British troops swarmed up the river bank, pressed on into the breaches, or hurled themselves to the top of the walls. Column after column melted back, under the torrent of fire from the parapet and from the batteries in the citadel. "In vain," says Napier, "the following multitude covered the ascent, seeking an entrance at every part; to advance was impossible, and the mass of assailants, slowly sinking downwards, remained stubborn and immovable on the lower part of the breach .

"The volunteers, who had been with difficulty restrained in the trenches, 'calling out to know why they had been brought there if they were not to lead the assault,' being now let loose, went like a whirlwind to the breaches, and again the crowded masses swarmed up the face of the ruins, but reaching the crest line they came down like a falling wall; crowd after crowd were seen to mount, to totter and to sink, the deadly French fire was unabated, the smoke floated away, and the crest of the breach bore no living man."

The British artillery, from a near elevation, now reinforced the attack with a raking fire, and new regiments plunged across the stream and rushed to join the attack. "The fighting now became fierce and obstinate again at all the breaches, but the French musketry still rolled with deadly effect, the heaps of slain increased, and once more the great mass of stormers sank to the foot of the ruins, unable to win; the living sheltered themselves as they could, but the dead and wounded lay so thickly that hardly could it be judged whether the hurt or unhurt were most numerous.

"It was now evident that the assault must fail unless some accident intervened, for the tide was rising, the reserves all engaged, and no greater effort could be expected from men whose courage had been already pushed to the verge of madness. In this crisis, fortune interfered. A number of powder-barrels, live shells, and combustible materials which the French had accumulated behind the traverses for their defence, caught fire, a bright, consuming flame wrapped the whole of the high curtain, a succession of loud explosions was heard, hundreds of the French grenadiers were destroyed, the rest were thrown into confusion, and while the ramparts were still involved with suffocating eddies of smoke, the British soldiers broke in at the first traverse. The defenders, bewildered by this terrible disaster, yielded for a moment, yet soon rallied, and a close, desperate struggle took place along the summit of the high curtain; but the fury of the stormers, whose numbers increased every moment, could not be stemmed. The French colors on the cavalier were torn away, by Lieutenant Gethin of the eleventh regiment. The hornwork and the land front below the curtain, and the loopholed wall behind the great breach, were all abandoned; the light-division soldiers, who had already established themselves in the ruins on the French left, immediately penetrated to the streets; and at the same moment the Portuguese at the small breach, mixed with the British who had wandered to that point seeking for an entrance, burst in on their side.

"Five hours the dreadful battle had lasted at the walls, and now the storm of war went pouring into the town. The undaunted governor still disputed the victory for a short time with the aid of his barricades, but several hundreds of his men being cut off and taken in the hornwork, his garrison was so reduced that even to effect a retreat behind the line of defences which separated the town from the Monte Orgullo was difficult; the commanders of battalions were embarrassed for want of orders, and a thunder-storm, which came down from the mountains with unbounded fury immediately after the place was carried, added to the confusion of the fight.

"Many officers exerted themselves to preserve order, many men were well conducted; but the rapine and violence commenced by villains soon spread, the camp-followers crowded into the place, and the disorder continued until the flames, following the steps of the plunderer, put an end to his ferocity by destroying the whole town."

It is beyond imagination, this sunny June afternoon, that the shining city about us has gasped in smoke and ruins, has been pierced with arrows unto death as was its patron saint of old; that this contentful droning of the shore and the street deepened once to the roar of war and rose to the shriek of suffering.

CHAPTER VI.

AN OLD SPANISH MINIATURE.

"When Charlemain with all his peerage fell,
By Fontarabia."
—MILTON.

The next day an indolent morning train draws us back to the frontier. The landscape is rather shadeless; "a Spaniard hates a tree." It should be but a twenty-minute ride, and so, it being short at the longest, we do not have time to grudge the additional twenty consumed in "indolencing." The time-table allowed for

that, and so prepared us. It is when larger times are involved,—when a four-hour ride is inflated to eight, and an eight-hour trip to fifteen, as in going to Burgos,—that the corporate deliberateness of the Spanish railways ceases to be a curiosity, and becomes a crime.

We are soon in Irun once more, and after change of cars, cross to Hendaye, and baggage is inspected for France. The train goes on its way north, but we stay in Hendaye, to lunch, and to make our projected excursion to Fuenterrabia.

In terms of logic, San Sebastian the modern has in Fuenterrabia the ancient its full "contradictory." The one, the resort, is affirmative and universal; the other, the old, strange town, is negative and individual. The one has told us little of old Spain; we turn hopefully to the other.

Fuenterrabia lies near the mouth of the Bidassoa, on the Spanish side of the stream, below Irun. It is but two miles, from Irun, and readily reached from that place by carriage; from Hendaye, on the French side, one reaches it by row-boat in about the same time, with the additional zest and boast of recrossing the river and of entering and leaving Spain once more.

II.

Luncheon past, we walk up the long, easy incline that leads from Hendaye station into its town; and with a turn to the left find our way through its streets down again to the river bank. Here are boats and boatmen, and we have to run the customary gauntlet of competition, as vociferous at Hendaye as at Killarney or the Crossmon. We elect two of the competitors as allies, and the rest become our sworn enemies forthwith.

The tide is low, the water still and shallow; and we are sculled smoothly out into the stream, restful in the soft sunshine, the full blue of the afternoon sky. The voices of our hundred enemies recede; the sounds from the town yield to the dripping oars; soon the stream stretches its silent width about us. Close-grouped on the opposite shore we see the dark walls of Fuenterrabia, domineered by the castle. The railway whis-

tle begins to seem a memory of another existence, the bustle of travel a thing remote. The quiet of the river, unlike Lethe, turns us to the past, and clouds the present in a dreamy haze.

"In that sunny corner where the waves of the Bay of Biscay wash over a sandy barrier and mingle with the waters of the Bidassoa stream,"—thus runs the legend so charmingly recounted in *The Sun-Maid*,—"they tell the ancient story that a favored mortal won from the gods permission to ask three blessings for Spain.

"He asked that her daughters might be beautiful, that her sons might be brave, and that her government might be good.

"The first two requests were granted,—the beauty of a Spanish woman is of world-wide renown; and if the men are rash, passionate, and revengeful, at least they are brave; but the last request was refused.

"'Impossible!' was the answer; 'impossible! Already she is an earthly paradise, and were this last blessing hers, the very gods themselves would desert Elysium and come down to dwell in Spain.'"

Of this we think, winding among the shallows, as the Spanish bank comes nearer, and the boat at last grounds lightly on its soil. Before us is the old town we are seeking,—a type perhaps of the nation itself, in its courtly unthrift, its proud misgovernance.

III.

There is a little custom-house on the bank, but our *impedimenta* are safe in Hendaye. I think our passports are there as-well, so bold does one grow upon familiarity.

We have scarcely traversed a hundred yards before we come upon the middle centuries. There will be no caviling at the satisfying antiquity of Fuenterrabia. We have passed in between the lichened walls which still guard the city, and a few steps bring us into the town and to the foot of the main street. We pause to look, and the sight is certainly striking. Beyond a doubt Fuenterrabia is old. It has a true Spanish tint, and one dyed in the wool; one might probably travel far in Spain before meeting a truer. This street seems utterly unmodified by modern formulæ. Wavering and narrow and sombre, it stretches upward on a gradual incline until it meets the cathedral stepping out from the line of the old houses and closing the vista. Even in the short perspective, the huge, blackened eaves of the opposite roofs seem almost to meet. Balconies, associated with moonlight and mandolins, serenades and señoritas, jut out from every window; dark bosses of escutcheons mark the fronts; and below, along the edging of sidewalk, are the dim little shops, curtained by yellow canvas, intensely and delightfully local, and wholly unknowing of outside demand or competition. One of these places does indeed cater to visitors with a humble supply of photographs and of clicking sets of varnished wooden castanets paired by colored worsteds; but the others of the store-keepers and the inhabitants in the streets are clearly unhardened to foreigners, and regard us solely with a deep and artless curiosity,—tempered, I hope, by admiration. As the town has been, so it is. It is an epitome of Spain and her past.

IV.

At the head of the street we enter the cool cathedral, and find, as always, wealth created by poverty. In places such as these one realizes the hold of the Romish system on mediæval Europe. One realizes its power also. No matter what the size of a town, it boasts its costly church; oftener, as here, its cathedral. Villages, houses, people, may be poor, their church stands rich; they may be unlearned in art and in culture, their church stands a model of both. There was their shrine, their finality,—in religion not merely, but in art and wisdom and authority.

At least, the Catholic system held its followers firmly in leash. Condemn its errors and excesses, yet, these apart, it was marvelously adapted to its mission. As an engine of unification it was almost omnipotent. Through the ups and downs of restless migrations and invasions,—of feudalisms and governments and the soberer commercial spirit,—it has kept its hold unbroken upon the mass of European humanity. Its priests and popes might sink out of respect; the Church did not sink. In the fiercest civil feuds, its abbeys were held inviolate. To the most brutal, the Church had an odor of sanctity. Its threats terrified; its mandates were obeyed; it was the one persistent, binding principle; it held men in check from a relapse into tribalism.

And its hold is firm to-day. Go into a Romish church, you shall find worshipers at every hour. Worn housewives, seamed and aged market-women, a chance workingman, an awed and tiptoeing child,—they are there in their silence. They kneel, they pray, their eyes are fixed on the altar. Formalism or not, a sincerity underlies it,—a belief and obedience absorbed from centuries of environment; implicit and unquestioning, and making for good.

V.

Beyond the cathedral is the broad square or plaza, and the half-alive streets wandering from this are even more Fuenterrabian than the one just past, for they are less well-to-do. The poorer houses may reveal the traits and traditions of a town far more faithfully than the richer. The latter can draw their models from a wider field. The former copy only the local and long-followed pattern.

Here at our right stands the castle. It is stern in its decrepitude; its very aspect is historic. It was built by a king of Navarre, Sancho Abarca, known as the Strong, so long ago as the tenth century; the façade facing the square is somewhat later, and the other façade was rebuilt by Charles V. We pass through the entrance-way and across a murky, earthen-floored atrium, and stand in silence in the roofless central hall.

It is at this point that our nascent impressions are brusquely shocked. Fuenterrabia is not all steeped in dreams of the past. It has waked for once into the business present as well. Its proud reserve has been broken. There is a rift in the lute. Here by the mossy court-yard, enclosed by historic walls and the spirit of an unworldly past, we are met by a sign-board, with the following English inscription:

FOR SALE!
THIS ROYAL PALACE
AND CASTLE OF THE EMPEROR CHARLES V.
appli for informations
to
PRIMO FERNANDEZ, FUENTERRABIA.
A preceding traveler saw this sign when here, and quotes it in part in a recent book. It still hangs, as we see it now, two years after his visit, still pathetically but vainly invoking the spirit of a worldly present.

For the lover of day dreams, given to designing his *châteaux en Espagne*, I seriously recommend this purchase in Fuenterrabia. The castillo is a real one and the most accessible in Spain, and all its surroundings are gratefully in harmony. It is presumably a bargain, and one might either hold it for a rise, or turn grandee and live in it.

Within the court, the daylight comes in over the dismantled walls. The ivy green climbs along the grey stones. We trace the old hearth and the outline of the stone staircase scarred upon the wall. We conjure up the rest of the structure, but the Northern Wizard is not with us here, as at Kenilworth, to repeople it with life and merrymaking, and it strains the imagination to depart far from the dull, dead present of Fuenterrabia. Perchance of old there came hither knights and ladies, pricking o'er the plaine, perchance here was dancing and wassail. We close our eyes and would fain image the scene. We banish the ruined walls, the sunlight creeping among the ivy. We see the sheen of cloth of gold and the gleam of greaves and breastplates. We catch the tale of battle, the passing of the loving-cup, the stately treading of slow Spanish measures. We hear,—we hear,—what is it that we hear?—the melodious sound of woman's soft voice, gently whispering: "Five sous each for the party, monsieur."

And as we awake and pay and depart, we turn and see again the disillusionizing legend:

CHAPTER VII.

AN ERA IN TWILIGHT.

"*Pour faire comprendre le caractère d'un peuple, je conterais trente anecdotes et je supprimerais toutes les théories philosophiques sur le sujet,*"
—STENDHAL.

Returning to Hendaye, a train takes us again to Bayonne, connecting there for Orthez and Pau. The ride to Bayonne needs an hour or less, and from thence to Orthez calls for two. It is not many decades since much of this journey had to be made by the diligence. Railways and highways have pushed rapidly toward the Pyrenees. When in the approaching fortnight we shall come to traverse the Route Thermale, the great carriage-way along the chain, we shall see modern road-making in its perfection; and the rail will keep anxious watch, over the road, running parallel along the distant plain and reaching helpful arms up the valleys to uphold it.

Toward Pau especially, the railroads converge. That city, a social capital for centuries, is a social capital still, and its winter influx of invalids and pleasure-seekers stimulates every facility of approach. Then, too, it lies on the way crossing southern France from the Bidassoa to the Rhone, and no line linking these rivers could omit from its chain the Gave de Pau.

From Bayonne, the train at first traverses an edge of a singular region. It is a part of the *Landes*. This great savanna, which flattens the entire space from Bordeaux to Bayonne, was crossed in coming southward from Bordeaux, and now as we strike eastward and inland we but briefly skirt its southerly portion. A sandy, marshy waste, infertile, unhealthful and poor, it lies in utter contrast with the fields and slopes of neighboring provinces. It is anomalous, incongruous,—
"A bare strand
Of hillocks heaped with ever-shifting sand,
Matted with thistles and amphibious weeds,
Such as from earth's embrace the salt ooze breeds."
Its inhabitants are meagre and stunted; it scants them both in food and drink. Its miserliness is deep-set: artesian wells sunk a thousand feet through its dull grey sands bring up only a brackish yellow water; a precarious rye and barley grow grudgingly.

The low stretches of furze and heath and fern are fringed only by mournful horizons of pines or broken by long files of gashed and wounded firs. This extensive tree-growth, however, which is comparatively recent, has at least lessened one terror of the Landes: sand-storms and snow-storms, which once swept across the wastes, have been shorn of their strength. Honor for this is due almost alone to one man, a M. Brémontier. Before his time, forest-making had here been deemed impossible; pine seeds planted in the lax hold of these sands had hitherto been unable even to take root, against the unbroken sweep of the winds. M. Brémontier, after many experiments, conceived the idea of planting with the pine seeds the seeds of the common broom, whose hardy tuft should protect the tiny sapling until it could stand by itself. The result surpassed hope; pine forests, protecting in their turn, have sprung up and endured throughout the Landes; they have broken forever the power of the wind-storms; and their pitch and timber are even a source of some riches to the Department.

Still it remains a region unsmiling and melancholy. A monochrome of sand, darkened everywhere by long blotches of sickly undergrowth or the dull reach of the pines; here and there are cork-trees and alders. The sheen of some slow lagoon is caught in the distance. There is a charm in the very charmlessness of the scene, as in some sombre-toned etching.

One striking specialty this district has, however; and from the train windows we watch closely for a specimen. This is the shepherd on stilts, the *Xicanque*, immortalized by Rosa Bonheur and mentioned by many travelers. He is peculiar to this region; perched on these wooden supports, at a perilous height above the ground, he stalks gravely over the landscape, enabled to behold a horizon of triple range and to outstride the fleetest of his vagrant flock. When so inclined, he is quite able, it is said, to skillfully execute a *pas seul* or even a jig,—with every appropriate flourish of his timber limbs and with surprising grace and *abandon*. His stilts are strapped to the thigh, not the knee, for greater freedom, and he mounts from his cabin-roof in the early morning and lives in the air throughout the day. A third stilt forms a seat, and makes of his silhouette a ludicrous and majestic tripod. This genius's chief amusement is startlingly domestic: it is knitting stockings; and engaged in this peaceful art he sits with dignity and whiles away the hours. How he manoeuvres when he accidentally drops a needle, I have not been able to learn.

A dignitary of Bordeaux arranged a fête and procession in these Landes on one occasion; triumphal arches were erected, hung with flowers and garlands; and the feature of the parade was a sedate platoon of these heron-like shepherds engaged for the occasion, dressed in skins, decked with white hoods and mantles, preceded by a band of music, and stalking by fours imposingly down the line of march.

II.

We are nearing the Pyrenees now, and entering the ancient and famous province of Béarn, once a noted centre of mediæval chivalry. Beam did not become part of France until almost modern times. For seven hundred years preceding, its successive rulers held their brilliant court unfettered and unpledged. "Ours," declared its barons and prelates in assembly, "is a free country, which owes neither homage nor servitude to any one." The life of the province was its own, separated entirely from that of the kingdom. It had its own succession, its own wars and feuds, its own love of country. It has a national history in miniature. "If I have excused myself from bearing arms upon either side," said one of its rulers, replying to the royal remonstrances, "I have, as I think, good reasons for it: the wars between England and France no way concern me, for I hold my country of Béarn from God, my sword and by inheritance. I have not therefore any cause to enter into the service or incur the hatred of either of these kings."

There is a pleasant old legend which touches the true note of Béarn. Toward the year 1200, three of its rulers, in turn misgoverning, were in turn deposed by the barons. The heirs next in line were the infant twins of one William de Moncade. "It was agreed," as Miss Costello relates it; "that one of these should fill the vacant seat of sovereignty of Béarn, and two of the *prudhommes* were deputed to visit their father with the proposition. On their arrival at his castle, the sages found the children asleep, and observed with attention their infant demeanor. Both were beautiful, strong and healthy; and it was a difficult matter to make an election between two such attractive and innocent creatures. They were extremely alike, and neither could be pronounced superior to the other; the *prudhommes* were strangely puzzled, for they had been so often deceived that they felt it to be most important that they should not err this time. As they hung in admiration over the sleeping babes, one of them remarked a circumstance that at once decided their prefer-ence and put an end to their vacillation: one of the little heroes held his hand tightly closed; the tiny, mottled palm of the other was wide open as it lay upon his snowy breast. 'He will be a liberal and bold knight,' said one of the Béarnais, 'and will best suit us as a head.' This infant was accordingly chosen, given up by his parents to the wise men, and carried off in triumph to be educated among his future subjects. The event proved their sagacity, and the object of their choice lived to give them good laws and prosperity."

III.

The past of Béarn, like an ellipse, curves around two foci. One is the town of Orthez, the other, the later city of Pau. The hero, the central figure, of one is Gaston Phoebus, Count of Foix; that of the other, Henry of Navarre.

These are the two great names of Béarn. Each lights up a distinctive epoch,—Gaston, the fourteenth century, Henry, the sixteenth.

In two hours after leaving Bayonne, the train has come to Orthez. There is little splendor in the old town as one views it to-day; yet in Gaston's time it was the capital of Béarn, successor of the yet older Morlaäs, and a centre for knights and squires and men-at-arms, a magnet for pilgrims and noble visitors from other countries, attracted by its fame. There were jousts, tourneys, hunts, banquets. The now broken walls of the old Castle of Moncade on the hill have sheltered more glittering merrymakings than those of Kenilworth or Fuenterrabia. But decay never surrenders an advantage once gained; the castle is dying now; dull modern commonplace has enfolded the once bright town below; and this Orthez is to-day at best but a lounging-place for the pessimist. We shall love better Pau, its rival and successor, still buoyant and prospering, rising not falling. "Good men study and wise men describe," avers Ruskin, in a more than half-truth, "only the growth and standing of things,—not their decay. Dissolution and putrescence are alike common and unclean . in State or organism."

For all that, Orthez and its traditions are too significant to hasten by. Nowhere is the picture of mediæval life more strongly illuminated; in no spot shall we more fitly pause to summon back the inner past of the Pyrenees we are approaching. But we would linger over it only as it was in its best days, and leave to others the drearier story of its decadence.

It is Froissart, the old historian and traveler, genial, story-loving Sir John, who tells us most about Orthez and Gaston. Orthez, as the capital of Béarn, was in his time, at its meridian, (it was afterward supplanted by Pau,) and Gaston Phoebus, known as the Count de Foix, was lord both of Beam and of the neighboring county of Foix. It was precisely five hundred years ago, come next St. Catherine's Day, that the old chronicler alighted from his horse here in Orthez. He was come on a visit to the count, well introduced, and seeking further material for his easy-going history of the times; knowing that foreign knights assembled in Orthez from all countries, and that there were few spots more alive to the sound of the world's doings or better informed in the varying gossip of wars and court-craft.

Froissart liked to write, "and it was very tiresome," he remarks, "to me to be idle, for I well know that when the time shall come when I shall be dead and rotten, this grand and noble history will be in much fashion and all noble and valiant persons will take pleasure in it and gain from it augmentation of profit." So, seeking fresh chapters, he had come to Orthez, where he was at once handsomely received by Count Gaston at this Castle of Moncade. Here he remained through the winter, affable and inquiring and observant, adding many pages to his history,—which, his host assured him, would in times to come be more sought after than any other; "'because,' added he, 'my fair sir, more gallant deeds of arms have been performed within these last fifty years, and more wonderful things have happened, than for three hundred years before. '"

"The style of Froissart," says Taine, who has so marvelously divined the inner spirit of those times, "artless as it is, deceives us. We think we are listening to the pretty garrulousness of a child at play; beneath this prattle we must distinguish the rude voice of the combatants, bear-hunters and hunters of men too, and the broad, coarse hospitality of feudal manners. At midnight the Count of Foix came to supper in the great hall. 'Before him went twelve lighted torches, borne by twelve valets; and the same twelve torches were held before his table and gave much light unto the hall, which was full of knights and squires; and always there were plenty of tables laid out for any person who chose to sup.' It must have been an astonishing sight to see those furrowed faces and powerful frames, with their furred robes and their justicoats streaked under the wavering flashes of the torches." And one of Froissart's characteristic anecdotes is cited, which merits giving even more in full: "On Christmas Day, when the Count de Foix was celebrating the feast with numbers of knights and squires, as is customary, the weather was piercing cold, and the count had dined, with many lords, in the hall. After dinner he rose and went into a gallery, which has a large staircase of twenty-four steps: in this gallery is a chimney where there is a fire kept when the count inhabits it, otherwise not; and the fire is never great, for he does not like it: it is not for want of blocks of wood, for Béarn is covered with wood in plenty to warm him if he had chosen it, but he has accustomed himself to a small fire. When in the gallery, he thought the fire too small, for it was freezing and the weather very sharp, and said to the knights around him: 'Here is but a small fire for this weather.' The Bourg d'Espaign instantly ran down stairs; for from the windows of the gallery, which looked into the court, he had seen a number of asses laden with billets of wood for the use of the house; and seizing the largest of these asses with his load, threw him over his shoulders and carried him up stairs, pushing through the crowd of knights and squires who were around the chimney, and flung ass and load with his feet upward on the dogs of the hearth, to the

delight of the count and the astonishment of all."

IV.

Gaston himself was a type of the time. He had its virtues and its vices, both magnified. Hence, hearing an eye-witness draw his character for us is to gain a direct if but partial insight into the character of his era. Froissart's moral perspective is often curiously blurred, and in the light of many of his anecdotes about the count his eulogium perhaps needs qualification: "Count Gaston Phoebus de Foix, of whom I am now speaking, was at that time fifty-nine years old; and I must say that although I have seen very many knights, kings, princes and others, I have never seen any so handsome, either in the form of his limbs and shape, or in countenance, which was fair and ruddy, with grey and amorous eyes that gave delight whenever he chose to express affection. He was so perfectly formed, one could not praise him too much. He loved earnestly the things he ought to love, and hated those which it was becoming him so to hate. He was a prudent knight, full of enterprise and wisdom. He had never any men of abandoned character with him, reigned prudently, and was constant in his devotions. There were regular nocturnals from the Psalter, prayers, from the rituals to the Virgin, to the Holy Ghost, and from the burial service. He had every day distributed as alms at his gate five florins in small coin to all comers. He was liberal and courteous in his gifts; and well knew how to take when it was proper and to give back where he had confidence."

There is an obverse to the medallion. "The Count de Foix was very cruel to any person who incurred his indignation, never sparing them, however high their rank, but ordering them to be thrown over the walls, or confined on bread and water during his pleasure; and such as ventured to speak for their deliverance ran risks of similar treatment. It is a well-known fact that he confined in a deep dungeon his cousin-german, the Viscount de Châteaubon, during eight days; and he would not give him

his liberty until he had paid down forty thousand francs."

And then in the very chapter with his eulogy, Sir John goes on to relate the count's brutal killing of his own son in a fit of rage and suspicion, and torturing fifteen retainers as possible accomplices of the innocent lad; and elsewhere tells of his stabbing his half-brother and letting him die in a dungeon of the tower, for refusing the surrender of a fortress. This was the other side of Gaston's character, and a side quite as representative. It was all in line with the time. His reign was turbulent, magnificent, cruel, devout,—everything by extremes. The man is characteristic of the mode, and Orthez in this summarizes much of the life of the France of the Middle Ages.

V.

These old annalists scarcely pause to censure this spirit of crime, this hideous quickness to black deeds. They view it as a regrettable failing, perhaps, and glowingly point to the doer's lavish religiousness in return. Absolution covers a multitude of sins. To a generous son of the Church much might be forgiven. "Among the solemnities which the Count de Foix observes on high festivals," records his visitor, "he most magnificently keeps the feast of St. Nicholas, as I learnt from a squire of his household the third day after my arrival at Orthès. He holds this feast more splendidly than that of Easter, and has a most magnificent court, as I myself noticed, being present on that day. The whole clergy of the town of Orthès, with all its inhabitants, walk in procession to seek the count at the castle, who on foot returns with them to the church of St. Nicholas, where is sung the psalm *Benedictus Dominus, Deus meus, qui docet manus meas ad proelium et digitos meos ad bellum*, from the Psalter of David, which, when finished, recommences, as is done in the chapels of the pope or king of France on Christmas or Easter Days; for there were plenty of choristers. The Bishop of Pamiers sang the mass for the day; and I there heard organs play as melodiously as I have ever heard in any place. To speak briefly and truly, the Count de Foix was perfect in person and in mind; and no contemporary prince could be compared with him for sense, honor or liberality."

VI.

As to liberality, these robber barons were able to afford it. Mention is incidentally made in conversation of Count Gaston's store of florins in his Castle of Moncade at Orthez. Froissart instantly pricks up his ears:

"'Sir,' said I to the knight, 'has he a great quantity of them?'

"'By my faith,' replied he, 'the Count de Foix has at this moment a hundred thousand, thirty times told; and there is not a year but he gives away sixty thousand; for a more liberal lord in making presents does not exist.'"

We can see the good Sir John's eyes glistening:

"'Ha, ha, holy Mary!' cried I, 'to what purpose does he keep so large a sum? Where does it come from? Are his revenues so great to supply him with it? To whom does he make these gifts? I should like to know this if you please.'

"He answered: 'To strangers, to knights and squires who travel through his country, to heralds, minstrels, to all who converse with him; none leave him without a present, for he would be angered should any one refuse it.'"

With such sums at disposal, Gaston might well indulge his passion for the chase and keep sixteen hundred hounds. His hospitality too was unbounded. When the Duke of Bourbon made a three-days' visit to Orthez, he was "magnificently entertained with dinners and suppers. The Count de Foix showed him good part of his state, which would recommend him to such a person as the Duke of Bourbon. On the fourth day, he took his leave and departed. The count made many presents to the knights and squires attached to the duke, and to such an extent that I was told this visit of the Duke of Bourbon cost him ten thousand francs. Such knights and squires as returned through Foix and waited on the count were well received by him and received magnificent presents. I was told

that this expedition, including the going to Castile and return, cost the Count de Foix, by his liberalities, upwards of forty thousand francs."

The King of France was entertained by Gaston at a dazzling banquet where no less than two hundred and fifty dishes covered the tables. But a succeeding Gaston outdid this in a lavish dinner, likewise to visiting royalty, of which a faithful record has come down to us from old documents. There were twelve wide tables, each seven yards long. At the first, the count presiding, were seated the king and queen and the princes of the blood, at the others foreign knights and lords according to their rank and dignity. There were served seven elaborate courses, each course requiring one hundred and forty plates of silver. There were seven sorts of soup, then patties of capon, and the ham of the wild boar; then partridge, pheasant, peacock, bittern, heron, bustard, gosling, woodcock and swan. This was the third course, concluding with antelope and wild horse. An *entremet* or spectacle followed, and then a course of small birds and game, this served on gold instead of silver. Next appeared tarts and cakes and intricate pastries, and later, after another spectacle, comfits and great moulds of conserves in fanciful and curious forms,—the whole liberally helped down with varied wines, and joyously protracted with music, dancing and tableaux.

VII.

Gaston Phoebus died suddenly as he had lived violently. He was hunting near Orthez, three years after Froissart's visit, and to ward evening stopped at a country inn at Rion to sup. Within, the room was "strewed with rushes and green leaves; the walls were hung with boughs newly cut for perfume and coolness, as the weather was marvelously hot even for the month of August. He had no sooner entered this room than he said: 'These greens are very agreeable to me, for the day has been desperately hot.' When seated, he conversed with Sir Espaign du Lyon on the dogs that had best hunted; during which con-

versation his son Sir Evan and Sir Peter Cabestan entered the apartment, as the table had been there spread." He called for water to wash, and two squires advanced; a knight, the Bourg d'Espaign, (the hero of the Christmas Day exploit,) took the silver basin and another knight the napkin. "The count rose from his seat and stretched out his hands to wash; but no sooner had his fingers, which were handsome and long, touched the cold water, than he changed color, from an oppression at his heart, and his legs failing him, fell back on his seat, exclaiming, 'I am a dead man: Lord God, have mercy on me!'"

It is a significant comment on the period, that amid the commotion at the inn the first thought was of foul play. "The two squires who had brought water to wash in the basin said, to free themselves from any charge of having poisoned him: 'Here is the water; we have already drank of it, and will now again in your presence,' which they did, to the satisfaction of all. They put into his mouth bread and water and spices, with other comforting things, but to no purpose, for in less than half an hour he was dead, having surrendered his soul very quietly. God, out of his grace, was merciful to him."

He was entombed before the altar in the little church at Orthez, with imposing obsequies. No epitaph remains, but this of a preceding Gaston, buried in the same church, deserves note for its curious, jingling Latin rhyme:

"Continet hæc fossa Gastonis principis ossa,
Nobilis ac humilis aliis, pulvis sibi vilis,
Subjectis parcens, hastes pro viribus arcens.
Da veniam, Christe, flos militiæ fuit isle,
Et virtute precum, confer sibi gaudia tecum,
Gastonis nomen gratum fert auribus omen,
Mulcet prolatum, dulcescis sæpe relatum,"

Two hundred years afterward, in the tumult of Protestant iconoclasm, Gaston Phoebus's tomb was broken open, its débris sold, piece by piece, and Montgomery's Huguenots derisively kicked the august skull about the streets of Orthez and used it for a bowling-ball:

"They hopped among the weeds and stones,

And played at skittles with his bones."

VIII.

There are a few gleams of humor among these grim recounts. It was always tinged with the sardonic. Pitard, moralist and pedant, staying at the Béarnais court, fell into a dispute with a poet, Théophile:

"''T is a pity,' sneered Pitard, finally, 'that, having so much spirit, you know so little!'

"''T is a pity,' retorted Théophile, 'that, knowing so much, you have so little spirit!'"

Often the jests take a religious turn. The chaplain of one of the counts of Orthez, defending his own unpriestly fondness for hunting, asserted that the ten horns of the stag (*cerf*) stood for the Decalogue; and that the stag was to be as ardently followed as the sovereign pontiff, the latter being himself *le cerf des cerfs,—servus servorum.*

If a husband were seriously rasped by his wife, or their tempers could not agree, he was wont to retire her to a convent. "He did not send her to the devil," remarks a sly annalist, "but he gave her to the Lord."

And read this whimsical epitaph on an organist of the cathedral at Lescar, a bishopric near Orthez. He died in the fifteenth century:

"As you pass, pray God for his soul, that having assisted in the music of this world, he may be received forever among the blessed to assist in the celestial music. Amen."

Orthez is known to our century as the scene of a spiteful battle between Wellington and Soult, engaging eighty thousand men, and ending in the victory of the former and the rout of the French. But the town is so deeply sunk in the past that its kinship with modern events seems almost cause for resentment; and we will leave it as it is, with its older glories and memories thickly crusted upon it.

CHAPTER VIII.

"THE LITTLE PARIS OF THE SOUTH."

When the Count of Foix made a hunting trip to his *château mignon* on the present site of Pau, he found it a goodly journey. There were quagmires and waste land to pass, and the visit and return were not to be made in a sun's shining. More greatly than avenging spirits from his dungeons the spirit of steam would affright him to-day, as it goes roaring over the levels in a hundred minutes to the same destination.

From Orthez, it is less than two hours by rail, and we are at last in Pau. The *Midi* line is accurately on time. These French railroads are operated by the State; they are not afflicted with parallel lines and bitter competition; they have no occasion, as our roads have, to advertise a faster schedule than can possibly be carried out. Consequently their time-tables aim to state the exact truth, and the roads can and do live up to it.

It is late in the evening when we arrive, and we seek no impressions. A comfortable omnibus winds us up an infinity of turns, through an apparent infinity of streets, and we are at the Hotel Gassion.

It is impossible to be entirely impressionless, even for travelers at ten at night. It is the hotel itself which makes the dent. Our vague misgivings as to the "dismal roadside inns" awaiting our tour have already been arrested at Biarritz and San Sebastian. They are sent into exile from Pau. The Hotel Gassion, whose name honors a stout old Béarnais warrior, is fitly a palace. It cost four hundred thousand dollars. A cushioned elevator lifts us smoothly upward to our rooms, which prove high-ceiled and unusually large and have dressing-rooms attached. The dark walls accord with a deep mossy carpet. The furnishings are massive in mahogany, polished and carved: a wardrobe, dressing-cases, a writing-desk; a sofa-couch, made inaccessible, as everywhere in Europe, by the barrier of a huge round table; padded arm-chairs, upholstered in silk damask; and, acme of prevision, a praying-chair. The beds seem beds of state, covered and canopied with some satiny material; and both silk and lace curtains part before the windows, showing separate balconies in the night outside. The dining-hall and the parlors, which we do not seek until the morning, prove to be on an equally expensive scale; paintings of the Pyrenees hang in the wide halls; and there is a conservatory and winter-garden opening on the terrace. The building is of grey stone, with corner towers and turrets and an imposing elevation, and has less the look of a hotel than of a royal *Residenz*.

Our estimates of the standards of comfort in the Pyrenees are perceptibly heightened by the evening's impressions alone, as we discuss our surroundings and the Apollinaris. With Pau thus rivaling Lucerne, we grow more confident for Eaux-Bonnes and Cauterets, Luchon and Bigorre. And as, from the balcony, we look in vain across the murky night to see the snow-peaks which we know are facing us, we agree that here at the good Hotel Gassion we could luxuriously outstay the lengthiest storm to view them.

II.

We are glad when daylight comes, as boys are on Christmas morning. The present we are eager for is the sight of the Pyrenees snow-peaks. The sun is shining, the sky clear. Even coffee and rolls seem time-wasters, and we hasten out to the terrace.

Yes, the Pyrenees are before us. There stretches the range, its relief walling the southern horizon from west to the farthest east, the line of snow-tusks sharp and white in the sunshine. They are distant yet, but they stand as giants, parting two kingdoms. Austere and still, they face us, as they have faced this spot since that stormy Eocene morning when they sprang like the dragon's white teeth from the earth.

The view is a far-reaching one. The eye sweeps the broadside of the entire west-central chain,—a full seventy miles from right to left. The view might recall, as the greater recalls the less, the winter summits of the Adirondacks, seen from the St. Regis mountain. It has been more equally paired with the line of the distant Alps seen from the platform at Berne. I may parallel it, too, again in Switzerland, with the view of the Valais peaks which bursts on one when, winding upward past the Daubensee and its desolation, he comes out suddenly upon the brink of the great wall of the Gemmi. But here there is a warmth in the view beyond that of Switzerland. Some one has said that "snow is regarded as the type of purity not because it is cold but because it is spotless." This distant snow-line is spotless, but to the eye at least it is not cold.

Here as there, the separate peaks have their separate personality. It is not a blur of nameless tips. Two especially arrest attention, south and southeast, for they rise head and shoulders above their neighbors. Each bears the name of the *Pic du Midi*. That opposite us, dominating the valley of Ossau, is the *Pic du Midi d'Ossau*. It is ice-capped and jagged,—

"A rocky pyramid,
Shooting abruptly from the dell
Its thunder-splintered pinnacle,"—
the Matterhorn of the Pyrenees. That on the left is the noted *Pic du Midi de Bigorre*, famed for the view from its top. Other prominent peaks are also pointed out. *Mont Perdu* and the *Vignemale*, two of the princes of the chain, are partly hidden by other summits, and are too distant to rule as they ought. The monarch *Maladetta*, the highest summit of the Pyrenees, is farther eastward still and cannot be seen from Pau.

It is a repaying prospect; a majestic salutation, preceding the nearer acquaintance to come. One thing we know instantly. There will be no lack of noble scenery in these mountains. We shall find wild views among their rocks and ice,—views, it must be, which shall dispute with many in the Alps.

This prospect from the terrace at Pau is a celebrated one. Icy peaks are not all that is seen. In front of them the ranges rise, still high from the plain, but smoothed and softened with the green of pines and turf. Between these and the Pau valley spread hidden leagues of rolling plains, swelling as they approach

us into minor ravelins of foothills known as the *coteaux*; and little poplar-edged streams, "creaming over the shallows," winding their way toward the valley just below us, are coming from the long slopes to join the hurrying Gave de Pau. Houses and hamlets are here and there, and the even streak of the railway; and over toward the coteaux we see the village of Jurançon, famed for its wines.

The terrace falls sheer away, a fifty-foot wall from where we stand, and at its base, as we lean over the parapet, we see houses and alleys and just beneath us a school-yard of shouting, frolicking children. We brighten their play with a few friendly sous, as one enlivens the Bernese bear-pit with carrots.

Behind us, the Hotel Gassion rises to cut off the streets beyond it; to the right, along the terrace a few hundred yards, stands a stout old building, square and firm, which we know at once for the castle of Henry of Navarre.

III.

"In most points of view," as Johnson observes, in his *Sketches in the South of France*, "we look down the valley and see on either side its mountain walls; or we are placed upon culminating points overtopping all the rest of the prospect; but here the view is across the depression and against the vast panorama, which opposes the eye at all quarters, and comprehends within it the whole of the picture. High up in the snow the very pebbles seem to lie so distinctly that, but for the space between, a boy might pick them up; lower down, from among the brown heather thin blue streaks stream aloft from some cottage chimney, winding along the brae-side till melted into air. We half expect to see some human figure traverse those white fields and mark the footprints he leaves behind, some shepherd with his dog crossing from valley to valley. Alas! it is twenty miles away, the pebbles are huge masses of projecting rock, precipices on which the snow cannot rest; yonder smoke is from the charcoal-burner's fire, which would take in a cottage for a mouthful of fuel, and a dozen

men piled on each other's shoulders might at this moment be swallowed up in these snow-beds and we never the wiser.

"With the warm sunlight upon it, and the pure, clear blue above, into which these great shapes are wedged like a divine mosaic, the scene looks so spotless and holy in its union with the heavens that one might fancy it a link between this earthliness and the purity above, 'the heaven-kissing hill' on which angels' feet alight. The great vision of marvelous John Bunyan seemed there realized, and we had found the Immanuel's Land and these were the Delectable Mountains. 'For,' said he, 'when the morning was up they bid him look South; so he did, and behold, at a great distance he saw a most pleasant mountainous country beautified with woods, vineyards, fruits of all sorts, flowers also; with springs and fountains very delectable to behold. It was common, too, for all the pilgrims, and from thence they might see the gates of the Celestial City.'"

IV.

At the other side of the hotel we are in Pau. There is not very much that is impressive in its general appearance. We go by a patch of park and through a mediocre street, and find ourselves in the public square,—the Carfax of the city. From this run east and south its two chief streets. All of the buildings are low and most of them dingy. We expected newer, higher, more Parisian effects. At the right of the square is the long, flat market-building, vocal, in and out, this early morning, with bustling hucksters superintending their stalls. The square itself is bright with the colors of overflowing flowers and fabrics and other idols of the market-place. Neat little heaps of fruit, apexed into "ball-piled pyramids," are guarded by characterful old women, alert and intent, whose heads, coifed with striped kerchiefs, nod a reward to the purchaser with a hearty "*Merci, monsieur!*"

Few of the streets in the town are well paved, and few of the villas seen in dri-

ving in the suburbs aid to raise the architectural average. Except for its palace-hotels, Pau seems to show little of artistic building enterprise.

This city, so popular with the English, is rarely spoken of in America. There, in fact, it is singularly little known. This is no truer of Pau than of the Pyrenees themselves; but even to Englishmen who may know as little as we of the latter, the former is familiar ground. Four thousand Britons winter here annually, besides French and other visitors, and Pau runs well in the hibernal race, even against Mentone and Nice. Its hotels alone would evidence this. Up to these, there are all grades of good accommodation,—the *pensions*, of good or better class; furnished apartments, or a flat to be rented by the season; whole villas to be leased or purchased, as the intending comer may prefer.

One can leave Paris or Marseilles by the evening express and be in Pau the next afternoon,—about the same length of time as required to reach St. Augustine from New York. This is certainly far from a formidable journey, and it is matter for surprise that the adventurous American does not oftener take it.

The favor of the spot, it owes to its climate. Something there is,—some meteorological idiosyncrasy in its location,—which guards its still, mild air, the winter through. Storms rage impotently down from the mountains or across the Landes; they cannot pass the charmed barrier of the coteaux. Winds are rare in Pau. Rain is not rare; but the atmosphere, even when damp, is not chilling, and the lines of rain fall soft and never aslant. There is a tradition of an old sea-captain who once made a brief stay here and who, as he took his daily walks, was noticed as constantly and restlessly whistling. He finally left in disgust, with the remark that there was not a capful of wind to be had in the place.

The winter colony takes full possession of the town. It passes thirty thousand inhabitants under the yoke, as Rome passed their forefathers the Aquitani. Pau in the season is a British oligarchy. Society fairly spins. There are titles, and there is money; there are drives, calls, card-parties; dances and dinners; clubs,—with front windows; theatres, a Casino, English schools, churches; tennis, polo, cricket; racing, coaching,—and, *Anglicissime*, a triweekly fox-hunt! For some years, too, the position of master of the hounds, a post of much social distinction in Pau, was held by a well-known American, so we are told,—a fact certainly hitherto unheralded to many of his countrymen.

Socially, there is a wide range of entertainment at Pau. What Johnson wrote of it thirty years ago is not materially inapplicable to-day: "One set, whom you may call the banqueteers, give solemn, stately dinners immediately before going to bed; another perform a hybrid entertainment, between the English tea-party, and the Continental soirée, where you may enjoy your Bohea and Souchong, play long small whist, and occasionally listen to ponderous harmonies solemnly performed. A third are the formal rout-givers, the white-kid-and-slipper, orchestra-and-programme, dance-and-sit-down-to-supper folks; so like home that it only requires Gunter's men to fancy oneself in Baker Street of olden times. Another is the delightful soirée *pur sang*, where everybody comes as a matter of course, and where everybody who does not sing, dances or plays, or is a phenomenon in charades, or writes charming impromptus, or talks like the last book, or can play at any known game from loto to chess, or knows all the gossip of the last six hours; and where everybody chats and laughs, and sends everybody else comfortably home in the best of humors just about the time that the great people are expecting the *coiffeur* to arrive."

Thus there is a stir in the Pyrenees the year around. In the winter, at Pau; in summer, at the twenty cures and centres among the mountains. The proprietor of a winter hotel here will own also

his summer hostelry at Bigorre or Cauterets. In the summer, it is the French and Spanish to whom he caters, for they have so far been the ones most appreciative both of the springs and the scenery of these mountains. And so, with the rise and dip of the seasons, the European element waxes as the English wanes, in a kind of solstitial see-saw. And the smiling landlord stands upon the pivot.

The clouds are closing in, after granting us that glittering panorama, and the morning grows dull and dark. We explore the book-stores, and finally find the old Library in the upper story of the market-building. Here two of us at least pass a long and contentful forenoon.

V.

In fierce Count Gaston's time, Béarn centred in Orthez, and Pau was but his hunting-box. Two hundred years later, Pau had become the focus, and Béarn and Foix not only, but French Navarre as well, were its united kingdom. Gaston's Castle of Moncade had aged into history,—

"Outworn, far and strange,
A transitory shame of long ago,"
and the hunting-box had grown in its turn to castle's stature.

The world had brightened during the two centuries. Constantinople had fallen and the Renaissance came. Luther had posted his theses on the Wittemberg church door and the Reformation took root. Men were older than when Froissart lived and wrote. And this active province of Béarn kept pace; it opened quickly to the new influences, was alive to the changing *zeitgeist*. There remained the chivalric still,—and a trace of the barbaric,—as with the outer world; in short, in its faults and fervor's, in its codes and standards, the sixteenth century is aptly summed up in Béarn-Navarre,—and Navarre in its famous Henry.

VI.

And so, on the following morning, we pass into the courtyard of his castle here at Pau with the feeling that in some sense we are evoking the shade of the era, not of the man. The feeling dies hard; but the robustious, business-like guide that herds us together with other comers, and shepherds us all briskly through the official round, goes very far toward killing it. There is little that one needs to remember of the successive rooms and halls; it is a confusion of polished floors, and vases, and tapestry, and porphyry tables, and the rest,— adorned and illumined by a voluble Gallic description. Later French kings have restored the old building, and stocked it with Paris furniture, and made it modern and comfortable. One is always divided in spirit over these restorations. The castle needed help painfully; it had been badly used by the Revolution; and it had been debased to a barrack by Napoleon's troops, who "stabled their steeds in the courts and made their drunken revelry resound in the chambers of Marguerite of Angoulême." Dismantled, half-roofless, its great halls, unsheltered and unsheltering, it was wasting fast under the elements into picturesque but irreparable ruin. And I suppose the pleasure of kings and the peace of utilitarians ought fairly to outweigh the disappointments of the touring impression-seeker.

In one apartment, however, we make a stand. The herd and its shepherd can pass along. This, he has told us, is the birthplace of Henry IV. The floor is polished like the rest, and the furniture has been in part renewed, but the room is the same which that alert baby first laughed upon. In the corner at the right is an antique bed of carved walnut, with four posts and a rich canopy. Around its side are cut in the wood an elaborate series of medallions, each a foot square, representing the heads of the kings of France. Across the apartment swings still a great tortoise-shell, which served the royal infant for a cradle,—saved afterward from the furies of the Revolution by the substitution of a false shell in its place.

In this room, Jeanne d'Albret sang a Béarnais song as the hero of Ivry was born, and so won the wager with her martial old father, the King of Navarre;

and the boy came into the world smiling and unafraid. And writers tell us how delighted the old king was, and how he took the infant into his arms, and rubbed its lips with a garlic clove, and tilted into its little mouth from a golden goblet some drops of the manly wine of Jurançon. When Queen Jeanne herself was born in this very castle, twenty-five years before, the Spaniards had sneered: "A miracle! the cow (of the arms of Béarn) has given birth to a ewe!" "My ewe," exclaimed the happy old father now, "has brought forth a lion! *Tu seras un vray Béarnais!*"

VII.

Henry's life was as martial and as merry as his grandfather sought to form it. He grew up on the coteaux in a hardy, fresh-air life, and at nineteen became King of Navarre,—the title including Béarn and Foix. Into this old room in the castle where we stand throng reminders of his career, its beginnings so closely twined with Pau. Independent still as under Gaston, the sovereigns of the stout little kingdom had lived friends but no subjects of the King of France; and the Court at Pau, always proud and autonomous as the Court at Paris, had become defiantly Protestant besides. And now if ever it had a sovereign after its own heart. Henry was kingly, but a king of the people. He had their spirit. His long, keen, grizzled face was alight with ready comradeship. "I want my poorest subject," he said, "to have a fowl for his pot on Sundays." He was a Béarnais from sole to crown,—in bravery and craft, tact and recklessness, in virtues, and—which pleased them as much—in vices. "He was plain of speech, rough in manner,—with a quaint jest alike for friend or foe; his hand upon his sword, his foot in the stirrup, his gun slung across his shoulder, the first in assault, the last in retreat. Irregular in his habits, eating at no stated times, but when hungry voraciously devouring everything that pleased him, especially fruit and oysters; negligent, not to say dirty, in his person, and smelling strong of garlic. A man who called a spade a spade, swore like a trooper, and

hated the parade of courts; was constant in friendship, promised anything freely, a boon companion, a storyteller, cynical in his careless epicureanism, and so profound a believer in the 'way of fate,' that reckless of the morrow he extracted all things from the passing hour."

Time had not jogged on so far, in journeying from Orthez to Pau, as to forget all his mediæval ways,—his promptings to strife and feuds, his liking for adventures. Henry had abundance of them, in his running fire against his neighbor-enemies, in his hot Protestant struggles against the Medicis, in his hotter fight for the throne of France. There are both meats and sweetmeats in his career,—strong deeds and knightly diversions. "These old wars are the most poetic in French history; they were made for pleasure rather than interest. It was a chase in which adventures, dangers, emotions were found, in which men lived in the sunlight, on horseback, amidst flashes of fire, and where the body as well as the soul had its enjoyment and its exercise. Henry carries it on as briskly as a dance, with a Gascon's fire and a soldier's ardor. This is no spectacle of great masses of well-disciplined men coming heavily into collision and falling by thousands on the field, according to the rules of good tactics. The king leaves Pau or Nérac with a little troop, picks up the neighboring garrisons on his way, scales a fortress, intercepts a body of arquebusiers as they pass, extricates himself pistol in hand from the midst of a hostile troop, and returns. They arrange their plan from day to day; nothing is done unless unexpectedly and by chance. Enterprises are strokes of fortune. To act, to dare, to enjoy, to expend force and trouble like a prodigal, to be given up to the present sensation, be forever urged by passions forever lively, support and search the extremes of all contrasts, that was the life of the sixteenth century."

Exciting incidents abound among Henry's dashing forays. He exposed himself to every risk he asked of his men, deaf even to their own entreaties that he should take more care of his life. More than once it was his personal leadership alone that carried the day. For example, there was a hostile city on the river Lot. Henry coveted it. Its garrison was strong; its governor scoffed: "a fig for the Huguenots!" Henry would brave defeat sooner than brook defiance. He marched to the town at once. "It was in the month of June," as Sully relates it in his *Memoirs,* "the weather extremely hot, with violent thunder but no rain. He ordered us to halt in a plantation of walnut trees, where a fountain of running water afforded us some refreshment;" and after a brief rest, he disposed his little army, and planned his attack:

"We had three gates to force; these we made haste to throw down with the petard, after which we made use of hatchets. The breaches were so low that the first who entered were obliged to creep through on their hands and feet. At the noise of the petard, forty men armed and about two hundred arquebusiers ran almost naked to dispute our entry; meantime the bells rung the alarm, to warn everybody to stand to their defence. In a moment, the houses were covered with soldiers, who threw large pieces of wood, tiles and stones upon us, with repeated cries of 'Charge, kill them!' We soon found that they were resolved to receive us boldly; it was necessary therefore at first to sustain an encounter, which lasted above a quarter of an hour and was very terrible. I was cast to the ground by a large stone that was cast out of a window; but by the assistance of the Sieur de la Bertichère and La Trape, my valet de chambre, I recovered, and resumed my post. All this time we advanced very little, for fresh platoons immediately succeeded those that fled before us; so that before we gained the great square, we had endured more than twelve battles. My cuisses being loosened, I was wounded in the left thigh. At last we got to the square, which we found barricaded, and with infinite labor we demolished those works, being all the time exposed to the continual discharge of the artillery, which the enemy had formed into a battery.

"The King of Navarre continued at the head of his troops during all these attacks; he had two pikes broke, and his armor was battered in several places by the fire and blows of the enemy. We had already performed enough to have gained a great victory; but so much remained to do that the battle seemed only to be just begun; the city being of large extent and filled with so great a number of soldiers that we in comparison of them were but a handful. At every cross-way we had a new combat to sustain, and every stone house we were obliged to storm; each inch of ground so well defended that the King of Navarre had occasion for all his men, and we had not a moment's leisure to take breath.

"It is hardly credible that we could endure this violent exercise for five whole days and nights, during which time not one of us durst quit his post for a single moment, take any nourishment but with his arms in his hand, or sleep except for a few moments leaning against the shops. Fatigue, faintness, the weight of our arms, and the excessive heat, joined to the pain of our wounds, deprived us of the little remainder of our strength; our feet, scorched with heat and bleeding in many places, gave us agonies impossible to be expressed.

"The citizens, who suffered none of these inconveniences and who became every minute more sensible of the smallness of our numbers, far from surrendering, thought of nothing but protracting the fight till the arrival of some succors, which they said were very near; they sent forth great cries, and animated each other by our obstinacy. Though their defence was weak, yet they did enough to oblige us to keep upon our guard, which completed our misfortunes. In this extremity the principal officers went to the king, and advised him to assemble as many men as he could about his person and open himself a retreat. They redoubled their instances at the report which was spread and which they found to be true, that the succors expected by the enemy were arrived at the bar and would be so soon in the city that he would have but just time to force the wall and secure himself a passage. But this brave prince, whose courage nothing was ever able

to suppress, turning toward them with a smiling countenance and air so intrepid as might have inspired courage into the most pusillanimous heart: ''Tis heaven,' said he, 'which dictates what I ought to do upon this occasion; remember then that my retreat out of this city, without having secured one also to my party, shall be the retreat of my soul from my body. My honor requires this of me; speak therefore to me of nothing but fighting, conquest or death.'"

There could be but one issue to such words. Henry fought till reinforcements came to him, and the town fell.

Anecdotes of Henry are in a very real sense anecdotes of Béarn. The one following, lines out two of the king's best qualities. He was besieging a strong city in Poitou. "We applied ourselves without ceasing to the trenches and undermining. The King of Navarre took inconceivable pains in this siege; he conducted the miners himself, after he had taken all the necessary precautions to hinder supplies from entering without; the bridges, avenues and all the roads that lead to the city were strictly guarded, as likewise great part of the country. The mining was so far advanced that we could hear the voices of the soldiers who guarded the parapets, within the lodgment of the miners. The King of Navarre was the first who perceived this; he spoke and made himself known to the besieged; who were so astonished at hearing him name himself from the bottom of these subterraneous places that they demanded leave to capitulate. The proposals were all made by this uncommon way; the articles were drawn up or rather dictated by the King of Navarre, whose word was known by the besieged to be so inviolable that they did not require a writing. They had no cause to repent of this confidence; the King of Navarre, charmed with a proceeding so noble, granted the garrison military honors and preserved the city from pillage."

VIII.

The great satisfaction in contemplating the career of Henry is in the fact that it succeeded. His ambitions, maturing in purpose, ended in result. The King of Navarre found himself at last the King of France.

The path had not been of roses. He had captured two hundred towns and fought in sixty battles on his way. He himself had strewed thorns for others as well. His wars spread suffering throughout France. His skirmishings, petty but many, add up to an appalling total of harm. Henry as a model of renounced ambition is a failure. Read what his Catholic enemies in Béarn said of him, in an address and appeal to the Catholics of France; as now first translated out of its Old French, it has an oddly Jeffersonian ring:

"Knowing long since, to our cost, the nature of the wolf who seeks to deceive and then devour you, we have deemed it duty to warn you of the character of the beast, (le naturel de la beste,) so that by our putting you on your guard he shall not have means to endamage you. Within twenty years he has summoned a round million of foreign mercenaries to pillage and rend your kingdom. He has sacked and demolished two thousand monasteries and twenty thousand (sic!) churches; he has wrecked no less than nine hundred hospitals; he has caused the death, by war and divers punishments, of nearly one million, six hundred thousand men. In the face of his assurances to the nobility in 1580 and of his reiterated protestations, he has put up our very priests at auction and sold them off to the highest bidder, in order that his Huguenots might have on whom to wreak at leisure their diabolic hatred. He thinks himself King of France; it is a malady common to the crack-brained to fancy themselves kings of the first realm they spy and to fashion them seigniories in the air. Beware trusting your fowls to this fox!"

Evidently the Béarnais hero had made some tolerably strong enemies in pursuing his ambitions. No less truly his ambitions had made some tolerably wide gaps in his ethics.

But the world pardons much to success. And this man had a certain high-mindedness in him which compels admiration. When the battle of Ivry was

commencing, "he remembered," relates Perefix, an old historian, "that the evening before the battle he had used some harsh expressions to Colonel Theodoric Schomberg, who had asked him for money, and told him in a passion that it was not acting like a man of honor to demand money when he came to take orders for fighting. He afterward went to him, when he was ranging his troops in order, and said: 'Colonel, we are now upon the point; perhaps I shall never go from this place; it is not just that I should deprive a brave gentleman as you are of your honor; I come therefore to declare that I know you to be an honest man and incapable of committing a base action.' Saying this, he embraced him with great affection."

He besieged Paris, but would not storm it. "I am like the true mother in the judgment of Solomon," was his famous declaration; "I would rather not have Paris at all than see it torn to pieces." "The Duke of Nemours sent all useless mouths out of Paris; the king's council opposed his granting them passage; but the king, being informed of the dreadful scarcity to which these miserable wretches were reduced, ordered that they should be allowed to pass. 'I am not surprised,' said he, 'that the Spaniards and the chiefs of the League have no compassion upon these poor people; they are only tyrants; as for me, I am their father and their king, and cannot hear the recital of their calamities without being pierced to my inmost soul and ardently desiring to bring them relief.'"

Take it good and bad, lion of ewe, the character of Jeanne's high son is crystallized in one saying of his: "I would give a whole finger to have a battle,—and two to have a general peace."

With delight Pau watched her merry monarch; backed his final claim to the throne of St. Louis, made on the death of the last of the Medici kings and traced back through nine generations; followed tensely his long contest for that high prize, his rivalry with the League and with Philip of Spain, his victories at Arques and Ivry, his coronation, and his wise reign as Henry the

Fourth of France. His fame was hers. The hour he died,—stabbed while in his state-carriage at Paris by the dagger of a fanatic,—"a tempest broke over the place of his birth, and lightning shivered to pieces the royal arms suspended over the gateway of the castle."

"Rubente
Dextera sacras jaculatas arces,
Terruit urbem"

IX.

A winter station such as Pau is a hub with many spokes. Excursions and drives are in all directions. Idle fashion enjoys its outlets to the air, and invalidism demands them. Each hamlet is a picnic resort. One has choice of time and space, from an hour's ramble in the park, to a day's long visit to the monster sight of the mountains, the Cirque of Gavarnie. The park, as we pass, deserves its hour's ramble. Its wide promenade, arched with great trees, is entered not far from the castle, and leads along the torrent of the Gave, whose source we are later to see in the snows around Gavarnie itself. It is the scene of the favorite constitutional of Pau,—a neutral ground for all social factions.

Four drives in particular point us each to its own quarter of the compass. One is long, with the watering places of Eaux Chaudes and Eaux Bonnes for its double destination. The others, nearer in distance, lead farther in event,—back through the centuries, ninety, fifty, thirty decades, in turn.

The first of these is to Morlaäs, the earliest capital of Béarn. The distance is seven miles. Though the road is flat and tame, the ride affords superb prospects of the line of the Pyrenees, and these culminate at the top of the hill just before descending to the village. Here the panorama is even finer than from Pau. Easterly ranges have come into the field. The sweep of the mountain barrier in sight is a full hundred miles, and the waste of intervening plains, no longer hidden by coteaux, increases the impression of distance without lessening that of height. The greater peaks rise now into better proportion. Mont Perdu and the Vignemale loom above their neighbors, and best of all is seen far away the crown at least of the great Maladetta.

You must enjoy Morlaäs wholly for its past. You cannot enjoy it for its present. It is a poor, dejected, straggling street, noticeable only for mud and stones and dun-coated hovels. It does not, like Fuenterrabia, retain the picturesqueness of its antiquity. There, it is the old town's to-day that carries us delightfully back into its yesterday. But at Morlaäs there is neither to-day nor yesterday.

For the prime of this place antedates old Fuenterrabia by many a hundred years. The latter may come to the former's estate as many centuries hence. Orthez is but in middle life, Pau a summer stripling, in the presence of this wreck of time. Poor Morlaäs! Thou hast seen thy long successor rise and reign and fall, succeeded in its turn by the brilliant capital that now sends hither its subjects to scoff at thy driveling old age.

To share the mood of this grey spot you must travel far back, down its dim retrospect. You must retrace long, successive eras, sensitive to the spirit of each as you pass. You must cross the sixteenth century, brightening into humanity yet still un-human,—the vivid, reckless King of Navarre its type. You must penetrate beyond the twilight where Count Gaston's armor flashes across from the brutal towers of Orthez, lawless and splendid; you must grope back farther into the gloom, four hundred years still, before you see the shadowy Morlaäs in its full stature, proud, powerful, rude, rich,—the capital of old Béarn.

Nine hundred years ago. Mohammed's name and power were still new. Charles Martel had just saved Europe from the Saracens. England had not been recreated by a Norman Conqueror. The Crusades were still undreamed of. Art, science, letters, were in custody in the East. These armed children ran riot,—passionate, intense, uncontrolled, loving fight and finery as the Trojans, or the Norse heroes of the Sagas.

A single fine portal of the original sanctuary is still to be seen. But of the old castle not a trace remains; only its name survives,—*la Hourquie*,—with its significant etymological story: *Horcæ,— furcæ,—- fourches patibulaires*,—the gibbet. For these viscounts of Morlaäs had recourse to a savage expedient to control the lawlessness of their day. They kept a gallows-tree erect before the castle gateway, a speaking symbol of vengeance, and there the blackened corpse, might hang until replaced, swinging in the winter wind. There was a mint here also, which stamped the metal of the little realm, and on the coins too appeared the device of the gibbet. There is a tradition that the executions took place only on market-days, and in the Pyrenees to this day the market-gathering is known as the *Hourquie*. Eleven miles west leads us four centuries forward again from Morlaäs. This is Lescar; with its ancient cathedral, the St. Denis of Béarn, the burial-place of generations of its rulers. Morlaäs has been deposed, and Orthez reigns in its stead,—with Lescar as primate. The gleam and glory of chivalry have grown with the years. Here was the seat of the church militant in its strongest manifestation. "The bishops of Lescar," writes Johnson, satirically, "are said to have been well suited to the times in which they lived; fighting when they could, and cursing when they could not. In the early history of the province, they are found lustily taking a part in the battles of the frontier country; and when peaceful times came, getting up a comfortable trade with the intrusive infidels they had so lately belabored. The reputation for wealth acquired by this astute community seems to have brought its troubles upon the enterprising diocesans, for tradition has it that in the eleventh century Viscount Dax laid sacrilegious hands upon their property. Whether he was too strong for the carnal weapon or spiritual

manifestations were deemed more appropriate to his particular case, history does not record, but certain it is that the rebellious noble, being deaf to expostulation, was excommunicated, and resenting that, was seized with a leprosy, of which he died. His successor, adopting the same line of policy as the deceased, was treated in the same way and with the same result. So that between the thunders of the church and the arms of the flesh, the Episcopality of Lescar waxed mightily, and its bishops took the position of premier barons in the province, sitting next to royalty in council and therein keeping to order all grumblers against their rights and privileges. If two of the venerable prelates themselves happened to disagree and logic failed them, then,—it being scarcely orthodox for the reverend men to fight the matter out personally,—they employed a couple of lusty varlets to settle the business for them, and upon the weakest shoulders fell all the consequent disadvantages; thus instituting a simple and expeditious method of cutting short disputes by which the ecclesiastical courts of the present day do not appear to have benefited."

Lescar was called the *ville septénaire*; for it had, it is said, seven churches, seven fountains, seven mills, seven woods, seven vineyards, seven gates, and seven towers on the ramparts. It is another senile hamlet now, and imagination must do all the work. Even the cathedral has been altered, and in its large, rather plain interior are few relics of its earlier state, few marks to tell of the after-despoiled tombs of Henri Quatre's ancestry. There is a satisfying legend about this sanctuary. One of the feudal rulers had a violent hatred for some neighboring seignior, and finally secured his assassination. His hatred was thereupon followed by a remorse equally violent,—these men were violent in good as in bad, which redeems much; and in atonement he rebuilt magnificently this cathedral, which was even then an old one, and added to it a monastery as well. And to complete the story of poetic expiation, the assassin he had employed became a penitent himself; was later appointed one of the monks by his penitent patron; and ended by rising to the reverend office of abbot itself.

Southeast from Pau lies our third landmark of the past,—Coarraze. It is a longer road and a dusty one, but a village will tell off each mile, the Gave de Pau brings encouraging messages along the way, and the far Pic du Midi de Bigorre keeps inspiringly in sight. Besides the commoner trees to be met in this and other directions from Pau, are occasional orange-trees, Spanish chestnuts, aloes, acacias, and here and there a magnolia; but this region is north of much tropical verdure, even now in July, and plain beech and oak play the principal parts. Coarraze can be reached by rail also, and preferably so when haste is an object, for it is thirteen miles by the highway, while the train covers the distance within the half-hour.

This spot too had its castle and its feudal barons, subject to the court at Orthez. A tower of the castle still remains. It is of Raymond, one of these barons, that Froissart tells the legend of the familiar spirit. This obliging bogey was wont to visit his host as he lay asleep, waking him to tell him what had happened during the day in distant countries. His mode of rousing his patron was unceremonious, not to say boisterous. In his first visit, he made a terrific tumult throughout the castle, pounded the doors and casements, broke the plates in the kitchen, appalled the sleeping servants, "knocking about everything he met with in the castle, as if determined to destroy all within it. On the following night the noises and rioting were renewed, but much louder than before; and there were such blows struck against the door and windows of the chamber of the knight that it seemed they would break them down."

The baron could no longer desist from leaping out of his bed, and proceeding to investigate matters; and in the end the bogey and he became fast friends. In fact, the former "took such an affection to the Lord de Corasse that he came often to see him in the night-time; and when he found him sleeping,

he pulled his pillow from under his head or made great noises at the door or windows; so that when the knight was awakened, he said, 'let me sleep.'

"'I will not,' replied he, 'until I have told thee some news.'

"The knight's lady was so much frightened, the hairs of her head stood on end and she hid herself under the bed-clothes.

"'Well,' said the knight, 'and what news hast thou brought me?'

"The spirit replied, 'I am come from England, Hungary or some other place, which I left yesterday, and such and such things have happened.'

"Thus did the Lord de Corasse know by means of this messenger all things that were passing in the different parts of the world;" and for years this invisible mediæval sprite kept his patron comfortably posted on all current events, in a ghostly adumbration of the modern newspaper press.

But Coarraze and its castle carry us on later than Froissart's days. Here young Prince Henry ran about in his hardy youth, and romped and played pranks on his future subjects. Nothing delighted him more in after life than to come back here and hunt up his old peasant playfellows, bashful and reluctant, and bewilder and charm them with his state and his *bonhomie*. Most of the old castle is gone now, destroyed by a storm and since replaced by a newer structure. The old baron's spirit-messenger or the "white lady" of the House of Navarre have only the single tower remaining, for their ghostly visits,— finding change over all save the far line of the Pyrenees glittering unearthly in the moonlight.

CHAPTER IX.

THE WARM WATERS AND THE PEAK OF THE SOUTH.

"And we who love this land call it a *paradis terrestre*, because life is fair in its happy sunshine,—it is beautiful, it is plentiful, it is at peace."—*The Sun Maid.*

It is a nineteenth-century sun that wakes

us, after all, each morning, through the Gassion's broad windows. We can reconjure foregoing eras, but we do not have to live in them. The hat has outlawed the helmet; the clear call of the locomotive is unmistakably modern. Throughout Pau, in its life, its people, its social rubrics; in its streets, shops, hotels,—the thought is for the present age exclusively. The past is appraised chiefly at what it can do for the present. Business and society pursuits are not perceptibly saddened by memories of the bear-hunt at Rion or the dagger of Ravaillac.

And thus we come into the instant year once more, as we take the mid-morning train from Pau. We point straight for the mountains. We are on the way to Eaux Chaudes and Eaux Bonnes, before mentioned as a fourth excursion from Pau; but we go not as an excursion merely, for they lie directly in our farther route. These resorts, the repute of whose springs we hear in advance, are south from Pau about twenty-eight miles; twenty-five are now covered by the new railway, and the remaining three are done by the diligence or by breack,—for the latter of which, we telegraph.

It is a brief journey by the rail. The longer post-road no longer controls the travel. The train hastens on, by the coteaux, past maize-fields and meadows, through odds and ends of villages, into valleys more irregular, and among hills higher and steeper. Of Bielle, a village where it halts for a moment, there is a well-turned story told against Henry IV. It is one of the few cases where he was at a loss for a retort. He admired the four marble columns in the church, and asked for them; a kingly asking is usually equivalent to a command. But the inhabitants made reply both dexterous and firm, and it proved unanswerable. "Our hearts and our possessions are yours," they said; "do with them as you will. But as to the columns, those belong to God; we are bound for their custody, and you will have to arrange that with Him!"

When the train reaches its terminus at Laruns, we are fairly among the highlands. Rising wedge-shaped beyond the town, dividing all progress, is a mountain,—not a hill. To the left and right of it pass the roads we are in turn to follow. On the left, two miles beyond the fork or three from the railway's end, will be found Eaux Bonnes; on the right, at the same distance, is its lesser equal, Eaux Chaudes, our first objective point.

In the distant direction of the former rises the snowy *Pic de Ger,* nearly nine thousand feet in height and conspicuous from where we stand at the station platform. Still leftward, east of the hills, is a notch in the mountains; through it, we are told, pierces the Route Thermale,—the great carriage-road on to Cauterets and Bigorre, which we are to take after visiting the Eaux.

Here at the Laruns station, we find our breack awaiting us,—a peer of the peerless Biarritz equipage. It has been sent down from Eaux Bonnes to meet us. Trunk and baggage are stowed away, and we are driven up the straight, sloping road from the station into the village of Laruns itself, where a stop is to be made for lunch.

The appearances are not prepossessing. Laruns is a small village centring about a large square. It looks unpromising, and one of its most unpromising buildings proves to be the "hotel,"—a low, dingy, stone building set in among its mates. At this the breack draws up. The splendor of the Gassion seems in the impossible past. The expectant landlady urges us within; her face beams pleasantly; her appearance promises at least more than does her environment. One by one and very doubtfully, we enter a dark, narrow doorway; pass along a dark, harrow hall, walled and floored with stone; catch a passing vista of a kitchen, a white-jacketed and white-capped cook, and a vast amount of steam and crackle and splutter near the stove; and going up the curving stairs are led into a neat little front dining-room overlooking the square. The carpet is of unpainted pine; so are the table and chairs; but both are clean, and this fact cheers. With misgivings we ask for a lunch for seven; without misgivings it is promptly promised, and the beam-

ing hostess hurries to the depths below. Whether her quest shall bring us chill or further cheer, we do not seek to guess.

We canvass the situation and idly look out on the square before us. The low houses edging it are of stone, faced with a whity-grey, and have a sleepy, lack-lustre air about them, even under the sun's rays. Women are grouped around the old marble fountain near the centre,—one drawing water, several washing and beating white linen. There are barnyard fowls in plenty, bobbing their preoccupied heads as they search among the cobbles. In the foreground stands the temporarily dismantled breack, begirt with awed urchins and venerable Common Councilmen. Behind all rise the mountains. There is a pleasing effect of unsophisticated dullness about it all, that seems queerly out of place in a rising railroad terminus.

But a bright-faced, rosy little girl bustles in presently and proceeds to set the table. She has an unconscious air of confidence in the doings of the chef below,—this fact cheers; and the cloth is indubitably clean,—this also cheers. We take heart. Napkins and plates appear, white as the cloth; knives, forks, glasses, rapidly follow, seats are placed, we gather around, and the old lady herself comes triumphantly in, with a huge, shapely omelet, silky and hot,—and lo, our three cheers swell into a tiger!

Well,—we shall always recall the zest of that lunch. It was perfection. The cuisine of the Gassion was more refined but not more whole-souled. The trout vie with the omelet; the mutton outdoes the trout. Course after course comes up as by magic from that dark kitchen,—*petits pois,* a toothsome filet, mushrooms, pickled goose, tartlets, cheese, fruit,—and each a fresh revelation of a Pyrenean chef's capabilities. Our doubtings vanish with the déjeûner, and we exchange solemn vows never hereafter to prejudge a Gascon boniface by his inn.

II.

Our road forth from Laruns brings us soon to the base of the blockading mountain, the *Gourzy.* There it divides,

and taking the right-hand branch, the breack strikes at once into the narrow ascending valley which leads southeast to Eaux Chaudes. Below, a fussy torrent splashes impetuously to meet the incomers. The driver has pointed out to me an older and now disused wagon-way, short and steep, over the hill at the right; it is tempting for pedestrianizing, and while the breack is pulled slowly around its foot by a broad, easy road, I climb by it for some twenty minutes, gain the crest of the ridge, and passing through a windy, rock-walled cut, come out on the other curve of the valley. Here the scene has become wholly mountainous. Grass and box cling to all the slopes; pines and spruces shoot upward wherever they have won footholds. They are not great peaks that we see yet, nor anything above the snow level; but the mountains in view, with their faces of rock, their massive flanks of green, are imposing notwithstanding. Far below, the breack has just come in sight, its forward route meeting mine some distance ahead.

Close at the side of the path stands a tiny roadside oratory. On the walls of this little shrine, which (or its predecessor) has stood here for three hundred years, one might formerly read in stilted French the following astonishing inscription, ignoble witness to human platitude, as M. Joanne calls it:

"Arrest thee, passer-by! admire a thing thou seest not, and attend to hear what it is thou shouldst admire: we are but rocks and yet we speak. Nature gave us being, but it was the Princess Catherine gave us tongues. What thou now readest we have seen her read; what she has said we have listened to; her soul we have upborne. Are we not blessed, passer-by? having no eyes, we yet have seen her! Yet blessed thou too, in having seen her not; for we rocks were lifeless and the sight transformed us into life; but as for thee, traveler, thy transformation would have been into lifeless rock!"

As our routes converge, mine descending, the other rising, the valley narrows to a gorge. In its depths, a hundred and fifty feet or more below, the torrent is noisily roaring, and at the other side, half way up, the carriage-road is built out from the almost perpendicular wall of the Gourzy. We draw nearer, and at length I cross, high above the stream, by a rude wooden bridge, and rejoin the main road. The slope I have quitted steepens now into a precipice, and the two sides of this ravine move closer and closer together, their bare limestone brows a thousand, two thousand, feet above the road. I vividly recall the Via Mala in Switzerland, as I lean over the stone parapet and push down a heavy stone to crash upon the rocks of the torrent far beneath.

The toiling breack rejoins me, and the road cuts in through the gorge for some distance farther. Patches of snow are now seen on some of the summits approaching. Then we round a corner at the left, the valley opens out, though very slightly, and soon we see ahead the closely set houses of the Baths of Eaux Chaudes.

We pause before a plain, fatherly hotel, and a motherly landlady appears at once to welcome us. We are won at once by Madame Baudot. Her benignant face is a benediction. She leads us in through the low, wide hallway, past the little windowed office at the end, and turning to the left into a short corridor brings us out to a set of rooms in the new extension. As we step out upon the tiny balconies at the windows, we cannot forbear exclaiming at the charm of their situation. We are directly above the torrent, which chafes along perhaps fifty feet below, and the balconies jut out over the water. Beyond it are the cliffs, rising huge before us, wooded high, but bare and bald near the top; up and down the valley the eye ranges along their fronts. The rooms, simple but exactingly clean, are dainty with dimity and netted curtains and spreads. The whole effect is so home-like and restful, the relief of the contrast so great from plain and city and the rush of trains, that involuntarily we sigh for a month to spend at Eaux Chaudes.

III.

We find but two streets, terraced one behind the other; quiet, heavily-built houses, a small shop or two, another hotel, a little church, and the bathing establishment. The latter, large and substantial, overlooks the Gave a few steps up the road. We stroll inquisitively down through the village, lighten a dull little shop with a trifling investment, strike out upon the hill above for the reward of a view, descend to the bed of the torrent, and finally drift together again into the streetside near the hotel. Most of the houses are *pensions* or boarding-places during the summer, and while the spot is much less fashionable and populous than its neighbor, Eaux Bonnes, it is instinct with a comforting placidity not easily to be attained in larger resorts. The waters are said to be specifically good for rheumatism. Both drinking and bathing are prescribed. In former times the simple rule was, the more the better; Thor himself could scarcely have outquaffed the sixteenth-century invalids. One of the early French historians relates his visit "to the Baths of Beam, seven leagues from Pau. " A young German, he says, "although very sober, drank each day fifty glasses of sulphur water within the hour." He himself was content with twenty-five, "rather from pleasure than need;" he experienced "great relief, with a marvelous appetite, sound sleep, and a feeling of buoyancy in his whole body."

An experimentally inclined visitor, a few years ago, heard of this exploit of the "sober young German," and attempted to repeat it. He very nearly lost his life in consequence.

The sovereigns at Pau were very fond of the Eaux. Marguerite of Angoulême loved to come to this stern, peaceful valley, and here found inspiration for her thoughts and her writings. One of her letters tells us that in these mountains, apart from the careless court, *"elle a appris à vivre plus de papier que d'aultres choses,"* Her daughter, Queen Jeanne, Henry's mother, found her health here when she was young, having been "meagre and feeble." She often visited them afterward. Her visits were costly, too; the expenses of the court were considerable, but she had to bring

an armed guard as well; Spain always stood ready to kidnap the Queen of Navarre if it had opportunity. Such were the times.

Later, for almost a century, these springs became neglected and forgotten; they were then again brought into notice, and now seem to have gained a permanent popularity.

As afternoon closes in, we reunite at the hotel, where Madame greets us graciously. Her visitors will begin to come with the coming week, but we actually have the house to ourselves. In the tidy parlor blazes a wood-fire; out of doors, in the dusk, it has grown a trifle chilly. Attentions are doubled upon us when it is known that we are Americans; Madame's daughter, who has married the chef and will succeed to the inheritance, will succeed to the kindly disposition as well, and with a sunny-faced waiting-woman looks after details of comfort with a personal interest. Our famous lunch at Laruns was both so ample and so recent that now we ask only for "tea and toast," and so, while the lamps are lighted, the trays are brought to us in the parlor, and around the centre-table and before the fire we nibble *tartines* in soothed content and plan tomorrow's excursion.

Later in the evening we pause at the little office in the hall, behind whose window sits Madame, busy with her knitting yet watchfully supervising all the details of the household. She chats with us freely, speaking slowly in her clear, low-toned French,—that southern French which sounds the vowels and the final *e* so lingeringly,—telling us of the village and its surroundings, of the people, of herself; questioning us about America, (where, she tells us, lives one of her daughters;) welcoming us evidently with the greater regard as being of the few she sees from that active, far-off land.

IV.

The low, steady, insistent rumble and rustle of the torrent below our windows becomes almost ghostly in the stillness of the midnight. It is coming from the dark and mysterious forests it so well knows, the same unchanging water-soul it has been in the days of the Pyrenees past. One almost ascribes to it the power of audibly retelling its past, as it intones its way onward below us; infusing our dreams with subtle imaginings of the spirit of dead times, the pathetic forgottenness of the mountain lives that have been lived within its sound, the roysterings of the knights who have hunted along its coursing.

For into these forests often rode Gaston Phoebus and his fierce men of Orthez, in pursuit of a fiercer than they, the now disappearing Pyrenees bear. At no time was superstition more rife than then; savage souls were imputed to these savage animals; the spectres of the killed brutes returned to trouble the dreams of the hunter-knights, as the growl of their familiar torrent penetrates ours. We seem to hear old Froissart's voice above the sound, believingly telling a legend of the hunt:

"'Sir Peter de Béarn has a custom, when asleep in the night-time, to rise, arm himself, draw his sword, and to begin fighting as if he were in actual battle. The chamberlains and valets who sleep in his chamber to watch him, on hearing him rise, go to him and inform him what he is doing; of all which, he tells them, he is quite ignorant, and that they lie. Sometimes they leave neither arms nor sword in his chamber, when he makes such a noise and clatter as if all the devils in hell were there. They therefore think it best to replace the arms, and sometimes he forgets them and remains quietly in his bed.'

"'Holy Mary!' said I to the squire, 'how came the knight to have such fancies, that he cannot sleep quietly in bed but must rise and skirmish about the house! This is very strange.'

"'By my faith,' answered the squire, 'they have frequently asked him, but he knows nothing about it. The first time it happened was on a night following a day when he had hunted a wonderfully large bear in the woods of Béarn. This bear had killed four of his dogs and wounded many more, so that the others were afraid of him; upon which Sir Peter drew his sword of Bordeaux steel

and advanced on the bear with great rage on account of the loss of his dogs; he combated him a long time with much bodily danger, and with difficulty slew him; when he returned to his castle of Languedudon in Biscay, and had the bear carried with him. Every one was astonished at the enormous size of the beast and the courage of the knight who had attacked and slain him.

"'But when the Countess of Biscay, his wife, saw the bear, she instantly fainted and was carried to her chamber, where she continued very disconsolate all that and the following day, and would not say what ailed her. On the third day she told her husband she should never recover her health until she had made a pilgrimage to St. James' shrine at Compostella. "Give me leave therefore to go thither and to carry my son Peter and my daughter Adrienne with me; I request it of you." Sir Peter too easily complied; she had packed up all her jewels and plate unobserved by any one; for she had resolved never to return again.

"'The lady set out on her pilgrimage, and took that opportunity of visiting her cousins, the King and Queen of Castile, who entertained her handsomely. She is still with them, and will never return herself nor send her children. The same night he had hunted and killed the bear, this custom of walking in his sleep seized him. It is rumored the lady was afraid of something unfortunate happening, the moment she saw the bear, and this caused her fainting; for that her father once hunted this bear, and during the chace a voice cried out, though he saw nobody: "Thou huntest me, yet I wish thee no ill; but thou shalt die a miserable death!" The lady remembered this when she saw the bear, as well as that her father had been beheaded by Don Pedro without any cause; and she maintains that something unfortunate will happen to her husband, and that what passes now is nothing to what will come to pass.'"

V.

White clouds scud away before the breeze, as we climb down toward the

torrent again before breakfast and cross a diminutive foot-bridge to a path on the other side. The sun is at his post. "All Nature smiles," here in the mountains as over the plains, and promises lavishly for the day. The ramble brings a sharpened appetite, and we come back to the sunny breakfast-room, to find flowers at the plates of mesdames and mademoiselle, and a family of Pyrenean trout, drawn out within the half-hour from a trout-well by the stream, in crisp readiness upon the table.

We have planned for a view to-day of the great Pic du Midi d'Ossau,—the mountain seen so sharply from Pau. It is not in sight at Eaux Chaudes; but it is the giant of this section of the range,—a noon-mark for an entire province. There is no mountain resort without its pet excursions, and there are three here which take the lead. One is to Goust, another to the Grotto; but the foremost is to Gabas and the majestic Pic.

Our breack comes pompously to the terrace by the hotel, and the hostess wishes us *"une belle excursion."* The road takes us on through the village, and pushes up into the valley with an ascent which is not steep but which never relaxes. Around us the scene grows increasingly wild and everywhere picturesque. We cross at some height the Gave, by the stone *Pont d'Enfer,*— Bridge of Hell, so named,—and keep along the westerly bank. On one side the ledges are bare, but the opposite slopes are greener, densely wooded, and ribboned by occasional cascades. Goats and cattle graze on the upper stretches of herbage; and the shadows of the clouds chase each other in great islands over the broad flanks of the mountain. Often, as the horses pause to rest, panting silently with the work, we climb down from our perches to walk on against the warm breeze, or clamber up from the roadway to add a prize to the ladies' mountain bouquets.

At a noted angle in the trend of the valley, the forked white cone of the great Pic comes suddenly into sight. The vision lasts but a minute. A cloud sweeps down upon it, and when it lifts again we have passed the point of view.

We anathematize the intruder openly; this is incautious, for our anathemas provoke reprisals. Other clouds rally around their offended sister in support, as we push slowly onward, and some of the nearer mountains are soon enveloped also. The blue sky is forced back, cut off in all directions; even the pusillanimous sun retires from the conflict; the heavens have darkened ominously.

In an hour and a half from Eaux Chaudes, we have come to Gabas, 3600 feet above the sea. The place consists of two or three houses, and a dull little inn by a patch of wooded park. It does not attract overmuch, but to go farther at present is manifestly unwise. Nature's smile has become a pout, and that is fast developing into a crying-spell. The guide and ponies sent on from Madame Baudot's must wait. The breack is tarpaulined and left to the pines in the park, the horses are led off into the stable, and we disconsolately enter the hotel, to chill the coming hour with spiritless lemonade and a period of waiting.

I believe it will always rain on you at Gabas. The few persons we had hitherto met who had been to Eaux Chaudes enthusiastically praised this trip toward the Pic du Midi,—"but we could not complete it, ourselves." they invariably added, "because it came on to shower when we reached Gabas." We had smiled commiseratingly, confident of being better favored. Now we find that the clouds, jealous body-guard of this regal summit, which is "first a trap and then an abiding-place for every vagrant vapor," can deny him alike to the just and the unjust,—that they trouble little to make distinctions, even where nationality is involved.

It is a dull hour. Within, we are in a murky, musty reception-room, and find no consolation save in ourselves, last week's Pau newspapers, and a decrepit French guide-book which tells tantalizingly of the magnificent trip on toward the peak. Without, the rain falls softly and maliciously, slackening at times in order to taunt us with glimpses of fugitive blue overhead. We wait and conjecture; plans and anecdotes and a good fire help wonderfully to hurry the time. The landlord offers but dubious prophecies; and the window-panes prophesy as dubiously, as we peer out into the grey mist and the dripping, shivering park. Nature's resentments are strong, and when she gives battle she fights to a finish.

At last, in full caucus assembled, we vote the war a failure and elect for a retreat.

VI.

The climb we were to take is to a plateau called Bious-Artigues. It is about three miles beyond Gabas by bridle-path, and its ascent needs an hour and a half. Here the full face of the Pic du Midi d'Ossau is squarely commanded. The view is said to challenge that of the Matterhorn from the Riffel. The plateau itself is nearly five thousand feet above the sea, and across the ravine before it, this isolated granite obelisk, with its mitre of snow, lifts itself upward more than five thousand feet higher,—a precipitous cone, "notched like a pair of gaping jaws, eager to grasp the heavens."

This formidable pyramid was first ascended in 1552, and afterward by Palma Cayet in 1591. It has often been climbed since, and affords a view over a veritable wilderness of peaks. From Bious-Artigues, without making the ascent but simply following the sides of the surrounding basin, one can go on to a second and even a third plateau, adding to the outlook each time, and may finally work his way entirely around the Pic and return to Gabas by another direction. At Gabas too one is but seven miles from the Spanish frontier, and there is a foot-pass that scales the high barrier between the countries and leads down to the Spanish baths of Panticosa. A great international highway over this pass has been in contemplation,—the carriage-road to be continued on from Gabas, upward over the crest of the range, and so descending to Panticosa and the plains of Aragon. It is a singular fact that at present, from the Bay of Biscay to the Mediterranean, there is not one such highway over any portion of the chain, but solely around the two extremities. The only midway access from country to country, (except a poor cart-road from Pau to Jaca,) is by mulepaths, or oftener difficult trails and passes known chiefly to the blithe contrabandista.

Mournfully, yet with philosophy, we muse on these withholden glories, as we drive rapidly homeward. Umbrellas shut off the scenery where the mists do not, and we are forced to introspection. We resort for comfort to praising each other for bearing the disappointment so well. We laud each other's cheerfulness under affliction. After all,
"Into each life some rain must fall,
Some days must be dark and dreary."
We solace ourselves with the most fulsome mutual adulation, uncriticised by the stolid coachman; and as we roll down the long descent back to Eaux Chaudes, our disappointment wears gradually away; at Hell Bridge, we have become quite angelic; and we respond to Madame Baudot's condoling welcome almost with hilarity.

VII.

The last wrinkles of regret are smoothed away by a sumptuous luncheon. It competes even with that at Laruns, which we have set up as henceforth the standard, the model, the criterion, the ultimate ideal, of all luncheons. Of a truth, this chef is proving himself a worthy son-in-law.

It has set in for a rainy afternoon, and this comforts us surprisingly. If it had cleared after all, on our return here to Eaux Chaudes, and the blue had opened into bloom overhead, I do not know what would have been said of the climate, but we should have held very strong opinions concerning it. As it is, we can lay the fault on Fate, not on any misplanning. This is an inestimable relief. We did *our* part. We went more than half way. The blame was Fate's, not ours. Fate is the one, therefore, that merits the abuse. It is a solace to put the blame squarely where it belongs, and a greater solace still to abuse the absent.

But need we spend the rest of the day at Eaux Chaudes? The hotel is cosy and seems almost a home, but the wet little street has nothing to invite us. We are not going to Gabas again. On that point we are resolved. The Pic du Midi has forfeited all claims. Goust we can return to visit. We call another caucus,—and in an hour, warm farewells have been spoken to Madame, and we are atop of our breack, on the watery way to Eaux Bonnes.

CHAPTER X.

THE GOOD WATERS OF THE ARQUEBUSADE.

"Tant que l'on est aux baings, il fault vivre comme ung enfant, sans nul soucy. "—MARGUERITE OF AN-GOULÊME.

The road toward Eaux Bonnes retraces its steps from Eaux Chaudes almost to Laruns, before it swings off into the other southward gorge. The ride in all is about four miles,—two on each branch of the V. Between the resorts is also a foot-path over the Gourzy, recommended in fine weather; it is steep and said to be toilsome, but the view is reputed a full compensation.

This whole valley, comprising the main depression running north from Laruns and the narrower fissures split through to Eaux Chaudes and Eaux Bonnes, was in Miocene times the bed of a huge glacier. It is known as the Val d'Ossau,—"the vale where the bears come down." Bears are still met with, it is said, in the vast forests about the foot of the Midi, but they are shy and scarce. The *izard,*—the chamois of the Pyrenees,—is more frequently seen and often hunted. This valley is individual in Béarn, as Béarn is in France. In past time it was a distinct principality, small but defiant, and it had its own line of hereditary viscounts entirely independent of the larger province enfolding it. The people still cherish some of the old local customs and costumes, their native dances, and a few other past differentia

of the valley; but railroads and time are great levelers, and the Ossalois is broadening into the Béarnais, as the Béarnais is broadening into the Frenchman.

We speed on in the persistent rain, down between the steep sides of the Eaux Chaudes ravine and out to the Laruns foot of the great Gourzy ridge; and having doubled this, turn into the gorge which leads southerly again to Eaux Bonnes. The incline is now upward once more, and progress is slower. An entirely new torrent is rushing to greet us. From what we gain of the scenery, between the showers, the valley, though narrow, is wider than the one we have left, but its mountains are as high or higher. There is a fine prospect behind us of the Laruns amphitheatre. But the drops still patter upon our umbrellas, and we are glad when our conveyance, after a half hour more, climbs the last hill and rolls down into the Grande Rue along the little park in Eaux Bonnes, to stop at the handsome Hotel des Princes.

II.

At the first, we are not sure that we are glad we came. We miss the cosiness of good Madame Baudot's. But we soon see that Eaux Bonnes has attractions of its own, though they be very different from the charms of Eaux Chaudes. It is larger, busier, incomparably more fashionable. The great entrance-hall of the hotel is hung with wide squares of tapestry, has columns of marble and a marble flooring, and is invested with an air of ceremonial which is rather pleasing. The rooms aid to reconcile us; they are on the first floor, large and finely furnished, and are directly over the entrance, their balconies overlooking the park. It is a transition from dimity and sweet pine, but travel, like life, should be prized sometimes for its transitions.

On the ground floor we find the parlor opening from the great hall; it is a long, frescoed apartment, with full Continental array of gilded mirrors and polished flooring, round, inlaid reading-tables and glossy mahogany furniture. Our readjusted ideas of Pyrenean hotels are sustained at their high level. The

season has already reached Eaux Bonnes, and the parlor has a refreshingly animated look with its groups or units of talkers and readers. Across the main ball is the dining-hall, equally long and frescoed, and beyond it a satellite breakfast-room; and when the afternoon has worn away and the hour announces the gastronomic event of the day, it is a goodly representation of guests that gathers itself together at the formal table-d'hôte.

III.

There is no mistaking the character of the next day. It is "settled fair." Probably Nature feels that she carried affairs a trifle too far yesterday. Everything is radiant, this morning; the leaves on the trees glow and are tremulous in this warm southern air. Eaux Bonnes appears to better advantage than at our rainy arrival. I cross the street to the diminutive park, which is triangular, its apex northward. It has paths and seats and leafy Gothic arches, fountains and a music kiosque; while in and about are promenaders, nurses and children, guides and idlers, already out of doors for sunbaths or business. The town mainly centres about this triangle, the houses facing it from across the streets in a similar triangle proportionately larger. The buildings are tall and uniformly handsome; other hotels resembling the Princes line the western side and the base, and opposite are diversified shops and *pensions* and still more hotels. Livery-stables are omnipresent, the sign, *"chevaux et voitures à louer,"* greeting one at every turn. Along the sides of the streets flow lively rivulets of water, led in from the mountain slopes and fresh and clear from their clean, rocky ways. The spring-house and Casino, a decorated structure, built against the mountain, stands on a low eminence west of the head of the park, and from this to our hotel extends a broad foot-way, lined with stalls and booths, "where bright-colored Spanish wools, trinkets and toys are sold, where bagatelle and *tir au pistolet,* round-abouts and peepshows,—all the 'fun of the fair,' in fact,—is set out for the amusement of idle Eaux Bonnes." These are sure indications of fashionable prosperity. Wherever these evanescent summer stalls appear, at Saratoga or St. Moritz or Eaux Bonnes, they tell of patronage to call them into being,— an idle, prosperous patronage that spends for gimcracks what the native would economize from necessaries.

Behind all, walling the square closely in on almost every side, are the cliffs; at the east is a lower curtain of rock shutting off the outer valley; and on the south, almost overhanging us, shoots up the Pic de Ger. The view of its rocky escarpments and silver peak may fairly be called stupendous, it is so sharply at variance with the smooth carpetings of the lower mountains about it.

I pass down through the park. At its base is a congress of single-seated donkey-carriages like those at Biarritz. They are officered by importunate though good-natured boys and women, but I persevere in unruffled declinations. The street slants up a short hill here and comes out upon another open place much smaller than the park and likewise bordered with stores and *pensions*.

This is Eaux Bonnes, as it is, as it was, as it will be. The place cannot grow, except into the air. Its area is little over half an acre. It stands wedged into the Gourzy, on a species of platform in a huge niche in the mountain, partitioned off from the main valley by the low ridge of rock behind the houses on the farther side of the park. Save this attractive little grove in its centre, every inch of ground is utilized. The torrent, tearing past along the lower bottom of the main ravine without, has cut away the level on that side; beyond it, the mountains rise sheerly upward again. And the Gourzy, as just said, hems us in on the sides remaining. From the rear windows of the Hotel des Princes you can put out your hand and touch the naked rock. A few additional houses are perched here and there on convenient projections or lodged in narrow crannies against the hill; and blasting and cutting have created space where it was not before; but the limit seems reached, and what is

must be Eaux Bonnes cannot afford to increase in popularity. Popularity has seriously incommoded her already. Like a full-bodied but tight-bodiced dowager, she devoutly hopes she will not have to grow any fatter.

As I saunter back through the park, I meet a striking individual. It is one of the local guides arrayed in full regimentals. His startling colors are designed to attract the wary but inquisitive tourist,—much as the waving of the hunter's colored scarf is said to attract the wary but inquisitive gnu. Still it is the true Ossalois dress, and as such claims inspection. I open a conversation, and find the man to be one of the four Eaux Bonnes guides having the honor of mention in Murray; Caillou Martin is his name. A broad, good-humored face, swarthy and strong, with the eyes dark and small and far apart, and shaded by the inevitable berret. Caillou's is scarlet, and so is his jacket, thrown open in flapping lappels and showing a white flannel waistcoat beneath. He wears knee-breeches of brown corduroy, and thick creamy-white leggings, coarsely knit and climbing up over ankle and calf nearly to the knee. He has hemp sandals, and around the waist circles a scarlet sash, equally inevitable with the berret.

Caillou grins as I tell him of Murray's encomiums, and wants us to go up the Pic de Ger. The day is *"magnifique"*, the ascent *"très facile"* the view *"ravissante."* And each adjective is set off with a rattling fusillade of crackings from his great whip. This weapon is a specialty of all Pyrenean guides and drivers. The handle, short and stout, is of wood, with a red plush tuft around the centre, and the lash is made of braided leather thongs, four or five feet in length, finishing in a long whipcord and a vicious little knot. This instrument will make a crack like a pistol shot, and under artistic manipulation will signal as far as Roland could wind his famous

horn. It is worn slung over the shoulder and under the opposite arm, the handle in front linking by a loop with the lash; and it fitly completes a highly picturesque costume. We bargain for the whip on the spot, a five-franc piece changes hands, and Caillou Martin graciously writes his honored autograph on the handle.

IV.

Some of us have planned a return to Eaux Chaudes for the day. One of its characteristic excursions we have not yet taken; the strange village of Goust is unvisited. This hamlet, situated on a mountain-side near Eaux Chaudes, is described by M. Moreau as "a species of principality, tiny but self-governing, similar to certain duchies of the confederation without their budget and civil list," a box within a box, it would appear,—a spot independent of its Valley of Ossau, as Ossau was of Béarn, and Béarn of France. It has lived always in the most utter aloofness from the world's affairs; it still so lives to-day. It is noteworthy too for its old people; Henry IV granted to one of them, born in 1442, a life pension which, it is credibly recorded, was not extinguished until 1605.

We have a strong curiosity to visit this unique settlement, solitary, indifferent to time and its new ways, Nature's "children lost in the clouds." So I gladden one of the anxious liverymen with an order, and soon a comfortable carriage is taking us back down the hills toward Laruns. We can dwell this morning on the view of that village and its green basin, as we glide down along the side of the valley with the distant specks of houses always in front. We dwell too with more comprehension on the heights and depths of the Eaux Chaudes ravine, as we turn the foot of the V and pull steadily upward and inward again. There is Madame Baudot at the doorway, hearing the distant wheels, ready to welcome us with all her heart; there appear her daughter, Madame Julie, and the rubicund serving-woman; and even the square, white cap of the chef bobs up and down behind them, within the hall.

The carriage is moored, the horses are unshipped, wraps and overcoats speedily unladen and left in bond. The good women promise us the best of lunches on our return, and we are fairly afoot down the road toward the Bridge of Hell,—hearts and highway equally paved with good intentions. The sun is full but not oppressive, a breeze is stirring, and there is a flood of vitality, a buoyancy and light-heartedness, about these bright mountain mornings, as one strides on, "breathing the free air of unpunctuality," which animates to high deeds and heroic resolve.

The deed now in prospect is high, but not superlatively heroic. The hamlet we seek is stowed away upon the mountainside across the ravine from Eaux Chaudes, 3000 feet above the sea, and will require a climb of perhaps three-quarters of an hour. We cross the diabolic Bridge,—*"facilis* ascensus,"

"The gates of Hell are open night and day,

Smooth the *ascent* and easy is the way,"—

and shortly strike off from the road and up among the bushes. There is a well-worn pathway, and it toils easily skyward, doubling back on itself to rest and unrolling wider and wider vistas of the valley. The Gourzy across the chasm enlarges its proportions as we rise. Here comes a peasant or two posting valleyward, going to his world-centre, the metropolis of Eaux Chaudes, or perchance even on to the universe-hub,—Laruns. Birches and beeches mingle everywhere with the darker, green of the fir-trees; alders and oaks and hazels are abundant; among all run the heavy growths of box. Tree life is profuse and rich on these warm lower flanks of the range, while wild flowers and butterflies tempt one to constant digressions. The path grows steeper. After all,

"to ascend, to view the cheerful skies
In this the task and mighty labor lies."

Virgil must have had this very occasion prophetically in mind:

"To few great Jupiter imparts this grace,—And
those of shining worth and heavenly

race!
Betwixt those regions and our upper light,
Deep forests and impenetrable night
Possess the middle space; the infernal bounds
Cocytus with his sable waves surrounds,"—

Cocytus being an evident euphemism for the Gave.

We meet another peasant, this time a woman, who stares and replies that Goust is very near. Another incline is mounted, we come out upon an uneven break of pasture-land, and our destination is at hand.

We are not positive as to this at first. Eight hoary, grey-stone hovels are before us, a few rods away, and the path passing along the side of a high stone wall goes on to their doors. We follow it, finding the way grown muddy and stony, and finally stop inquiringly before the cellar-like opening of the most prominent "hutch." So this is the principality of Goust! A woman has been peering at us from over the wall we have passed by, and now our arrival brings other women to their respective doors, to stare in the unison of uncertainty. Approaching, I doff my hat, and politely explain that we are visitors, that we have come from America to see this settlement, and that any courtesies they may extend will be considered as official by the nation we represent. The dumb neutrality of the beldames, at this, is soon dispelled by our friendly interest, and they gradually come out and group around us in the mud of the path, with interest no less friendly and even greater. Their faces are intelligent and shrewd and practical; there is abundance of wise if narrow lore lined out in those strong, crude features. Their frames are brawny; they are used to work. They are those who fill, and fill faithfully, their single niches, living moveless, as the trees; change, new surroundings, the world, they have not known. Their life has cut its one deep dent and there it is hidden,—as boulders sink their way into the glacier-fields.

But evidently it is we who are the chief curiosity,—not they. The dresses

of the ladies are unobstrusively but openly admired,—gloves and hat-pins discussed in detail, in an unintelligible patois. I inquire how many people there are in the village; what they find to do; whether they are not lonely, so far from the world. They answer my queries in unconfused French, speaking both this and their patois, and even ask respectful questions in turn. There are about seventy people who live here, they say, but most of them are away in the fields during the day; the women at home weave silk, to be taken to the valley for sale. They are nearly all related by marriage (alliés) or by blood to each other; they are governed by a little council of old men; there is no chief, nor anyone superior to the authority of the council; it regulates the duties of each. They know of no taxes of any kind to pay; they always marry within the village, except where the patriarchs may grant a dispensation with an outsider; yes, they have many old people here, one or two very old indeed, though none so old as a hundred and sixty-three,—the age of King Henry's ancient pensioner.

But the other questions we put are too large or too novel to grasp. They do not apparently know what I mean by being lonely. The conception has never occurred to them. Nor do they think they are far from the world. They go down to the valley beneath, at times, they tell us; and on feast-days and for the rustic August dances they have even been to Laruns; the men cross the Gourzy to Eaux Bonnes, and they have all often heard long descriptions of Cauterets and Pan.

The interest of our hostesses in their unwonted visitors is manifestly as great as ours in them, and there is a curious zest in gratifying it. Yes, we are traveling in France; we have come from America to travel; we have been to Pau and Eaux Bonnes, and are going on to Cauterets and through other parts of the Pyrenees,—it was a bold undertaking! They do not find a reason for it at all. One of them is familiar with America, she says, for she once knew of some one who went there—to Buenos Ayres. They are well-intentioned and free and happy, and never think of envy as they query these cometary strangers.

The camera focuses their wonder. We show them the reflections on the ground-glass,—the houses, the waving leaves, each other's faces. It is incredible! We open the box and explain the structure of the monster. Finally we boldly ask for a sitting, and after some urging and bashful demurring, these belles and dames of Goust coyly group themselves by a felicitous doorway, and—veritable "flies in amber"—are perpetuated for posterity.

"Will messieurs and mesdames come within?" A matron speaks. It is what we have been hoping, and we follow eagerly, escorted by the troupe. Inside the door it is blackness. We tread an earth-floor, and by sounds and scents infer that this is the stable. We pass up some dark, uncertain stairs, and stand in the living-room of the family. It is long, dark and low-ceiled. The rafters are discolored with smoke, the board-floor with wear, the walls with strings and festoons of onions and native herbs. Ears of maize and great sides of beef and pork hang drying from above. In the dim rear are two pine bed-frames, with spreads of sackcloth and plaid canopies; nearer are sets of shelves lined with trenchers and earthen crockery in formal array, while a wood-fire smoulders on the wide hearth in front between the window-openings, fortified with a primitive crane and kettle of strange designs and unrecorded antiquity, and with various pots and pans. Everything seems clean. Our hostess, pleased at entertaining distinguished and appreciative visitors, draws out a wooden bench for us, and attempts to rouse the sleepy flames.

It is a significant, a typical scene. These peasants of France, with their honest, unspiritualized faces, are showing their life,—frugal and voiceless; bounded, but rarely pinched; in dusk, but seldom in dark; and with all, contentful, industrious, religious, and wishing no ill to any of mankind. This hamlet and home is an over-accented instance; the lowland French peasants have more interchange, wider thoughts and interests, and many of them more

prosperous abodes. Yet the scene before us stands for thousands of meek cabins in solitary places scattered through France. This exile-life of Goust tells its patient lesson, touching, and at the same time reassuring; and I am very certain that in all its limitations it is higher, as it is happier, than that of a poverty-soured mécontent of the Quartier Belleville in Paris.

A younger woman of the family is now commissioned to produce their treasured adornments for inspection. From an obscure adjoining room a small chest is brought out and placed upon the floor before us, and the eager girl, kneeling by it, proceeds to display the contents. Carefully she takes out and unfolds a headdress of bright striped silk, to be passed admiringly around; and two or three other head-dresses follow, also of silk or of sharp-colored wools. We ask when these are worn, and learn that they are chiefly hoarded for gala-days and saints'-days. The large scarlet capulet comes next, and one of the women dons it to show the effect. Then appear a scarf and two light shoulder-mufflers, made of the true Barèges wool, a specialty of the Pyrenees, soft and fascinatingly downy. These are followed by a few neatly-rolled ribbons, brought over at different times from Spain, which are duly unstreamed; some silver pins and a chain, and a rosary; worsted mittens, and a pair of men's white knee-stockings, similar to Caillou's. But the gem of the collection, reserved for the climax, is a brocaded silk shawl, a really handsome article and handled with great reverence. The proud owner assures us that it is valued at seventy francs and has been handed down in the household for many years; and her listening neighbors, standing respectfully behind us, murmur their assent and admiration.

We not only show but feel a warm interest in every detail, and praise each article as it is produced. Our new friends are clearly as much pleased as we; they seldom see strangers, and more seldom any who sympathize thus with their privations and prides, and this will be a long-remembered event in their small community. Our hostess is much gratified when we give her little boy a silver piece,—we can see that she had no thought of favors; and before we take leave we present her with a crimson handkerchief of India silk, owned by one of the party, at which she is fairly overjoyed. That, we tell her, is to go into the treasure-chest, as a little reminder of her foreign visitors. They press on us offers of milk and other refreshment, but we are mindful of the lunch preparing for us in the valley, and inform them why we must decline. We promise to send our hostess a print of the photograph, and bid a cordial adieu; and as we descend the stairs and move off down the path, we are given a half-wistful and most earnest farewell from them all.

Madame Baudot is true to her word. On her table is the most appetizing of tiffins; and after it we have another talk through the office window. As she knits, she asks us about our plans, makes suggestions for the coming ride over the great Route Thermale, and wishes us not only a prosperous journey but a return in later years to Eaux Chaudes and the Pic du Midi. For herself and her household, they are here the winter through, as there may be always a few comers; but it is dull and bitterly cold; they are often shut away for days from the lower valley, and she is glad with the coming of summer.

And so we drive away again from genial Eaux Chaudes, waving, as we turn the corner, to the warm faces at the doorway, the bouquets they have given us at parting.

V.

We find Eaux Bonnes at its best as we return. The early afternoon siesta is over, and every one is out of doors. The sunshine pours over the little park, filled with fashionable loungers. Uniforms and afternoon toilettes add their tart hues to the sombrer garb of the male civilian. The little donkey-carriages or vinaigrettes are in great demand, and one by one are coming or going with their single occupants, the attendant Amazon, if desired, running by the side. Saddle-horses are also in requisition; the sidewalks have an animated air; booths and gaming-stalls are in-good swing; the springs are being dutifully patronized; motion, Heraclitus' flux and flow, is the mark of the hour. The transition seems even greater than yesterday's, from Eaux Chaudes; and, glad in the charms of the latter, we are glad too to return again to the world and its harmless vanities.

After the evening dinner, we explore the street on the other side of the triangle. We find a narrow cut in the rocks behind the houses, and, passing through, a few steps bring us out upon the view of the main ravine, from which this narrow curtain of rock shuts off the town. The contrast is instantaneous. From the hemmed-in nest of streets we have suddenly emerged upon the long sweep of the valley below us, finely commanded by the ledge where we stand. The level plunges off abruptly down to the Gave, which speeds toward Laruns, "leaping through a wild vegetation and 'shepherding her bright fountains' down a hundred falls." A few houses cluster on the hill as it goes down and at its base, but the torrent is again banked in by the mountain opposite, which climbs high above our own level. There is a long view up and down the valley, still and quiet in the gloaming. The night falls almost while we linger, and at length we turn back through the cut and saunter again across the park.

Passing the line of booths, we keep on toward the Casino, which is elevated some feet above the street in front. Its windows are lighted up; people are entering the building; a concert is about to commence. Before following them we pause for a while upon the terrace to turn and face the Pic de Ger. Erect and regal, its height throws it, alone among the surrounding mountains, into the full evening after-light; its precipices and white summit are all aflame still with the red sun, already lost to the valley. The great peak glows like the sacred pillar of fire by night, and we cannot but gaze at it long and reverently.

VI.

Sunday is more quietly kept by Eaux Bonnes than might be expected. The little French chapel has its service, and there is a certain staidness about the morning which is unlooked-for and refreshing. The shops, however, are open as always; the vinaigrette-dragowomen as energetic as commonly; and in the afternoon the band plays in the kiosque as it does on week-days. In fact, except for this certain staider air, the place like other Continental resorts does on Sunday very much the things which it does on other days of the week.

The springs of course are as regularly sought. Their routine cannot yield to religious institutes. These waters are chiefly useful in throat and lung diseases, though the baths are healing for abrasions and wounds. Both hot and cold waters are here; at one spot, oddly enough, the two temperatures well up close together. The springs have long been known, and anciently, as now, they were more popular than those of the sister valley. One of the kings of Navarre sent hither disabled soldiers from his wars in Italy; many had been wounded by the arquebus, then a new weapon, and from the cures effected, the waters were called after its name. They are seven in number, ardently sulphureous and officiously odorous. They are not to be dealt with in the spirit of levity of Eaux Chaudes' "sober young German": fifty glasses are not lightly to be tossed off. "Caution is necessary," warns Murray, "in using these waters; bad consequences have arisen from a stranger taking even a glassful to taste. It is usual to begin with a table-spoonful and a half!"

Habit, however, makes even the lion-tamer fearless: these invalids buy their course tickets, entitling to cure, concert and écarté; and they bathe and gamble and engulf their deadly draughts with the immunity of long familiarity.

A distinctive attraction of Eaux Bonnes is its abundance of promenades. There are walks of all grades of difficulty. One can mount to a summer-house or to the summit of the Pic de Ger. If he does not want to mount at all, he can walk for half a league along a perfect level,—the Promenade Horizontale. This walk is unique among walks. It was artificially laid out for precisely such people,—those who do not want to ascend and descend. It runs back around the bend of the Gourzy overlooking the Laruns hollow, the carriage-road grooving its way down far below it. In this region of angles and slants, this marvelous path moves leisurely forward, plane as a spirit-level, broad and well kept, shaded with trees, relieved with benches, and affording inspiring views throughout. Each of the promenades has its view and its cascade and almost its hour. With so many idlers, it is easily believed that each is duly popular. And when one tires of promenades or of liveliness or even of fine weather,—can he not easily drive to Gabas?

"We are all kept in good order here," observes Blackburn, in his account of the Pyrenees resorts; "everything is *en règle* and *au règle,* and if we stay a whole season we need not be at a loss how to get through the days. It is all arranged for us; there is the particular promenade for the early morning, facing the east; the exact spot to which you are to walk (and no farther) between the time of taking each glass of water; the after-breakfast cascade, the noon siesta, the ride at three, another cascade and more water or a bath at four, promenade at five, dinner at six, Promenade Horizontale until eight, then the Casino, balls, 'société,' écarté, or more moonlight walks,—and then decidedly early to bed."

Caillou and the liverymen predict a fine to-morrow for the long carriage-journey we have planned. The breeze is resolutely east, they say. This fact seems anything but convincing to us, accustomed to the weather signs of the west Atlantic seaboard. But here, as is quickly explained, the reversed signs prevail, and it is the *west* wind that dampens feathers and the spirits of rheumatics.

The band on Sunday plays at night as well as in the afternoon, and as the music, though secular, cannot be excluded, we throw open the windows and frankly welcome it as we sit in our balconies overlooking the lighted park in the mild evening air. The band plays well, and people throng the paths and listen appreciatively. Two overtures, a waltz movement, the *Melody in F*, a march, and a cornet obligate which is vigorously applauded, may serve as index of the unpartisan scope of selection. Music is enjoyed to the full in Europe; many a well-to-do city fosters its orchestra and has its public music-stand in the square or in the Volksgarten. In Bordeaux, workmen and mechanics, small urchins and sailors from the quays, fringed the more aristocratic circle of chairs, and listened as intently and as seriously as a Thomas audience at home. It cannot but have a humanizing effect. These listeners below us,—and so with the rough populace of Bordeaux,—have become tranquilized, soothed, softened; the buzz of harsh or random talk dies down; all faces are turned for the time to the common centre, all thoughts mingle in a common stillness of enjoyment.

CHAPTER XI.

OVER THE HIGHWAY OF THE HOT SPRINGS.

"Like a silver zone,
Flung about carelessly, it shines afar;
* * *
"Yet through its fairy course, go where it will,
The torrent stops it not, the rugged rock
Opens and lets it in; and on it runs,
Winning its easy way from clime to clime."
—ROGERS' *Italy*.

It is Monday morning at Eaux Bonnes. The dome of the sky is of unspecked blue. The departing diligence for Laruns has just rolled away down the road, and now a landau with four horses, and a victoria with two, stand before the Hotel des Princes. A formal contract, wisely yet ludicrously minute in detail, bristling with discomforting provisos for contingencies, and copied out in the usual painstaking French handwriting, has been discussed and gravely signed. We are to be conveyed to Cauterets as the first day's stage, and thereafter to have the carriages at command, for an agreed price per day, if we wish to retain them. Thus we can journey on to Luz, Gavarnie, Barèges, Bigorre and even Luchon. The memorandum is handed us; it provides for delays and breakdowns, disputes, damages, sickness; it stipulates for return prices from the place of dismissal. The average price for two such conveyances in this region, "keep" included but not *pourboire*, will be found to hold within from seventy-five to ninety francs a day,—thirty-five to forty-five francs for each carriage; I record it as matter of information for possible comers. The carriages, the horses and the drivers are all strong and all well-cushioned, and the drivers are resplendently tinseled besides.

We are now to enter oft the *Route Thermale*. This carriage-road is one of the marvels of modern engineering. The chief resorts in the French Pyrenees are imbedded each at the head of a north-and-south valley running up from the plain against the crest of the range. Between them, the huge mountain ridges, like ribs from a Typhon's spine, stretch down in irregular parallels from the backbone of the chain. Before this road was built, these resorts could only be visited successively by a tedious double journey in and out of each separate valley, or by high foot-paths over the ridges between. Thus the traveling from one to another had its serious drawbacks. The railroad came, skirting the plain, though not yet provided with the offshoots which now run partway into the valleys; but even by rail the détours needed would be circuitous and wasting, and they missed utterly the out-of-door fascinations of true mountain travel. Something yet was called for.

The Route Thermale was the result; it is another of the wonders of Louis Napoleon's régime. It has revolutionized the comforts of Pyrenean summer travel; the ridges need no longer be skirted, for they can be luxuriously crossed,—and by one of the best carriage-roads in Europe. Beginning at Eaux Bonnes, and running in the main parallel with the central crest, it rears itself serpent-like over four of these great intervening barriers, attaining and crossing in turn the broad valleys between them, connecting northward with the stations, southward with the springs. This immense band, sinuous and unbroken, uplifting itself to the snow, plunging again from snow to the maize-fields, stretches along the central Pyrenees a full hundred miles. Four days' journey away lies its distant end at Luchon. The hostile mountains shower it with earth and stones. Winter buries it in ice, spring assaults it with freshets; it is rarely passable before June, and mountain storms even in summer measure their strength against it. But Napoleon III inspired this road, and it emerges, quickly rejuvenated, from tempest and torrent, to laugh unconquered. Of the undertakings of the Bonaparte family, only two were ever baffled by opposing forces.

Such an enterprise as this gives a new light, for the stranger, upon the popularity of the Pyrenees. This costly road-building could only have arisen from a demand great enough to require and sustain it,—from an amount of summer traffic, a multitude of summer visitors, commensurate in part at least with the outlay. Evidently, figments of lonely settlements and dark paths belong in limbo with those of dismal inns.

The next great synclinal, adjoining the Valley of Ossau, is the Valley of Lavedan, and at its head in the mountains lies Cauterets, our next point of attack. The notch of the road in each intervening ridge is called a *col*, that which is in the ridge that now bars us from Cauterets being the Col d'Aubisque. Over the Col d'Aubisque, accordingly, opposite the Pic de Ger, our way to-day lies.

II.

We abandon Eaux Bonnes, almost reluctantly, to its summer's festivities, and drive down the broad street and around the end of the park and so out through the curtain of rock into the road of the main valley. The slow ascent begins almost at once. We rise gradually along a wooded hill, stopping once to enjoy a cataract which, like a happy child, is noisy for its size and entirely lovable nevertheless. A long reach of valley is then entered, bottomed by the Gave, the road well up on the side. In an hour or more, we finally turn to cross the valley, and commence the serious ascent of the opposite side. Facing us now from the side we have left is the mass of the Ger, very near, very high, and uncompromisingly precipitous. All the morning this Pic looms stonily above us; the sunshine brightens its snows but cannot soften the stern rock-features. Steadily, though with frequent rests, the horses toil higher, and the Pic seems to rise as we ascend. Often we are walking, by the side of the carriages. Other peaks are now coming up into view; the road mounts in long zigzags, shaded plentifully at times and always astir with a trace of breeze. Our admiration at its skillful construction increases hourly. Patiently surmounting all obstacles, it moves surely upward, unvexed by resistance, broad and smooth and firm, and protected by parapets wherever the paternal solicitude of the Department could possibly conjecture a need for them. The trees become scanter as we near the top. Road-makers are at work cutting stones or repairing here and there; they doff their faded berrets in greeting. They have frank, hardy faces, marked with belief that life is worth living:

"*Les tailleurs de pierre*
Sont de bons enfants;
Ils ne mangent guère
Mais ils solvent longtemps!"

By eleven o'clock the top is gained. We are on the Col d'Aubisque, 5600 feet above tide-water. The horses pause for a well merited breathing-spell, and we step to the ground for a survey. Across the valley towers the Ger, still apparently as high above us as at the start. Farther to the right, the Gourzy, though still in the near distance, has dwindled to a moderate hill, and Eaux Bonnes has throughout been niched from the field of view. To the left, other peaks, several heretofore unseen, stand silently out; their rocks and snow "of Arctic and African desolation," as Count Russell has observed of another scene, "since they are both burnt and frozen." The Pic du Midi d'Ossau, which should lie to the southwest, is not in sight, being hidden by intervening heights.

We turn for a view to the east. Here barren pastures sprawl over the hills, dotted in places with herds of cattle or flocks of mountain sheep. But the Valley of Lavedan, which we expected now to overlook, is not yet in sight. After a long descent before us, there is another though lower col to surmount before we can point out the villages of the new valley.

We seat ourselves by a snowbank, and enjoy the pleasures of rest for a season. Enter to us, a peasant upon the scene,—a woman, crossing the col from the Lavedan side. The large bundle magically balanced upon her head-cloth wavers never a trace as she steps lithely up the last acclivities and comes upon us. From a stick held over her shoulder depends another bundle, and over all she is carrying a war-worn and ludicrous umbrella. The interest is mutual. Promptly I spring up and pull off my cap in introduction. Her round face, simple and good-tempered, a comely type of her neighborhood, opens gradually from a stare into a smile, as the ladies add their greetings. She seems rather glad of the excuse to rest and lay aside her bundles, and in a few moments has grown quite communicative. She has come, this morning, she tells us, from Arrens, a small village on the way down toward the Lavedan valley and to be our destined halting-place, we recollect, for luncheon. She is taking to Eaux Bonnes a few woolen goods, stockings and hoods and shawls, knit by herself and her old mother during the long winter. They are not for fine people; oh, no, but the guides and the hotel maids like them.

"And your husband," we ask,—"what is he?" "A charcoal-burner, monsieur; he has his pits in the forests of the Balaïtous; it is a hard life."

"It is hardest in winter, is it not?"

"It is hard always, monsieur,"—this very simply; "but we have enough, though not more.—On the left of the road, madame,—our home,—as you walk out from the inn at Arrens toward the monastery."

Again the conception of discontent is a stranger; the idea puzzles her; her life has always been thus; she did not expect anything otherwise. It is a genuine forest-nature, mute yet never inglorious, reciting uncomplainingly its lesson of passiveness and endurance.

Her dress, coarse in texture, well worn but well cared for, appears to differ little in detail from the costume of the Ossau valley we have now quitted, but is more strictly, so she tells us, that of the peasantry of the Lavedan district next to be met with. The pleasant face is framed in by the ever-favorite hood or head-mantle. This is sometimes, as here, a kerchief, of conspicuous colors, peculiarly coifed,—the precise twist varying according to the mode of each locality. Often, as with the women of Goust, the kerchief is of plain white, tied below the chin, and set off with a short outside cape, black or colored, over the crown. At times the cape alone is worn without the kerchief, and on occasion the larger capulet of red supersedes them both.

Artfully we lead the conversation into a philosophical discussion, while the camera is secretly made ready,—when, from the side we have come, enter also another peasant, an old man this time, quite as good-humored and quite as characteristic as the first comer. He has dispensed with jacket or blouse, and displays the loose, baggy-sleeved cotton shirt often worn in substitution, an outlawed pair of *ouvrier's* trousers, and the local berret and *spadrilles*. His features have the true Gascon cast of shrewdness and tolerance. We formally introduce the two to each other, and the camera is trained upon the pair. But now the woman, discovering the plot, evinces that bashful disinclination, common among women the world over, to pose for immortality when without her best finery; though the old man, I am pleased to record, does not appear in the least sensitive about his. Silver, however, is a great persuader; now it proves a worthy adjutant of its nitrate; the drivers, who are greatly absorbed in the situation, add their encouragements to the reluctant one, and finally agreeing and ably supported by her new acquaintance as leading man, accoutred as she is, she plunges in; conscious attitudes are unconsciously taken,—as taken they always are for photography, be it in Paris or the Pyrenees, by all humankind; and the two wights, humbly and happily serving their separate lives, valued items in Nature's wide summation, stand forth together in the dignity of humanity to mark this trifling meeting in permanent remembrance.

There they talk together on the road, as we finally drive down the hill, their figures silhouetted against the sky. They have been on the whole pleased and awakened by their adventure; they will discuss and compare their emotions, finger their silver, wonder and speculate, and go their separate ways, convinced anew that the ways of the world and its worldlings are verily strange and inscrutable.

III.

The noonday heat has now become noticeable, and seems greater on this easterly shoulder of the ridge. We are grateful for the rapid downhill trot, which makes two breezes blow where one breeze blew before. Even that one is less marked on this side of the col, and as we descend, turn by turn, beyond the limits of snow patches and into the zone of undergrowth and then of greener vegetation, the air grows perceptibly oppressive. The view has wholly changed since leaving the crest. The Ger and its associates have fallen from sight; their valley is gone, and we face a scene entirely new. We climb again, to surmount the secondary col; and then commence the final descent.

It is now that the Route Thermale shows its mettle. This section of the road was among the most difficult portions encountered by the engineers. Nature stood off and refused all aid. "Beyond is the valley," she curtly told them; "between are the ravines; make what you can of them!"

A hopeless task it seemed. But Nature reckoned without Louis Napoleon. The road is here, serene and self-sufficient. It literally carved its way down to the valley. Slopes often greater than forty-five degrees have been cut into intrepidly; arches and viaducts thrown over gaping clefts, bridges over unbridgeable chasms. The road turns on itself; it doubles and twists and dodges; it crawls midway along the ledges, gouges a path into the hill around a landslide's groove, looks over uncomfortable brinks with easy unconcern, and in short outplays Nature at every point. And all the while it continues wide and firm, and we trot ceaselessly downward with not one pause. The parapets are less frequent than nearer Eaux Bonnes; often there is but a low line of heaped-up earth between us and the verge, and sometimes even this is wanting; but nowhere is the way too narrow for teams to pass, nowhere is there danger, save from a drunken driver or a thunderbolt.

We look back from the moving carriages, and the camera is pointed toward the ledge of road we have just traversed. The picture proves an eloquent witness to all that can be said of the Route Thermale.

Far below and in front, a patch of grey and brown has come into view; the drivers point out its clustering houses: it is Arrens. Many kilometres are traversed before that patch grows larger,—more still, before we have curved and dropped at last down to its level and are speeding along on a straight line toward the village. We find a ragged little street, and attract the usual waiting audience of Arcadians, and drawing up before the door of the inn are glad to escape for a time from the outside heat and glare.

IV.

The shady patch of garden at the side of the inn is an unqualified blessing. Roses overhang the paths, and green branches bend over its plot of grass. We have found the little dining-room dark and rather stuffy, have thrown open the windows and shutters, have confidently spoken for an artistic meal, and can now ruminate approvingly upon rest and refreshment, the sweet restorers of life. How should one tolerate its zigzaggings without the gentle recurrence of these its aids?

The kitchen opens invitingly from the hallway, and presently some of us drift indoors and group around its entrance. There is a hospitable stir of preparation within; a blazing and clattering that charm both eye and ear. The landlady and her daughter are busy with a fiery fury. We grow bolder. We crave permission to enter and watch operations. The old woman pauses and looks up as she cracks an egg on the edge of a plate, and then assents, willingly enough, but with unmistakable astonishment. She is used to predatory raids of visitors but evidently not to this inquiring spirit. Yet purposeful travel, we might tell her, is hundred-eyed and has glances for just such matters as this. It seeks out cities and scenery and history; but it seeks out life no less. We are gaining impressions which cannot be drawn from books, as we come close to these homely ways and habits, questioning, appreciating the people we meet, understanding their capacities and objects and limitations. One sees the breaking of an egg; he can see, besides, a thousand accompaniments to the event,—a biography summed up in an act.

At present, we note the breaking with rather more concern than the biography. Egg after egg is being deftly chipped, and its lucent content dropped first upon a plate,—a thrifty half-way station for possible unsoundness,—and then slid off into a clean-looking oval saucepan. The pan is then hung from an unfamiliar variety of crane close over the fire, and the contents wheedled and teased by a skillful spoon and bribed with salt and butter and a sprinkle of parsley. And even as we watch, the golden mass melts together; sighs and quivers, and thickens into wrinkles; bodies itself slowly into form and shape, under crafty oscillation; and is at last dexterously rolled out, a burnished ingot, upon the long platter, with a flourish that bespeaks practice and confidence. The stiff face of the old woman involuntarily relaxes with honest pride; she looks up half unconsciously for approval, and we all applaud galore.

Manifestly, externals vary, fundamentals persist. Barring details of place and process, the culinary art follows much the same laws and works out much the same results in this remote Department of the French Republic as in the Middle States of the American.

The kitchen itself is roomy and neat; the floor is of large, flat stones, the square embrasures of the windows are relieved with earthen pots of flowers. Full panoply of tins and trenchers and other implements of cheer hang in order against the walls or line the worn wooden shelves,—many of them strange in shape and of unconjectured use. Over all, there is that deft, subtle knowledge of place displayed by its busy inmate, a lifelong wontedness to surroundings, indefinable and unconscious, which fascinates us, and which reminds us that the same scene may be to one habituated to it the most iterated of commonplace and to new-comers often alive with novelty and interest.

At the window, meanwhile, other tragedies are enacted. The daughter is not idle. Here is a low, tiled shelf, with three square, sunken hollows, each lined with tiling and bottomed by an iron grating. Into these have been thrown small embers from the fire; the draught fans them into a flame, and above, three flat pans make their toothsome holdings to sizzle and sputter with infinite zest. This arrangement serves to the full every purpose of an oven, and does away with the range and all its cumbrous accompaniments. One is impressed with its obvious but effective simplicity.

In very brief time an appetizing déjeûner of seven courses is being ceremoniously served in the now airy dining-room,—interrupted throughout, to the good woman's unlessened wonder and our own enjoyment, by the journeys of some of us across to the kitchen at the end of each course to watch the preparation of the next.

The dame thaws out momently under our evident good-will, and as she brings in the cherries and cakelets, she ventures in turn to stand near the door, and is even pleased when we renew the conversation. Her husband, we learn, used to have charge of a little customs-station near the frontier; now they have this inn; it is pleasanter for him; one offends so many in a customs-post. They put by something each year; it is not much; many pause here during the summer, coming from Eaux Bonnes or Cauterets. Some seasons there are diligences running, which is better; for without them many go around by the railroad.

"But you, madame," I ask,—"you have traveled too by the railroad?"

"Yes, monsieur, a little; we have been several times to Pau; once we were at Bayonne."

"And do you prefer the cities?"

"We like better the mountains, monsieur; one can breathe here, and is not dependent."

The charge for the luncheon would be three francs each; she is glad that her visitors have been pleased; and our extra gratuity is the more appreciated because it seems wholly unexpected.

There is a monastery just out from the town. It is but a short walk, we are told, so while the horses are brought around, two of us explore. We follow a shaded avenue, triply garnished at the left with a brook, a foot-path and a long-row of small cottages; and soon mount a short hill, pass through an open gateway, and are before the churchly pile. Not a soul is about the place, and we have to look into the building entirely unciceroned. An apartment opening wide from the main hall is evidently some priest's oratory. We venture to peer tentatively in through the doorway. The room is plain, containing beside other furniture a small crucifix, a shrine, and a praying-chair,—and nearer us a recent number of *Figaro* open on the table. Thus it goes: the secular blending harmoniously with the spiritual.

The place is known as *Poey le Houn* or Hill of the Fountain; its site commands an extensive view, but otherwise there appears little about it that is distinctively interesting,—save as it is one of the fortunate Catholic institutions of the Lavedan spared from Montgomery's Huguenot raids. The chapel, entered from without by another portal, is sombre and rather large. We feel lonesome and intrusive without some guide, and do not examine it very carefully. A few towels are bleaching in the sun, on the paved court before the chapel,—the only sign of recent human presence. It is the home of brotherly deeds, and we piously turn the towels to bleach on the other side.

V.

We start again on the afternoon's drive with renewed zest. The hostess allows herself the luxury of several friendly smiles as the carriages move, and we give her farewell and good wishes in return. Umbrellas and parasols quickly go up to screen from the sun, and we lean restfully back, in contented anticipation of the remaining half of the day's ride.

At our right, for a while, at the far end of a valley, we have a mountain in view, whiter than common with excess of snow. This is the *Balaïtous*, craggy, irregular and weird, too far off to be imposing, yet one of the highest of the range. It is not an easily accessible mountain, nor is it often climbed. There is deemed to be something uncanny about it. Its ascent is very dangerous, they say. Accidents have occurred there; a strange ill omen, it is believed, invests those ghostly snows; the death-clutch of the Balaïtous holds many a brave mountaineer. As seen from here, it has an indefinably spectral, repellent look; there seems something almost hideous in its white and wrinkled cerements.

The road has now an easy course before it. We are but eight miles from the town of Argelès, where we shall be on the floor of the Lavedan valley; and the downward slant is slight. From Argelès, it will be but ten miles more to Cauterets. The scenery has softened greatly; cliffs and peaks are out of view, and we have rounded hills and easy, green, swelling curves and here and there a basking village.

Argelès is reached sooner than we expected. There is nothing to detain us here; it is a bright town, tidy and rather attractive, and we see it and all its inhabitants as we drive through. Here the journey from Eaux Bonnes to Cauterets over the road we have come, twenty-seven miles in all, is often broken for the night; many travelers and all the drivers advise a day and a half for the transit. We had seen that it could be as readily made within the day, the additional ten miles counting but little in mid-afternoon; and the horses after their long rest at Arrens now trot on, fresh and willing as in the morning.

At Argelès we meet the railroad once more. It is the Lavedan branch; it has left the main line at Lourdes, and runs southward up the valley, passing through Argelès and penetrating as far on the road to Cauterets as the town of Pierrefitte. The arrangement is a counterpart of the branch from Pau to Laruns. Our road now turns south also, going likewise to Pierrefitte, and running mainly parallel with the tracks though at some distance away. One could take the train from Argelès to Pierrefitte, and there connect with the diligence; but very little would of course be gained.

VI.

We are now out of Béarn, and have entered the ancient province of Bigorre.

In modern terms, we have passed from the Department of the Low Pyrenees to that of the High Pyrenees. One watering-place in this Department,—Bagnères de Bigorre,—which we shall visit in its turn, still preserves the old name of the province.

This county was not a principality like Béarn; though it had its own governors and government, it belonged to France and was held from the king. Béarn would not have tolerated a like state of dependence. When our old friend Gaston, Count of Foix, was living, the French king, grateful to him for previous aid in arms, offered him the control of Bigorre. The king "sent Sir Roger d'Espaign and a president of the Parliament of Paris, with fair letters patent engrossed and sealed, of the king's declaration that he gave him the county of Bigorre during his life, but that it was necessary he should become liege man and hold it of the crown of France." But the high-spirited Count of Foix declined. He was "very thankful to the king for this mark of his affection, and for the gift of Bigorre, which was unsolicited on his part; but for anything Sir Roger d'Espaign could say or do, he would never accept it. He only retained the castle of Mauvoisin [on its extreme confines] because it was free land and the castle and its dependencies held of none but God."

As France and Béarn seldom quarreled, Bigorre should have been a peaceful neighbor. But its northerly portion was held for a long time by an English garrison for the Black Prince, and this kept the county in constant disturbance. The strong post of the English was the town of Lourdes, (anciently Lourde,) eight miles north of us. "Garrisoned," says one, "by soldiers of fortune in the English pay, part of whose duty and all of whose inclination it was to harass the adjoining French possessions, Lourdes became the wasps' nest of the Pyrenees; whose fierce occupants were constantly buzzing about the rich hives of the plains for thirty leagues around, and leaving ugly stings behind."

"These captains,"—hear Froissart,

who traveled through Bigorre on his way to Béarn,—"made many excursions into Bigorre, the Toulousain, the Carcassonois and on the Albigeois; for the moment they left Lourde they were on enemy's ground, which they overran to a great extent, sometimes thirty leagues from their castle. In their march they touched nothing, but on their return all things were seized, and sometimes they brought with them so many prisoners and such quantities of cattle, they knew not how to dispose of nor lodge them." Thus, "these companions in Lourde had the satisfaction of overrunning the whole country wherever they pleased. Tarbes, which is situated hard by, was kept in great fear and was obliged to enter into a composition with them. On the other side of the river Lisse is a goodly enclosed town called Bagnères, the inhabitants of which had a hard time of it. In short, they laid under contribution the whole country,—except the territory of the Count de Foix; but there they dared not take a fowl without paying for it, nor hurt any man belonging to the count or even any who had his passport; for it would have enraged him so much that they must have been ruined."

The count showed less respect for Lourde than Lourde for him; and he even aided the French on one occasion by a scheme to capture the place and oust the intruders. This—it is a cruel story—was when he summoned its governor, his own half-brother, Sir Pierre Arnaut, to Orthez, under pretense of desiring a visit. Sir Pierre was holding Lourde stoutly in fief for the English prince, and was in considerable doubt about going, for he knew his man and had suspicions; however, "all thynges consydred, he sayd he wolde go, bycause in no wyse he wolde displease the erle." He left the castle with his brother Jean under strict injunctions, and proceeded to Orthez, where he was handsomely received by the count, "who with great ioye receyued hym, and made hym syt at his borde, and shewed hym as great semblant of love as he coude."

For the sequel, let us go back for once

to an earlier translation of the Chronicles than the one best known. The cruel story gains in effect of cruelty from the quaint, childlike telling.

"The thirde daye after, the Erle (Count) of Foiz sayd aloude, yt euery man might here hym:

"'Cosyn Pierre, I sende for you and ye be come; wherefore I comaunde you, as ye wyll eschewe my displeasure, and by the faith and lignage that ye owe to me, that ye yelde vp the garyson of Lourde into my handes.'

"Whan the knyght herde these wordes, he was sore abasshed, and studyed a lytell, remembringe what aunswere he might make, for he sawe well the erle spake in good faithe; howebeit, all thynges consydred, he sayd:

"'Sir, true it is, I owne to you faythe and homage, for I am a poore knyght of your blode and of your countrey; but as for the castell of Lourde, I wyll nat delyuer it to you; ye have sent for me to do with me as ye lyst; I holde it of the Kyng of Englande; he sette me there; and to none other lyueng wyll I delyuer it.'

"When the Erie of Foiz herde that answere, his blode chafed for yre, and sayd, drawyng out his daggar:

"'A treator! sayest thou nay? By my heed, thou hast nat sayd that for nought,'—and so therwith strake the knight that he wounded hym in fyue (five) places, and there was no knyght nor barone yt durst steppe bytwene them.

"Than the knyght sayd:

"'Ah, sir, ye do me no gentylnesse to sende for me and slee me!'

"And yet, for all the strokes that he had with the daggar, therle (the earl) comauded to cast him in prison, downe into a depe dyke; and so he was, and ther dyed, for his woundes were but yuell (ill) loked vnto."

It is a satisfaction to record that Gaston gained nothing by his dastardly act. Pierre's brother, Sir Jean, stood to his post in Lourde as stoutly as Pierre had done; and the count did not obtain the fortress. In fact he does not seem even to have pursued his attempt upon it farther. He doubtless thought he had done

enough to clinch Lourde's respect for his pugnacity.

It was in return for this well-meant assistance that the French king offered Gaston the whole of Bigorre, Lourde and all, which he so politely declined. He was shrewd as well as high-spirited; he was not covetous for the garden if the wasps' nest remained undemolished. So Sir Jean and his robber band buzzed merrily on in their castle.

Our chronicler naturally asks his informant:

"'Dyde this Jean neuer after go to se the Erie of Foiz?'

"He answered and sayd: 'Sithe the dethe of his brother, he neuer came there; but other of his company hath been often with the erle,—as Peter Danchyn, Ernalton of Restue, Ernalton of Saynt Colome, and other.'

"'Sir,' quod I, 'hath the Erie of Foiz made any amendes for the dethe of that knight or sorie for his dethe?'

"'Yes, truely, sir,' quod he, 'he was right sorie for his dethe; but as for amendes, I knowe of none, without it be by secrete penauce, masses or prayers; he hathe with hym the same knighte's sonne, called Johan of Byerne, a gracyous squyer, and the erle loueth hym right well.'"

VII.

Lourdes itself can be shortly reached by rail, here from Argelès, or from Pau. It would undoubtedly deserve the visit. Besides its robber reminiscences, it has developed another and contrasting specialty: it has become one of the most famous places of religious pilgrimage in Europe. Thirty years ago it was made the scene of a noted "miracle." At a grotto near the town, the Virgin appeared several times in person to an ardent peasant-girl; caused a healing spring to burst from the rock, and stipulated for a church. The girl published the miracle; its repute instantly spread far and wide, and the bishop of Tarbes, after examination, publicly declared it authentic. Since that time, devotees throng the town annually; Murray states that one hundred and fifty thousand persons visited the scene in the six months

following the apparition. The character of the place has been transformed; a tide of enthusiastic pilgrimage has swept over it like a whirlwind; everything in and about the city has taken the garb of this religious fervor. The grotto is lined with crutches cast away by the cured; the church is built, and is rich with votive offerings; every house lodges the shifting comers, a thousand booths sell souvenirs of piety; and,—last impressive mingling of mercantile and miraculous,—the waters are regularly bottled and shipped for sale to all parts of the world!

The castle still stands, on a pointed hill above the town. Its founding goes back far beyond the days of its thieving English garrison; the Saracens once swarmed into it long before, flying before Charles the Hammer; and there is another story about it in this connection, as related by Inglis, which ends more happily than that of its murdered governor. Charlemagne, some years after the Saracens captured it, laid siege to recover it; surrender grew inevitable; but its Moorish commander, Mirat, though an infidel was, for his nobility of character, in special favor with the Virgin,— Notre Dame de Puy. In this extremity, she sent to him an eagle bearing in its beak a live fish; and Mirat promptly sent it to Charlemagne, to show his heavenly succor. The king, knowing that there was no possible fishing on the castle hill, perceived that it was a miracle; and lessening his rigor in the face of this sign, proposed less hard terms: the Moors were allowed to depart in safety, Mirat on his part agreed to be converted and become a good Catholic, and the castle was formally surrendered not to Charlemagne but to Notre Dame de Puy.

VIII.

But meanwhile we are moving toward Cauterets, not toward Lourdes. This part of the Lavedan valley is known as the "Eden of Argelès." It expands about us in long, delicious levels; occasional eminences wrinkle its even lines; and the hills roll up from each side, rounded and gentle and often cultivated to their tops. Squares of yellow maize-fields chequer them, alternating with darker patches of pasture or orchard, while along the wide centre run the rails and the high-road, and the new Gave, fresh from Gavarnie and the Lac de Gaube,— new, yet an old friend, for it flows forth by way of Lourdes on to the Château of Pau. Walnut, lime and fig trees, twisted with vines, stand near its borders or about the chalets and hamlets on the slopes. Women and men are at work over in the fields, and often pause to look at our distant carriages and bow a response to our wavings of greeting; while on the road itself, here much traveled, we meet teams and ox-carts and a carriage or two with travelers coming from Cauterets.

Up on a bluff at the right is an old building: it is the abbey of Saint Savin, some of whose stones also could tell us of Charlemagne and perhaps of young Crassus. Farther on, we see, on an opposite slope across the valley, other ruins: a castle; an old tower; and higher still an ancient chapel of the Virgin, cared for to this day, it is said, as in the time of earlier travelers, by the trio of aged women voluntarily pledged to its guardianship and to solitude. Their number remains always the same; upon the death of one, the remaining two make choice of a third to fill her place. It has been thus from unknown periods. Thither repair the women of the valley, on days consecrated to the Virgin, to pay their devotions at this lonely shrine.

Thus together, peace and war, holiness and crime, have dominated this fair region; and with these shivered fortalices and ancient cloisters actually before us, their past seems nearer to possibility. Their relics, attesting the days of feudalism, seem to mourn its departure; the old order has indeed changed and yielded place to new. "It was sweet here to be a monk!" writes Taine, in his warm sympathy with the spirit of this valley; "it is in such places that the *Imitation* should be read; in such places was it written. For a sensitive and noble nature, a convent was then the sole refuge; all around wounded and repelled it.

"Around, what a horrible world!

Brigand lords who plunder travelers and butcher each other; artisans and soldiers who stuff themselves with meat and yoke themselves together like brutes; peasants whose huts they burn,. who out of despair and hunger slip away to tumult. No remembrance of good, nor hope of better. How sweet it is to renounce action, company, speech, to hide one's self, forget outside things, and to listen in security and solitude to the divine voices that, like collected springs, murmur peacefully in the depths of the heart!"

Farther on still, on another eyrie, is a ruined monastery, St. Orens. This saint came to the Pyrenees from Spain at an early age, and founded this retreat, loving solitude and meditation and austere living. His piety made him widely revered. He long refused the offered archbishopric of Auch; till, doubting his duty in this, he prayed to God for a sign. He was directed to plant a sapling in the earth, and it instantly bloomed into leaves and blossoms; whereupon the hermit wisely inferred that life was designed to bear fruit, not to wither itself away.

Montgomery, Queen Jeanne's ruffian Protestant general, tore through this Catholic valley in 1569, with his devastating mercenaries. It recovered heart, flowered afresh, and was swept again by enemies from a neighboring province. Often a winter storm will expose bedrock throughout precious roods of sloping harvest-land, and the farmer must carry up from the valley many painful baskets of soil to replace the loss. So that, though it smiles so happily in this afternoon warmth, there have been serpents in this Eden,—serpents of want and of suffering; and judging by the faces of the people, all have not yet been scotched.

But we are at Pierrefitte. It is five o'clock in the afternoon, and the innkeeper is rejoiced to find that we are thirsty.

IX.

Pierrefitte ends the branch railway from Lourdes, as Laruns ended that from Pau. In fact, it is all strikingly like Laruns.

A similarly uncompromising mountain, the *Viscos*, 7000 feet high, walls up the valley behind it, and here again the carriage-roads divide, one going up the gorge on the right to Cauterets, the other up that on the left to Luz and Gavarnie. The broad Argelès vale has been fittingly described as but the vestibule to the wild dwelling of the clouds, and Pierrefitte as the beginning-point for the narrow stair-flights which lead up to the interior.

As at Laruns, we are now to take the road to the right, at a later day returning to take the other. The Route Thermale goes on up the latter, passing through southeast to Luz, and then stretching eastward again to Barèges and over successive cols to Bigorre and Luchon. This we are progressively to follow in its entirety.

The train has come in, here at Pierrefitte, and the diligence for Cauterets is just leaving, attended by a wagonload of trunks. Horses and travelers refreshed, we soon move after it, and rising from the valley by half an hour's steep zigzags upward and forward, we pass the great yellow vehicle as it is entering the defile. Looking back, we have one brilliant view of the wide Eden of Argelès, and pass from light into twilight.

The road to Cauterets is a duplicate of that to Eaux Chaudes. Possibly the scenery is a trifle more impressive. We have the straight-cliffed gorge, with the torrent at its bottom and the road buttressed out or cut into the ledge; the turns in the ravine as we pull steadily higher, the bare slate and limestone precipices, the higher peaks. At times there is only width for the road and the torrent beneath, and the torrent seems uncomfortably crowded at that. The road does not allow itself to be crowded. It is hard and wide as always, and lavishly decorated with kilometre-stones. The stream is crossed, back and forth; the air has grown quickly cooler, and sunshades need no longer shut off the full view. "Upon nearing Cauterets, the carriage-way would seem as though it had grown phrensied from the mountainous opposition, for it curls and writhes and overcomes the difficulties only by the most desperate exertions; and at one spot, in its effort to compass a barrier of rock, it actually recoils within half-a-dozen yards of its former path. " Throughout, however, the same easy, imperturbable gradient is preserved. The old road was greatly rougher and steeper; four horses and three pairs of oxen, it is said, were once required to drag up each carriage.

Finally the valley widens slightly, and rather suddenly opens out upon an incline. At its farther end is a white-crested mountain, and below nestles the mountain resort of Cauterets, six miles in from Pierrefitte.

It is seven o'clock, as our wheels strike the stones of the pavement. We drive into the main street, pass through a neat, irregular little plaza, and, some distance beyond, turn to the right from a larger square, toward the Hotel Continental. The town is waiting for the diligence, and shopkeepers are at their doors, guides and touters and loungers and visitors in the streets, all expectant for the daily gust of arrival. The lamps are just twinkling out, against the dusk, and the general impression,—often a long determinant of like or dislike,—is of an animated and welcoming scene. The hotel proves to be nearly on the scale of the Gassion, and other equally pretentious ones have been passed in approaching it. We drive under the high entrance-way and into its great court, with the flourishes dear to the drivers' hearts; and the long and varying tableau of the day's ride is over.

CHAPTER XII.

MIRRORS AND MOUNTAINS.

"All along the valley, stream that flashest white,
Deepening thy voice with the deepening of the night."
—TENNYSON'S *Cauterets*.

Cauterets confirms its first good impressions. The next day proves cloudy and foggy, and we spend it lazily, re-reading and answering letters, or wandering about the town, absorbing its streets and shops. The season is fairly

afloat, and all sail is set. At the angle of two thoroughfares, a stretch of ground has been brushed together for a park or promenade, and this, sprinkled with low, flat-topped trees and a band-stand, naturally attracts us first. Booths and cafés and nicknack stalls reach around its sides, and across from us stands a fine official-looking structure of marble, which we learn is the Thermal Establishment. We stroll toward this, through the groups of promenaders, run the gauntlet of the booths, inspecting hopelessly their catchpenny wares and games, and find ourselves before it. It is well placed, and architecturally effective. To judge from the goodly patronage, it is pathologically effective as well. Within, the large, tiled hall conducts right and left to wings containing rows of white-tiled bath-apartments and two full-sized swimming-rooms. An imposing marble stairway leads upward to reading, billiard and gaming apartments, café and restaurant and a theatre-hall. Evidently the Thermal Establishment is the pivot of Cauterets. The serious use of these waters is carried to a science. You can be steamed, suffused, sprayed, sponged, showered, submerged or soaked. You can seek health from a teaspoon or a tub. Make choice, and buy a season ticket. Rather, the attendant physicians make the choice, for all is by rule here and no one moistens lip or finger without due prescription.

These springs are celebrated among French doctors. The systems of treatment are kept abreast of all modern theories. The waters are sulphureous, very hot, and abundant. They serve in throat and stomach troubles and for a wide range of ailments "where there is indicated a powerfully alterative and stimulating treatment."

We ramble back across the esplanade and out into the streets. The stores, al-

ways friendly in their hostile designs, conspire to be especially attractive in Cauterets. We waste much time—from a masculine standpoint—in an enticing lace store, where really fine Spanish nettings are purchased at tempting prices. They sell too, in Cauterets, the woolly stuffs called Barèges crape, marvelously delicate in texture, woven in various tints for mufflers and capes and shoulder-wraps. Farther up the street, we are allured during the forenoon into buying a woollen berret or two, and scarlet sashes, the badge of the country, for to-morrow's mountain excursion; and yield in the plaza to the fascination of barley-sugar candy and toothsome cakes of Spanish chocolate. But all entreaties to buy young Pyrenean dogs warranted bred in the region, are manfully resisted.

We invest too in a strange variety of umbrella, which can be folded into wondrously small compass and put into the pocket or the traveling-bag,—invest in it after a long struggle of rates, wherein each side gains the satisfaction of victory by a compromise. The eagerness of the Frenchy vendor,—his dramatic acting-out of the umbrella's workings,—his voluble deprecation of a possible lower price, and his gradual sliding down from his end of the scale as we rise in it from ours,—these accessories fully double the zest of the transaction for both. One must be wary and alert to properly enjoy European shopping; but if one is thus prepared, it can be made to furnish very solid enjoyment indeed. "As a rule," as the genial author of *Sketches in the South of France* observes, "the British purchaser must offer one half the price asked. Everybody does it, and it is in no way offensive, because the sum has been pre-arranged accordingly. The British costume springs the market at least ten per cent, bad French ten more, and an apparent ignorance of both market and language cannot be let off at less than thirty or forty. Expostulation is useless, even when convenient; the torrent of 'impossible', 'incroyable,' 'que c'est gentil,' 'ravissant,' 'beau' would drown any opposition. The only chance is to be deaf to argument, dumb to solicitations, to place the sum proposed before the merchant, and if it be not accepted, retire in dignified silence. Ten to one you will be followed and a fresh assault commenced; be resolute, and the same odds you get your bargain."

Variety marks the stores not only, but the streets and saunterers. All these Pyrenean resorts put on the motley. There is of course the substratum of plainly-garbed humanity; but as at Eaux Bonnes, it is set off with scarlet-coated guides, Spaniards in deep-colored mantles, peasant women with red capulets or bright-hued shoulder-wear, and the satin finish of fashion in its passing carriages. Hucksters are pleading their varied wares in the plaza, and here and there a shovel-hatted priest is given reverential right of way. We meet scarcely an English face, however, and of our own travel-loving countrymen none at all. At noon the band plays in the music pavilion, and by degrees the idle world drifts in that direction. The round café-tables under the trees gradually sort out their little coteries, and white-aproned gentry skate about with liqueur-bottles, clinking glass beer-mugs, baskets of rolls, and the inevitable long-handled tin coffee-pots. The outdoor scene tempts us more than a hotel luncheon; we cast in our lot with an alert-eyed waiter, and the syrups and chocolate he brings are doubly sweetened with the strains of *Martha*.

II.

Here is an old letter concerning these waters, which brings the dead back in flesh and blood. It leaves its writer before us in vivid presence, a womanly reality. It is Marguerite of Angoulême who writes it,—the thoughtful, high-souled queen of Béarn-Navarre, whose daughter was afterward mother of Henry IV. She is at Pau, and is sending word about her husband's health to her brother, Francis I of France.

"Though this mild spring air," she tells him, "ought to benefit the King of Navarre, he still feels the effects of the fall he met with. The doctors have ordered him to spend the month of May at the Baths of Caulderets, where wonderful things are happening every day.

"I am thinking of going with him," she adds,—how domestic and personal these little royal plannings seem,—"after the quiet of Lent, so as to keep him amused and look after him and help him with his affairs; for when one is away for his health at the baths, he ought to live like a child, without a care."

Hither they came accordingly, and the court with them. How royalty put up with the then primitive accommodations is not recorded; standards of comfort, if not of lavishness, were lower then. Here, surrounded by her maids of honor, Marguerite passed the pleasant days of the king's convalescence and wrote many of her *Contes* in the long summer afternoons upon the hillsides.

Rabelais used to come to Cauterets, and one of the springs is said to be named from a visit of Caesar's. Eaux Chaudes and Eaux Bonnes have had eclipses of popularity, but Cauterets has always been in vogue. It was not always luxurious, however. Invalids were brought here by rough litters or on the backs of guides or horses. A monk and a physician lived near the bath-enclosure, and narrow cabins or huts, roofed with slate, were let out to the sick and their attendants. How greatly the dignified Marguerite and her war-bred husband would marvel, if they could walk with us to-day from the Thermal Establishment, across the park and through the streets and squares,—to pause from their astonishment in the polished and gilt-mirrored drawing-room of the Hotel Continental!

III.

There are walks and promenades and mountain nooks in all directions from the town, but the afternoon grows misty and we do not explore them. The Gave running noisily on, hard by, has its stiller moments, up the valley, and the trout-fishing is reputed rather remarkable. In fact, one ardent angler who came here is said to have complained of two drawbacks: first, that the fish were so provokingly numerous as to ensure a nibble at every cast; and second, that they were so simple-minded and untactical that every nibble proved a take.

Besides affording these milder joys, Cauterets is a centre for larger excursions. There are three especially noted. The first and finest is the trip to the *Lac de Gaube*, a high mountain tarn at the very foot of the Vignemale. This we plan in prospect for to-morrow. It is four hours away by a bridle-path, passing on the way several much-admired mountain cataracts. The second excursion is by the foot-pass over a shoulder of the Viscos to Luz, a counterpart of the path over the Gourzy from Eaux Chaudes to Eaux Bonnes. As we purpose going to Luz by carriage, passing down to Pierrefitte and so up the other side of the V, we strike the Viscos from the list of necessaries. The third is the ascent of the Monné, the mountain overhanging Cauterets and 9000 feet above the sea; reported as long but not difficult and as giving a repaying view. But there is a mountain near Luz, the *Bergonz*, from which the view is held equally fine, and it is, we learn, simpler of ascent; there is even a bridle-path to the summit. Since we are to go to Luz, we decide for the Bergonz, and so cancel the Monné.

Cauterets might be likened to St. Moritz in the Engadine. It has no lakes so close at hand, but in its springs and baths, in its fashion and in its general location, a fair parallel is offered. Some of the important peaks of the range, Mont Perdu and the Vignemale, for example, are near us here though invisible from the town, as is the Bernina chain from St. Moritz. The Monné will stand for the Piz Languard. In hotels, Cauterets is hardly outgeneraled even by St. Moritz, though in expensiveness they will yield gracefully to the Engadine. The Hotel Continental, we find, has rather a pathetic story. It was built by a widow who had been left rich,—built only a few years ago, as a hobby, it would seem, and with little care for cost or judicious investment. It represented nearly three hundred thousand dollars, was extravagantly run, and lost money from the beginning. She also built a great café and music-hall across the street from the hotel, and the losses of the two together swelled in the end to an unbearable burden. Her fortune was sponged up, to the last franc; the property was bought in by a stock-company, and its unfortunate projector is now, we are told, in a charitable institution at Bordeaux. One hardly wonders at the result, in admiring the hotel. Its patronage may be large and rich, but no mere summer season,—at least without the English and Americans,—could recoup the interest on its costly outlay. The Gassion at Pau is profitable if at all because its yearly season is three times longer than this at Cauterets.

There is an evening conjuring performance at a café in the town, and some of us desert the ladies and enter its chaos of mirrors and tobacco smoke. The prestidigitator, a nervous, restive Frenchman with an astonishing rapidity of tongue, stands near the centre of the room and juggles and struggles with hats and rings and eggs and his own overmastering fluency. Now he will dart across the floor to borrow a listener's handkerchief; now he assaults our corner with the plea that we verify a card; later the hat is passed for the harvest. It is an interesting scene, European to the core; the men about the tables sip and smoke, intent on the performance or on their dominoes, grave and contemplative, finding uniformly in this contented café-life the needful finis of the day.

IV.

The son renews his acquaintance, the next morning, with Cauterets, as we start for the Lac de Gaube. It is the Fourth of July; the hotel manager has good-naturedly procured some firecrackers for the small boy of the party, and thus our national devotions are duly paid and we are shrived for the day. Carriages can be taken for part of the way toward the Lac; it is good policy, so saddle-horses for the ladies are sent on to wait for us at the point where the road ends and the bridal-path begins.

The first mile in the road is perhaps the most frequented bit in the Pyrenees; it is the route to a second large springhouse known as the *Raillère*, which is even more sought than the one in the town. We find the wayside everything but dull. Omnibuses meet us frequently, wealthier drinkers pass in light carriages, while many, going or coming, are enjoying the journey on foot. Each is armed with his or her individual drinking-cup, worn by a strap over the shoulder like field-glasses. The road is somewhat shadeless, and at noon will be hot; but this is an early-morning route. These are sunrise waters. Such is the dictum or the wont. The faithful even work up a mild daily rivalry in early waking. This may aid to make them healthy; improbably, wealthy; but it does not show them to be wise. Time is always quoted under par at a summer resort; why should the idlers heedlessly load up with too much of the stock? These people have come out here, many of them, at six and seven o'clock, a few even earlier; they have sipped their modicum of sulphur and scandal, have prolonged the event as fully as possible, and must now ripple irregularly back toward the town, objectless entirely until the noon music and the atoning siesta.

The building itself, a large, prominent structure, stands out on the slope of a sterile mountain side, the road sweeping up to its level in a long, elliptic curve. We find much people here congregated, and omnibuses and footfarers are still arriving and departing. Among the throng are three veritable Capuchin monks, thickly weighted with enfolding hoods and brown woolen gowns, the latter heavy and long and girdled at the waist,—a light, airy costume for a warm day. Our drivers stop here while one of them repairs a broken strap, and we contentedly watch and speculate upon the assemblage.

Three other smaller spring-establishments are passed in turn, farther up the valley. Each has its specialty and its limited but believing clientèle. Then the road becomes solitary, and ephemeral humanity is left behind. Soon the slow, even strain of the horses tells of stiffer work than along the easy, inclines nearer the Raillère. The Gave comes jumping downward more and more hurriedly, and presently its restless mutterings deepen into a dull growl, which grows louder. It rises by degrees to a roar, the road makes a last energetic bend,—and we are looking down upon the famed *Cerizet* cascade. It is a broad rush of the stream, thundering beneath the bridge; there is an unexpected body to the fall; the massed water bounds down a double ledge, and swirls angrily away down the gorge. The scene is strikingly set, with slippery rocks and dark-green box bordering the torrent, and the cliffs rising sharply around, naked and bony or furred with box and pine. This is the favorite short drive from Cauterets. Pedestrians seek it, as well. The Cerizet holds the charm of its wildness alike for the idler and the lover of nature.

Here the road ends, in a confined level across the bridge. At the bend above stand a rough shanty and a shed, and near by our waiting saddle-horses are unobtrusively browsing. Drivers and carriages now leave us and turn back, and the guide helps us to roll wraps and coats into cylinder-form and straps them snugly behind the saddles. The shanty is not too primitive to vend refreshing drinks, and the ancient Frenchman in the doorway vainly lures us to lemonade and sour wine. The guide hands out sticks for those of us who walk, swings the camera strap over his shoulder, and we all wave a friendly hand to the old mountain-taverner, who grins a forgiving *au revoir*.

We strike at once into the thicket. There is only the footway to pierce it, crooked and steep and stony from the start.

"The winding vale now narrows on the view,"

and the crowding trees at times shut out all sight of the cliffs opposite and above, though we always hear the noise of the torrent. The sun can rarely find the path, which is damp and at places muddy. The slant of the gorge has grown steeper, and when we come to breaks in the forest, we see the water tearing down toward us along its broken trough in increasing contortions, often in great flying leaps. No path could hold this incline directly, and this one gracefully yields and adopts the usual expedient, ricochetting upward in short, incessant lacings, tracing up in the main the run of the Gave, but often diverted, zigzagging, always mounting, quadrupling the distance while it quarters the angle.

Two other cascades are passed. The horses, used to the work, strain forward uncomplainingly, the guide leading the foremost; they toil quietly along the easier spots, but tug themselves rapidly, almost convulsively, up over the hard ones. The jolting, pitching motion is severe and somewhat trying; and at intervals the ladies dismount and join us in walking,—relieving the effort of rest with the rest of effort.

An hour or less of this, and then another roar presages another cataract, and soon we emerge upon the scene. This is the *Pont d'Espagne*, a bridge of long logs stretching across the torrent at the spot where two streams unite and throw themselves together into the hollow, twenty-eight or thirty feet below. We pause on the rough bridge and gaze down at the plunging water and foam and upward at our surroundings. The entire picture, framed in by the sharp blackness of the pines and the broken escarpments of cliff and mountain, has been well compared to a scene in Norway.

At the other side of the bridge stand another shanty and another shed; also another refreshment-vendor. A cool beverage has an attraction now which it had not earned an hour ago, and we feel that a breathing-spell will not be wasted.

Here paths unite as well as streams. We have been nearing the Spanish frontier-line again, and the trail following the right-hand stream would lead up toward its source and pass on over the crest of the mountain down to the Spanish baths of Panticosa, as did the path from Gabas in the Ossau valley. The top

of the pass is three hours away, and the view, it is said, is very extensive. These passes over the main chain are known as *ports*, as those over its branches are called cols. They are generally simple notches in the dividing ridges, massive but narrow, and the winds blow through them at a gallop. In a storm or in winter the danger is extreme. The Basques and Pyreneans have a saying that "he who has not been on the sea or in the *port* during a storm knows not the power of God."

The path following the leftward stream leads to the Lac de Gaube, two miles farther on, and is the one we now take. The way continues much the same as before, but the trees become sparser and the outlook wider and more desolate as we ascend.

Our guide is a sunburnt, athletic Frenchman of middle age, noticeable so far chiefly for his huge grey mustachios and for his silence. He has been willing but laconic,—taciturn, in fact. But I have felt sure he has a "glib" side. Can I find it? The stillest of men are fluent on their loved topics; there is some key to unlock every one's reserve. Can I hit upon the key to his? Which of possible interests in common will bring us into talk?

I am ahead with him now, in front of the horses, stepping up the crooking staircase of stones, sounding him on the weather and the way. Unexpectedly the key is hit upon. A chance comparison I make of a view in the Alps lights up the old fellow's face, and when I happen to mention an exploit of Whymper, his tongue is loosed. It is not merely a name to him,—this of Edward Whymper, scaler of mountains, the first to stand on the summit of the Matterhorn, one of the three who descended it alive out of that fated party of seven. This man knows him, he tells me joyously; he has been his guide here in the Pyrenees. It was many years back; he does not recall the year. It is evidently his proudest recollection, and he is more than willing to talk of it. In fact, I am as interested as he; for the pages of my copy of Whymper's *Scrambles among the Alps* have been very often turned.

Whymper came here, it seems, with his usual desire to conquer, and the guide tells me of some of the peaks they stormed together. The more familiar giants, the Vignemale, Mont Perdu and others, were climbed as a matter of course. Their ardor was greatest, however, in assaulting some uncaptured summit; and several such fell before their conquering attack. Monsieur Wheempair, the guide goes on, was "*très intrépide*"; not stout, but firmly compacted, lithe and very active, and he never asked a hand. "He told me," adds my companion, "that some time we would go to the Alps together;" and the man turns to me as we work onward, and questions me about those mountains. That is his ambition now,—to visit Switzerland and the rivals of his Mont Perdu and Maladetta.

I tell him, too, something of the greater peaks his hero has subsequently rendered subject among the Andes,— Chimborazo, Antisana and others; of his passing twenty-six consecutive hours encamped with his guides on the summit of Cotopaxi; of the difficulties of route and dangers of weather he everywhere experienced. The guide had heard that Whymper had been in the Andes, but knew no details of his doings nor of the heights and nature of the mountains. He greedily adds these new facts to his collection of Whymperiana.

These guides make little. To be sure, they spend little. Probably they want for little, as well. Living is low, and the Frenchman is thrifty. Yet a guide's occupation is particularly uncertain; there are long gaps of enforced idleness even in the season, and wages of seven or eight francs a day when he is employed are not only little enough at best, considering the toil and occasional danger, but must be averaged down to cover the unoccupied days besides. For ascents among the greater peaks the pay is better, but they are much less frequent. My friend of the mustachios lives in Cauterets, he tells me, during the season; he has a family; in winter he can work at logging and wood-hauling, in summer he earns most as a guide. Many persons too come to hunt, not to climb, and sportsmen are always liberal; but the hunting is growing poor; the bouquetin is extinct, the bear is almost gone, the wolf is a coward; of large game, only the izard remains.

V.

Meanwhile, we have all been clambering up the pathway, calling out at points of view, expecting at each rise to see the lake in the level above. At length, a short hour from the Pont d'Espagne, we press up the last curve, come out suddenly upon a plateau, and the lonely basin of the Lac de Gaube is before us.

Just ahead is the low-roofed house built at the side of the lake for the purposes of a restaurant; and we enter, to unroll the wraps and make some important stipulations regarding trout and a soufflet. Though the lake is not even with the snow-level, the cool air makes a light overcoat most acceptable after the warm morning climb. Then we hurry out to see our surroundings.

The great Vignemale, the central feature in the picture, at first disappoints us. This, the fourth in height of Pyrenees mountains, confronts one squarely from across the lake, effectively framed between two barren slopes,—the highest of its triple peaks somewhat hidden by the hill on the right. But the giant does not seem to tower in the least, and appears from this spot little else than a huge but disjointed mass of rock and glaciers, in the latter of which the Vignemale abounds. The view improves, a few yards on around the lake. But it requires an effort to believe that of those "three mountain tops,
Three silent pinnacles of aged snow,"
the loftiest is ten thousand, eight hundred and twenty feet above the sea; it is still harder to grant that its knobby tips are a full mile in perpendicular height above us at the Lac de Gaube. It is only by degrees that the distant form seems to grow and mount, as we come to realize its true dimensions.

This mountain was never ascended until 1834, when two guides from a neighboring valley, Cantouz and Guilhembert by name, finally mastered it. The ascent was marked by a signal ex-

hibition of pluck. The men had attained, after perilous work, the large glacier of Ossoue. They were traversing it, toilsomely and carefully, when an ice-bridge gave way beneath them and plunged them both into the depths of a crevasse. They were made insensible by the fall. Cantouz at last came to himself, stiffened and bruised; to his joy Guilhembert also was after some effort brought back to consciousness. For hours these men picked their icy way along the bottom of the crevasse and its branches, through the water and melted snow, seeking some opening, some way of escape to the upper surface of the glacier. Effort after effort failed. The day was waning. At length a narrow "chimney" was found, more promising than the rest; and by painful and dangerous degrees, wearied, sore and half-frozen as they were, the two slowly worked a zigzag way upward to the light.

Did they turn thankfully homeward and leave the grim Vignemale to its isolation? They did not. They grimly went on with the attack. Before darkness had fallen, they stood upon the summit,—the first human beings to accomplish the feat. They had to spend the night upon the mountain, but it was as their subject realm.

The lake itself is perhaps a mile across, and is exceedingly deep. The mountains crowd close to its edge, here wooded, there running off in long sweeps of rubbly waste, again starting sharply upward from the water. Close by the path, a tongue of rock runs out into the lake, and on this still stands the little shaft, enclosed with iron palisades, "A broken chancel with a broken cross, That stood on a dark strait of barren land,"—
a monument to a young Englishman and his wife, who were drowned here more than fifty years ago. They were on their wedding trip, and had come to the Lac de Gaube; they took a small boat for a row, and by a never-explained accident lost their lives together. The pathetic inscription reads:
"This tablet is dedicated to the memory of William Henry Pattisson, of Lin-

coln's Inn, London, Esq., barrister at law; and of Susan Frances, his wife; who, in the 31st and 26th years of their age, and within one month of their marriage, to the inexpressible grief of their surviving relations and friends, were accidentally drowned together in this lake, on the 20th day of September, 1832. Their remains were conveyed to England, and interred there at Witham, in the County of Essex."

A party of jolly, black-garbed priests have been journeying up the path behind us from the Pont d'Espagne. They now come out from the inn upon the scene of action. Their cordial faces attract us at once; they approach our little summer-house, and conversation opens on both sides,—with nation, tongue and creed soon in genial comity. Two of these men are young; their features, refined and thoughtful, are those of students; all are as fun-loving as boys out of school. They investigate the camera with great interest, and ask about our plans and travels, and tell us about their own. They invite us to join in a row on the lake, but we are mindful of the soufflet in near readiness; so they finally push out from the shore, charmed to oblige by forming the foreground for a photograph.

Other arrivals, two or three, are now at the inn, for the Lac de Gaube is a "required course" for all visitors to Cauterets. We are guilefully glad we preempted the trout. It is a very substantial little meal they serve, in this wilderness of rock and fir, where every supply except fish must be carried up, as it were, piecemeal. The proprietor does well in the catering line, but less well, he mourns to us, on his boats. It is that monument. The pale shaft is a constant *memento mori*. It suggests tragic possibilities. It always chills the tourist's enthusiasm for a row, and generally freezes it altogether. With good reason, it seems, may mine host complain bitterly of its flattening effects on the boat-trade; and there is a dark whisper in Cauterets that, were the shaft not so closely enveloped both in religious sanctity and in municipal protection, it would some night mysteriously disappear.

VI.

The sun still blazes down upon the motionless lake, as we walk out once more for a long gaze toward the snows of the Vignemale. We try to trace out the route to its perilous summits, and conjecture the direction taken by Cantouz and Guilhembert when they made that grim first ascent; and our guide, approaching now with the horses, points out the direction afterward taken by Whymper and himself. We settle our account for the repast,—an account by no means exorbitant; wraps are re-cylindered and re-strapped, and we are soon on the return path downward through the woods. The saddles pitch like skiffs at sea. These Pyrenean horses are far more pronounced in their motions than the lowly Swiss mule. One by one the ladies dismount, and for the steep portions at least the horses go riderless, and no doubt secretly exult in their own shortcomings.

We pass the Pont d'Espagne, the roar of whose cataract is cheering the waiting hours of its solitary refreshment-seller. We plunge into the thicker leafage below, striding fast, or staying to lend hands from stone to stone or around the patches of wet ground. The woods echo with the noise of the brook, and now and then with the crack of a distant rifle; and finally we are down again to the first hut and taverner and the Cerizet fall. Now the ladies can spring comfortably up to their saddles once more, and the carriage-road is a welcome change from the lumpy bridle-path which we are leaving behind.

We keep on in the mid-afternoon along the road, the horses led by the guide and ambling placidly along, the rest of us briskly afoot. The spring-houses are reached in due succession, and finally we are at the Raillère once more, where we have planned to take the omnibus which runs half-hourly to Cauterets. And so we buy our tickets, pay the guide,—with a double douceur for his mountaineering reminiscences,—and are soon rattling down the hill toward the town, and studying another priest, a fat, stubby friar on the opposite seat, who is conning his breviary, murmuring his orisons, and glancing wickedly about with his beady little eyes. There is also a gorgeously attired French dowager aboard, and a sprightly soldier; and in the interest of watching them all and the joy of repose against the padded leather cushions, we lose the idea of time until we draw up in the little plaza of Cauterets again, 'at half-past four by the meet'n'-house clock.'

CHAPTER XIII.

A COLOSSEUM OF THE GODS.

"Pyrene celsa nimbosi verticis arce,
Divisos Celtis late prospectat Hiberos
Atque æterna tenet magnis divortia terris."
—SILIUS ITALICUS.

"Parting is such sweet sorrow." Thus it is at Cauterets. The hotel manager evinces it as well as we. But the hour has come to leave him, and the tinseled supernumerary enters, left centre, with, "Milord, the carriages wait." The hotel bill here comes naturally to the front, and we find the charges very much on the average of all Continental resorts. So it has been at Biarritz, so at San Sebastian, Pau and Eaux Bonnes. Pyrenean hotel-keepers are not, as we had formerly mistrusted, an organization for plunder. The expense question is always timely, and experience works out the conclusion that, in the main and speaking generally, one pays at about the same scale of prices for the same accommodation, throughout Europe. In both, of course, there is customarily a wide range of choice. It must be said

that charges for travelers are out of all proportion with the cost of living to the peasants; and the morning hotel-service of coffee and rolls is fixed at a price at which a thrifty native would support his family for a day or more. The *National Review* recently stated that the average expenditure of the peasant freeholder in the south of France upon his food has been accurately computed and that it amounted to the astonishingly small sum of only four sous daily,—this sum having reference to a family, say, of four or five, and where the children are under the age of seventeen or eighteen years. This statement presumably refers to rural freeholders only,—where cattle and farm-land supply the staples without purchase; but even so, one finds difficulty in crediting it in full. The housewives are minutely frugal; they will claim a rebate on a lacking pennyweight in the pound; but it is scarcely to be admitted that any economy could lower the expense of necessary outside provisioning to such a sum. Still, quintupling it even, the hotel, at the spa a mile away, will charge you the same twenty sous for a cup of coffee, and considerably more for the lightest meal. The disproportion is thus seen to be enormous.

Yet at its highest it is not burdensome to a comer from richer countries. The hotel prices themselves halt at a certain mark, and marbled buildings and aristocratic prestige cannot force them higher. Wealthy idleness, Continental idleness in particular, knows to a nicety the sums it is willing to pay for its pleasures. It pays that cheerfully. A centime beyond, it would denounce as imposition.

Extortion is rare; we have not met one instance in these mountains. Oftener we find items to be added to a charge than erased. In this respect, the Pyrenees will prove less expensive than Switzerland, for they are so little touched by the money-reckless Anglo-Saxon. That ubiquitous tourist has not yet come, to brush with o'er rude hand the silvery dust from their butterfly wings. Nor—to complete the statement—have they yet learned to brush with o'er rude hand the golden dust from *his* butterfly wings. The latter fact is perhaps as important as the former.

II.

The road to Luz, whither we are now bound, will take us back along the shadow of the Viscos to Pierrefitte, and then up the left side of the angle under the other haunch of that dividing mountain. We start in the cool of the afternoon, preferring that time to mid-day for the drive. The ride down to Pierrefitte is quick and exhilarating. The six miles seem as furlongs. One enjoys more than doubly the double traversing of fine scenery, and this review of the splendors of the Cauterets gorge many degrees intensifies its effect. At Pierrefitte, the same innkeeper shows the same gladness to find that the same travelers are still thirsty, but there is nothing else to detain us in the little railway terminus. Here we take up again the thread of the Route Thermale, dropped for the visit to Cauterets; and trend again up into a mountain valley, the Viscos now on the right. The valley soon becomes a gorge in its turn, but the sides gape more widely and the incline of the road is slighter than of the one we have left. At times the horses can trot without interruption. It is an aggressive, inquiring road, is the Route Thermale, and thinks nothing of heights and depths nor of stepping across the Gave to better its condition. We cross that stream several times on the way to Luz. Each time, the passage is so narrow as to be spanned by a single arch, the keystone three hundred feet or higher above the water.

It is fourteen miles around from Cauterets to Luz, eight from Pierrefitte. In all, less than three hours have passed when we come out from between the cliffs into a wide, level hollow, carpeted with green and yellow, patterned with fields and orchards and thatched roofs, seamed with rills, and altogether happy and alive. Maize and millet rim all the foot-hills, and forests the higher mountains around. We trot across the level meadows through a poplar-marked road toward the foot of the Pic de Bergonz, and run up into the little town of Luz.

This Luz valley, once part of a miniature republic like the Valley of Ossau, is in the form of a triangle. We have just entered by the northern corner. From the angle on the right runs the defile leading southward to the far-famed Gavarnie, our to-morrow's excursion. On the left, through the opening of the remaining angle, the Thermal Route passes on eastward to Barèges and Bigorre, and that we are to resume on returning from Gavarnie.

The Widow Puyotte, at the Hotel de l'Univers, proves almost as winsome and quite as cordial as good Madame Baudot. The hotel has a châlet-like appearance which is unconventional and pleasing. Here too, as at Eaux Chaudes, our rooms overlook the Gave, but this stream is running sedately through the town itself instead of rollicking down a mountain gorge.

III.

We find Luz as lovable as its location. It is not fashionable and it has no springs. There are few objects of interest to clamor for recognition. Yet its appearance is so tidy, its bent streets so multifariously irrigated, its people so open-faced and respectful, that the town has an immediate charm. We are impressed everywhere in these mountains with the geniality of the people. Human nature, considering its discouragements, is wonderfully good at bottom. Kindliness seems a universal trait in the Pyrenees. It shines out in every nature. One has only to meet it half way. Innkeeper, guide, shopkeeper or peasant, all are unaffectedly good-tempered and well-disposed. A discourteous return would puzzle them; a harsh complaint would wound deeply. The sunshine comes from a nearer sun than in the north. A polite nation, the French are reputed to be; but always underlying this good repute has been the suspicion that the politeness serves mainly to cover self-interest; that it is simply an integument, a rind. In the cities there is a certain truth in this; but the provinces are not thus tainted. In these southern mountains the core is sound and sweet. The response to our advances is so hearty and direct, the interest taken so friendly, that its sincerity is unquestionable. Beggars abound; but your evidently self-respecting husbandman talking willingly with you in the millet-field is not of that class; he is not expecting a coin at parting. In some parts of Europe, he would be disappointed not to get two. On the Route Thermale, a small brace under one of the carriages gave way; it was near a village; we were promptly surrounded by six or eight pleasant-faced villagers, who turned their hands at once to help: one held the horses, three joined to lift the carriage, one or two crept under to assist the driver in repairs, and the others, while we talked with them, looked anxiously on, as relieved as all of us when the difficulty was finally adjusted. There was a raising of berrets, there were bows and good wishes, there was a hearty "*Bon jour, mesdames et messieurs*" as we started, and the men moved back down the road without a thought that their aid should have been sold for a price.

The wealthy French and Spanish, who are the chief visitors to these resorts, are judicious travelers; they injure neither the dispositions nor the independence of the natives. The Anglo-Saxon will come in time; he will regard these natives, as everywhere, as a lesser humanity; he will throw them centimes and sous; he will find imperious fault; he will cut off this ready communicativeness, miss all touch with these friendly lives, and knock their confiding "feelers" back into the shell. But the advance-guard at least of our countrymen will find here a human nature poor and narrowed but right-minded, true, unwarped either by feudal lordliness or modern superciliousness. Reciprocity of treatment, let us hope, will endeavor to keep it so for years yet coming.

IV.

There is a famous old church of the Templars at Luz, which we go to see. It stands at the top of a hilly street, shut off behind a stout fortified wall and between two square flanking towers. We pass through the gateway, and the old sacristan lets us into the church. There is a curious gate, a turret rough in traced carving, and inside, in the dim light, we are chiefly impressed with the rude-gilded altar and the grotesque frescoes on the walls. Yet there is a certain solemnity about the darkness and stillness, after coming from the warm daylight outside. It preaches silently of devotion, of the mystery of religion, of the power and the poetry of worship. "It is a superstition of the place that at a certain time the dead warrior-priests rise from their graves and sit in ghostly assembly, remembering the time when they had raised these rafters and piled these stones together and worshiped therein and died and were buried beneath them.

"The old church lies in the shadow of the Pic de Bergonz and within ear-shot of a mountain's torrent; and the moonlight plays all sorts of fantastic tricks, throwing strange shadows, until it is not difficult to fancy that unearthly forms are near. At the hour of vespers, there are as many as two hundred women in the church, [their heads always covered with their brown or scarlet capulets,] and its ancient, sombre interior appears filled with hooded figures, such as have often troubled our childish dreams, kneeling and crouching in the uncertain twilight to the sound of the Miserere."

No one knows the age of this church. Some accounts give the year 1060, but as the Templars' order was not founded until 1117 or 1118, this is improbable. They were warlike in their religion, these Templars, quite as able to fight as to pray, pledged "never to fly before three infidels even when alone," and with a stirring touch of romance about all their history. They were planted here, as is stated, to guard the frontier in those troublous times, keeping vigilant watch against both Saracens and Spaniards; and few will say that the Christian valley of Luz could have been more efficiently defended.

After we have looked over the interior, the sacristan conducts us out into the mouldy little burying-ground at one side, and crossing the grass, proudly points out in the surrounding wall the chief historic ear-mark of the place,—a scar among the stones, where was once a narrow opening through the wall. This was the despised entrance set apart for that singular race, the Cagots. The Cagots were a once-distinct tribe dwelling in corners of all these Pyrenean valleys, similar to the Cacous or Caqueux of Brittany and Auvergne, and for some reason held as outcasts and in universal detestation. The popular abhorrence of them was phenomenal. Their origin is not known: of Goths, Alans, Moors, Jews, Egyptians, each theory has had its propounder. Even the taint of descent from lepers has been ascribed to them. But whoever their ancestors, the people would none of them. They were pariahs, proscribed and held infamous. They lived in separate hamlets, shunned and insulted, their lives desolate and joyous, without hope, without spirit, without ambition. Laws were passed against them, one at Bordeaux as late as 1596,—many earlier; by these they were even denied the rights of citizens; they could not bear arms, nor engage in any trade save wood-working or menial occupations, nor marry out of their race; they were obliged to wear a scarlet badge on the shoulder, in the shape of a goose's foot; they were not to go barefoot in towns lest they contaminate the streets, and the penalty was branding with a red-hot iron; they were not to touch the provisions in the market-place nor the holy water in the font; they must creep into the church corners through contemptuous side-doors, as at Larroque and Lannemezan and here at Luz. The priests would hardly admit them to confession; the tribunals required the testimony of seven to equal that of a citizen; and hatred pursued them even to the grave and compelled their dead to be buried in lonely plots of ground, separate and remote from the Acre of God.

Did a burgher sicken and die, witchcraft was charged to the Cagot; did a reckless mob seek to vent its spite, it fell upon the Cagot. Despite popular report, most of them had the appearance of ordinary humanity, though rarely its spirit; a few even held their own intellectually; but very many, bred in by constant intermarriage of kin, seem to have become as the Swiss cretins,—deformed,

idiotic, repulsive.

The Cagots were cursed "on four separate heads and on four separate and opposing propositions: for being lepers, for being Jews, for being Egyptians, and for being Moors or Saracens;" and they were persecuted "as though the objectionable points of all four races were centred in them." As lepers, they were reputed to be descendants of the cursed Gehazi; as Egyptians, they were ascribed the *jettatura* or evil eye; as Saracens, they were held unclean and descended from infidels; and as Jews, their enforced pursuit of the carpenter's trade was considered as proving that their ancestors were the builders of the Cross!

Few of the race are to be found in these happier days; the old laws were softened during the first quarter of the eighteenth century, and the Revolution did away with them altogether. The Cagots as a separate tribe have gradually disappeared or been absorbed. Yet the antipathy to the name and the tribe even to-day in some of these regions, though now chiefly a tradition, is still alive and implacable. M. Ramond, the Saussure of the Pyrenees, carefully studied these outcasts over seventy-five years ago, and made this touching statement concerning them:

"I have seen," he wrote, "some families of these unfortunate creatures. They are gradually approaching the villages from which prejudice has banished them. The side-doors by which they were formerly obliged to enter the churches are useless, and some degree of pity mingles at length with the contempt and aversion which they formerly inspired; yet I have been in some of their retreats where they still fear the insults of prejudice and await the visits of the compassionate. I have found among them the poorest beings perhaps that exist upon the face of the earth. I have met with brothers who loved each other with that tenderness which is the most pressing want of isolated men. I have seen among them women whose affection had a somewhat in it of that submission and devotion which are inspired by feebleness and misfortune.

And never, in this half-annihilation of those beings of my species, could I recognize without shuddering the extent of the power which we may exercise over the existence of our fellow,—the narrow circle of knowledge and of enjoyment within which we may confine him,—the smallness of the sphere to which we may reduce his usefulness.".

V.

Coming out again upon the street, we stray down into one of the shops,—a shop local and naïve, a veritable French country-store. We have noticed the hemp-soled sandals worn by many of the mountaineers, and incline to test them for the approaching excursion to Gavarnie. The dark-eyed little proprietor and his wife spring to greet us; foreign customers, especially English or American, are with them a rare sight,—St. Sauveur, a mile away, being a more usual stopping-place for travelers than Luz; and soon the floor is littered with canvas-topped footwear, solicitously searched over for the needed sizes. A running fire of conversation accompanies the fitting. They show the usual French interest in ourselves and our country; we enlarge their views considerably on the latter score, though heroically refraining from romancing. They make a fair livelihood from their store, they inform us; many farmers and peasants outside of the village come to buy at Luz. In fact, the small shopkeepers such as these are generally the prosperous class in a place like Luz, though the standard of prosperity might not coincide with that of the cities. But as compared with that of their customers among the peasantry of the district, it seems to include not only necessity but comfort.

For notwithstanding the luxuriance of these valleys, little of their luxury, even to-day, goes to the tillers of their soil. The Pyrenean farmer or mountaineer has to support his family now, as in past ages, in poverty. Little beyond the most meagre of diet can he commonly provide them, and it is the joint anxiety of ensuring even this, that wears and disfeatures him and them, as much doubt-less as its meagreness. Bread, of barley or wheat or rye, is the great staple, supplemented by what milk can be spared from the town's demands. Eggs and butter go oftener to the market. Vegetables, such as lentils and beans, are also important, a few potatoes, occasional fruits and berries, and above all the powerful and omnipresent onion or garlic stew, signaling its brewing for rods around. In the summer, if he moves with his family to the higher pasture-lands to better pasture the herds, his daily menu expands in some directions and contracts in others. Fête-days and Sundays and trips to the town are usually the occasions of some indulgence, and a thin wine and perhaps macaroni or a pullet or a cut of beef or pork make the event memorable. But the chief fact is that he is fairly contented under all. His life has work and poverty and care, but it has its freedom in addition; he accepts it as it is, fully and without envy; it is not his class who are first to swell the numbers of the sans-culottes. When Henry IV pressed his old peasant playfellows to ask some gift or favor at his hands, their modest ambition stopped at a simple permission to "pay their tithe in grain without the straw."

Often there is even a little fund put by, or anxiously invested; France is noted for the number of abstemious husbandmen who add their mite of savings to her financial enterprises, and the distress and discouragement caused when one of these fails is easily conceivable. On the whole, the French small proprietor or peasant is thrifty and uncomplaining to a rather surprising degree, considering the national trait of restiveness. The revolutions of France are bred in her great cities, not in the provinces.

"But pastoral occupations form only a small part of the business of the Pyrenees," observes a recent writer in *Blackwood's*, in a summary so compact and accurate as to merit quoting. "There are large, various and constantly increasing industries, all special to the country. As water power is to be found everywhere, there are flour-mills and saw-mills in many of the villages. In certain valleys,—round Luz, for instance,—almost every peasant has rough little grinding stones and converts his own barley, buckwheat and maize into flour. Handlooms are numerous, and coarse woollen stuffs for the peasants' clothes are largely made. At Nay, near Pau, are factories where blue berrets for the Pyrenees and red fezzes for Constantinople are woven side by side. The scarlet sashes that the men wear round their waists are produced at Oloron. The manufacture of rough shoes in jute or hemp (*espadrillas*) is a growing element of local trade. Marble and slate works are plentiful, mainly concentrated round Lourdes and at Bagnères de Bigorre. Persons who are insensible to marble can turn to the knitted woollen fabrics of which such quantities are made at Bagnères; many of them are as fine as the best Shetland work, with the additional merit of being as soft as eider-down. The barley-sugar which everybody eats at Cauterets must also be counted; for it rises there to a position which it possesses nowhere else in the world,—it is regarded as a necessity of life; the commerce in it attains such proportions that 10,000 sticks are sold each day during the season. The little objects in boxwood which are hawked about by peddlers must be included too; and the list of special Pyrenean industries may be closed by bird-catching, which is carried on in the autumn months, especially round St. Pé and Bagnères de Bigorre.

"There remains one trade more, however,—the greatest of all,—the traffic in hot water. Numerous as are the natural beauties of the district,—varied as are its attractions and its products,—it owes its success, its prosperity and its wealth to its mineral springs. Some two millions of gallons are supplied each day by them. Fifty-three towns and villages exist already round the sources, and others are being invented each year. The inhabitants of the valleys are making money out of them in every form; for though the harvest is limited to the warm months, it is so various, so widespread, and so productive while it lasts, that everybody has a share in it, from the land-owner who sees his grass converted into building ground, to the half naked boy who cries the Paris newspapers when the post comes in.

"That hot water should become a civilizer and should mount in that way to the level of religion, education, monogamy, wealth and the fine arts, is a new view of hot water; but it is a true one in this case, for nothing else could have evolved the Pyrenees so widely or so fast. Neither commerce nor conquest has ever changed a region as hot water has transformed these valleys."

VI.

"There are corners here and there," remarks the same writer in another connection, describing this valley of Luz, "which have about them such an atmosphere of purity and innocence that people have been known in their enthusiasm to proclaim that they felt inclined to repent of all their favorite sins and to exist thenceforth in total virtue. They produce on nearly every one a softening effect; indeed they almost *make* you better. The vale of Luz is certainly the most winning of these retreats. Its soothing calm, its welcoming tenderness, its look of friendship and of wise counsel, wind themselves around you; and the beauty of its grassy shades, of its leafy brakes and color-changing hills, delights and wins you. Its babbling, laughing streams fill the whole air with life and melody; every chink of the old dry walls is choked with maiden-hair; from the damp rocks amid the dripping streams hang strange, fantastic mosses,—orange, grey and russet,— and with them grow wild flowers, white and purple, and emerald ferns with brilliant deep-notched leaves that glisten in the wet; and mixed with all stretch out the tangled rootlets of the beeches, bathing their bright red, yellow-tipped fibres in the splashing drops. The meadows are so intense in color, they are so supremely, so saturatedly, so bottomlessly green, that you recognize you never knew green until you saw it there; and while you gaze, you feel instinctively that you have reached a promised land."

VII.

The most noted excursion in the Pyrenees,—its *coup de théatre*,—is now before us. It is to *Gavarnie*, whose giant semicircle of precipices has been called "the end of the world." Luz and St. Sauveur constitute the most available headquarters for this trip, which is taken by every traveler to these mountains. "In the popular [French] imagination," writes a lively essayist, "the Pyrenees are composed of carriages-and-four, of capulets and berrets, of mineral waters, rocky gorges, Luchon, admirable roads, bright green valleys, two hundred and thirty hotels, and the Cirque of Gavarnie."

The cliffs of Gavarnie form the Spanish frontier. A village of the same name lies near their feet on this French side, thirteen miles up the defile leading south from the valley of Luz. There is now a carriage-road for almost the entire distance, and if fame is true, never did a destination better merit a road. We count on a memorable day, as the landau and the victoria carry us away from Luz,—where voluntary promise of a super-excellent table-d'hôte on our return has just been given by Madame Puyotte and thus every care removed.

The road crosses the valley, under the sentinel poplars, leaves on the right the road by which we came in from Pierrefitte, and shortly comes to the opening of the defile to Gavarnie. At the immediate entrance across the ravine stands the white street of hotels and lodging-houses which constitutes the Baths of St. Sauveur. We shall cross to it on our return, and now scan it only from the distance as we pass. It joins itself to our highway by a superb bridge, over two hundred feet above the chasm,—a single astonishing arch, one of the longest in existence, its span being 153 feet across, and its total length 218. It is of marble, a gift of Louis Napoleon and Eugénie to commemorate their stay at St. Sauveur; its cost was upward of sixty thousand dollars.

From this on, the scenery becomes again increasingly wild. The gorge now opens and now narrows, the mountains above us here approach over the road,

there draw back in a long, sweeping glacis of wood or pasture. The ledge of the road is at times four hundred feet above the frothy watercourse, which in some spots disappears entirely from sight in the chasm. Tiny mills are seen standing tremulously near its fierce supply, and there is room for a hamlet here and there, sheltered in a clump of ash or sycamore, on the mountain or at a widening of the valley. When the road nears the cliffs of Gavarnie, it will expire, from the simple impossibility of proceeding farther; so it is scarcely a thoroughfare, and we meet only infrequent bucolics or a few wood-carts coming down toward Luz. One fair-sized rustic village is passed through; and, two hours after the start, a second one, Gèdre, our more-than-half-way house, is finally seen ahead.

The mountain wall we are approaching begins now to show its battlements, far ahead. The snowy *Tours de Marboré* overtop it, and at their right can be plainly seen two small, rectangular nicks, embrasures in this mammoth parapet. Small they seem, as we sight them from this distance, but these notches are 9000 feet above the sea, and the greater of the two is a colossal gateway into Spain, no less than 300 feet in width and 350 feet deep. This is the famous *Brèche de Roland*, familiar to all lovers of Gavarnie. When Charlemagne made his invasion into Spain,— the invasion from which he was afterward to withdraw by Roncesvalles,—he sought to enter it, tradition says, by this defile to Gavarnie. Finding all progress blocked by the walls of the Cirque, he ordered Roland to open a way; and that lusty paladin with one blow of his good sword Durandal opened this breach for the passage of the army. There is another version of the making, which links it with the throes of Roland's defeat and death at Roncesvalles, at the end instead of at the beginning of the invasion; but even under unbounded poetic license, the mind refuses to admit that the wounded hero, bleeding and gasping for breath, could have made his way a hundred miles over the mountains from Roncesvalles, to shiver his sword against the cliffs of the Cirque and end his death-struggles at Gavarnie.

At Gèdre the horses pause for a rest and a drink, and travelers can do likewise. From this village, the main defile cuts on to Gavarnie, and another opens off to the left toward another cirque,—the Cirque of *Troumouse*. Thus each branch ends in a similar formation, peculiar to the Pyrenees, a semicircle of cliffs, sudden and blank and impassable. The Cirque of Troumouse is larger around than that of Gavarnie, but its walls are not so high and its effect is reported to be less imposing. To reach it from Gèdre requires perhaps three hours, the drivers tell us, by a good bridle-path. We feel tempted to revisit this point from Luz, another day, and explore the route toward Troumouse.

To-day, however, this is not to be; Gavarnie beckons, and we gird us anew and press from Gèdre on. The carriages twist their way up an unusual incline, and it is ten of the clock as we stop to face a long cascade which is jumping down from a cut across the chasm and not too busy with its own affairs to give us an answering halloo. The great Cirque is now coming more and more distinctly into view, though still some miles ahead. The two breaches are no longer seen, but snow-walls are becoming visible on all sides, and the distant precipices are constantly crowding into line and assuming shape and form. Even Louis the Magnificent's haughty proclamation, "*il n'y a plus de Pyrénées*," could not erase this impassable barrier. It was made for a wall of nations.

Already our destination sends out to welcome us. We have hardly left Gèdre, with several miles still to drive, before we are assaulted by peasants on horseback, advance-agents from Gavarnie. The carriage-road will end at the village, and the Cirque itself is three miles beyond; it is reached on foot or on horseback, and these peasants lie in wait along the road for visitors, to forestall their rivals in the letting of saddle-horses, and each to offer his or her particular animal for the way. In vain we assure them that we shall make no choice until

we come to the inn at Gavarnie. They turn and ride by the side of the carriages, urging their claims in incessant clamor, pressing about us, intercepting the views, good-tempered enough but decidedly an annoyance. We speak them fair, and request, then direct, them to abandon the chase. It has no effect whatever. They continue their pestering tactics, now falling behind, then ranging again alongside, hindering conversation, interrupting constantly with their jargon. Plainly it is a time for firm measures. We call a halt, and, standing up in the carriage, I tell them once for all and finally that we will have nothing to do with them either now or hereafter, either here or at the village; and order them shortly and decisively to "get out." Even when translated into French, there is a peculiar tang to this emphatic American expression that is impolite but unmistakable; it takes effect even here in the Gèdre solitudes, and we ride on without escort.

The road now passes into a remarkable region,—a famed part of this famed route. This is the *Chaos*, so-called and justly. The side of the mountain overhead appears to have broken off bodily and fallen into the valley, and its ruins almost choke the bottom. Huge masses of granite and gneiss are scattered everywhere in savage confusion, and the road barely twines a painful way through the labyrinth. Scarcely a blade of grass, a tint of green, is to be seen about us; the tract is given over to utter desolation.

"Confounded Chaos roar'd
And felt ten-fold confusion in their fall
Through his wild anarchy; so huge a rout
Incumbered him with ruin."

Some of these fragments, it is said, contain a hundred thousand cubic feet, and the blocks lie in all directions, uncount-

ed tons of them, grotesque and menacing, piled often one upon two, bulging out over the diminished carriages or entirely disconcerting the hurrying torrent.

"That block bigger than the church of Luz," points out Johnson, writing of this spot, "has been split in twain by the other monster that has followed in its track and cracked it as a schoolboy might do his playfellow's marble. We cease to estimate them by their weight in tons, as is the manner of hand-books, but liken, them to great castles encased in solid stonework; or calculate that half-a-dozen or so would have made up St. Paul's; or speculate upon the length of ladder we would want to reach the purple auricula that is flowering in the crevice half way up."

Beyond this, as we draw near the end of our course, there is an opening in the mountains on the right. A peak and a long bed of ice and snow are seen high beyond, and the drivers tell us that we are looking at a side glacier of the Vignemale, whose face we saw from the Lac de Gaube when we climbed up the parallel defile from Cauterets.

But here is the village of Gavarnie. We are in the courtyard before the inn, bristling with an abatis of mules and horses in waiting row.

VIII.

Negotiations for transport now begin. The black walls of the Cirque rise beyond the village, closing the valley, seemingly just before us; but it is a full league from the inn to the stalls of that august proscenium. The ladies recall their unrestful saddle-ride to the lake, and decide this time for sedan-chairs. The entire village is put in commotion by the order; for three men, one as relief, are required for each chair, (four on steeper routes,) and it takes but a very few times three to foot up a quick and difficult total, where the call is sudden and the supply small. The chairs themselves are promptly produced; they have short legs, a dangling foot-rest, and long poles for the bearers, as in Switzerland, but are ornamented besides with a hood or cover which shuts back like a miniature buggy-top. Soon the additional men are brought in, called from different vocations for the emergency; all of them broad-shouldered and sturdy and with a willing twinkle in their eyes. The ladies seat themselves, the first relays take their places before and behind the chairs, pass the straps from the poles up over the shoulders, bend their knees, grasp the handles, and with a simultaneous "*huh!*" lift the litters and their fair freight from the ground. This automatic performance is always interesting and always executed with military precision. They pass down the village road with rhythmic, measured tread, the substitutes carrying the wraps; the *petit garçon* of the party journeys forth on a donkey; and the rest of us, duly disencumbered and shod with hemp, resist the importunities of the youth at the inn to order a lunch for the return, and follow after on foot.

The sole interest of the walk is this stupendous curve of cliffs ahead, roofed with snow and glistening with rime and moisture. It fascinates, yet we try not to look, reserving a climax for our halting-place. The pathway is well marked though somewhat stony and irregular; the valley-bottom is wider here and we are close by the side of the Gave. The hemp sandals prove surprisingly useful. Their half-inch soles of rope utterly deaden the inequalities of the ground, and the pebbly, hummocky path is as a carpet beneath the feet. The bearers tramp steadily onward, the chairs sinking and rising in easy vertical motion, much more grateful than the horizontal "joggle" of the Pyrenean saddle-horse. We are an hour in approaching the Cirque, which looms higher at every step. The halting-place is reached at last. It is a small plateau almost in the heart of the arena, and here there is a restaurant,—the last house in France,— and the inevitable group of idlers to ruin the effect of solitude.

IX.

They cannot ruin the effect of sublimity, however. That term, not freely perhaps to be used in all terrestrial scenes, is beyond question applicable here.

The Amphitheatre of Gavarnie, in which we stand, surpasses easy description. It is a blank, continuous wall of precipices, bending around us in the form of a horseshoe, a mile in diameter, and starting abruptly from the floor of the valley,—perhaps the most magnificent face of naked rock to be seen in Europe. Its cliffs rise first a sheer fourteen hundred feet without a break; there is a narrow shelf of snow, and above this ledge they rise to another, and then climb in stages upward still, perpendicular and black, in a waste of escarpments and buttresses, terraced with widening snow-fields tier on tier, until their brows and cornices are nodding overhead almost a mile above the arena. Higher yet, the separate summits stand like towers in the white glaciers on the top; the Cylindre, at 10,900 feet above the sea, is partly hidden at the left by its own projecting flanges, and nearer the centre of the arc the Marboré, with its Casque and Turret, is but as an outwork concealing the greater Mont Perdu, the highest mountain in the French Pyrenees and next to the Maladetta the highest of the range.

A dozen slender waterfalls, unnoticed Staubbachs, are showering from the heights; over a ledge under the Mont Perdu streams the loftiest, known too as the loftiest fall on the Continent. It comes over slowly, "like a dropping cloud, or the unfolding of a muslin veil," falling steadily and with scarcely an interruption a quarter of a mile in vertical height, before it is finally whirled into spray against the rocks at the base. And the Gave which these cascades unite to form, and which we have been following thus toward its source this morning, is no other than the Gave de Pau, which will hurry on and down through the valleys till it is flowing below the old château of the kings of Navarre, and later joining the Adour will pass on through Bayonne to the sea.

It is a silencing scene. The effect it gives of simple largeness,—a largeness uncomprehended before,—may be fairly called overpowering. There is something almost of the terrific in it, something even oppressive. We are as a fact at the end of the world. The eye does not seem to be deceived here, as it often is in great magnitudes; it belittles nothing; it realizes to the full this strange impression of simple, hopeless bulk, immovable and pitiless as the reign of law.

The floor of the Cirque, far from being level, is blocked with snow and the débris of falling rock. Our halting-place is near the left curve of the arc; and a half hour's toilsome scramble across its chord to the opposite side would take us to the foot of a darker streak in the wall which seems from here like a possible groove or gully and in fact is such. Unscalable as it seems, that is the magic stairway which leads up out of this rocky Inferno to the higher ledges and finally over glacier-fields to the Brèche de Roland, (which is invisible from the Cirque itself,) and through this gateway on into Spain. Mountaineers and smugglers make the trip with unconcern, and it is entirely practicable for tourists, though needing a sure foot and a stout pulmonary apparatus. The Mont Perdu is also ascended from this direction; first climbed in 1802 by the intrepid Ramond, who seems to have been as true a mountaineer as a savant, it has been occasionally ascended since; its ledges are notably treacherous and difficult, and the trip demands proper implements and practiced guides. It is a striking fact that its upper rocks have been found to be marine calcareous beds. That proud eminence has not stood thus in the clouds for all time; it was once buried fathoms deep under the Tertiary ocean.

An interesting anecdote attaches to this mountain. It was assaulted some years ago by a French lady, a Mme. L., who vowed that she should be the first woman to stand upon the summit. She was accompanied by four guides, pledged to carry her body to the top alive or dead. No carrying was needed, however; the lady climbed with the coolness and hardihood of a born mountaineer; they camped for the night on the way, 7500 feet above the sea, at the base of the main peak, and in the morning she triumphantly gained the top. But now the fair climber undid all the glory of the exploit: a bottle had long been left in a niche of rock at the top, opened by each rare new-comer in turn to add his name and a sentiment or some expression of his admiration; our heroine opened this, scattered the precious contents to the winds, and inserted her card in their place, declaring that there should be but one name found on the crest of the Mont Perdu, and that her own.

Great was the indignation in the valley when this ungenerous act became known. A young stranger was staying at St. Sauveur at the time; no sooner had he heard of the occurrence than he started up the mountain himself. It was but a few days after Mme. L.'s ascent; the despoiled bottle was there, with its single slip of pasteboard; and a day or two later, the lady, then in Paris, received a polite note enclosing the card that she had left on the summit of the Mont Perdu, 10,999 feet above the sea!

X.

The restaurant, no less than the idlers, ruins the effect of solitude, but we find that we bear this with more equanimity. We are glad we resisted the village inn's importunities and can remain here for lunch instead. While we are at the table, our jovial porters, grouped near the path outside, while away the time in stentorian songs. We walk out afterward some space farther toward the base of the cliffs; but the foot of the fall is still two furlongs away, along the left wall,—a distance equal to its height; and over the broken boulders of the bottom it seems useless toil to clamber. So we sit and gaze again at the scene, seeking to crowd this sensation of immensity even more deeply into the mind. We cast about for some comparison to the scene. The sweep of the Gemmi precipices rising around the village of Leukerbad in Switzerland is like it in kind; but almost another Gemmi, mortared with ice and glacier, would need to be reared upon the first, to overtop the snows of the Gavarnie Cirque.

We turn back to the porters at last, and the cavalcade of chairs forms again. The men are earning three francs each by this noon holiday, and they are in good spirits. They do not think the sum

too little and we certainly do not deem it too much. When we regain the inn at the village, they wait about unobtrusively for their pay, and after arming ourselves with coin for the division we come out among them. At once we become the centre of a large and respectful assemblage, all other loungers drawing near to witness the coming ceremony. Our informal words of appreciation become rather a speech when delivered before so many. The leader now approaches, and we publicly entrust him with the division of the fund, adding, as we state aloud, our good-will and a *pourboire* for each. Instantly, and with, almost startling simultaneousness, every, cap in view comes off in unison; the movement is so general, so, immediate, and so gravely uniform, as to be somewhat astonishing; and a satisfied and metronomic chorus of "*Merci, Monsieur, merci bien*!" rises like a measured pæan around us.

This little performance over, the carriages come to the fore, and we retrace the road in the pleasant afternoon, under the Pimené, through the Chaos, by Gèdre and the opening of the Troumouse gorge, and on down the ravine out to the Bridge of Napoleon which leads us over to St. Sauveur.

The long, trim street of St. Sauveur backed against the mountain is a resort much in favor. It is not large enough to be noisily stylish, but in a quiet way it is select and severe. It is patronized by ladies more than by the sterner sex. Its springs are mild, helpful for cases of hysteria and atonic dyspepsia; and the nervous, middle-aged females who frequent it find a grateful sedative in the air and surroundings as well as in the springs. The hotels have the garb of prosperity, and the location, commanding both the Gavarnie gorge and the valley of Luz,-could not have been better chosen; in fact, headquarters for the trip to the Cirque might be and usually are fixed here quite as comfortably as at Luz.

We spend a half hour about the hotels and shops as the twilight comes on, while the carriages wait, down the road. In an unpretending shop an old lady has

just trimmed and lighted her lamp; she peers up through her glasses as we enter, and readily shuffles across the room for her asked-for stock of Pyrenean pressed-flowers. The dim little store proves a treasury of these articles, and part of our half hour and part of our hoard of francs are spent over the albums spread open by her fumbling fingers. Then we drive off again into the dusk, join the main road, and run restfully across the valley to end the day's ride before the lighted windows of our chalet-hotel at Luz.

The trip to Gavarnie can thus be readily made during a day, and it is indisputably one of the finest mountain sights in Europe. As Lord Bute, (quoted in the *Tour Through the Pyrenees*,) cried when there, many years ago, in old-time hyperbole, "If I were now at the extremity of India, and suspected the existence of what I see at this moment, I should immediately leave, in order to enjoy and admire it." Perhaps this sentiment should merit consideration from, other seekers of noble scenery; it was founded upon a justly sincere enthusiasm.

To-morrow, the Pic de Bergonz shall be our goal.

CHAPTER XIV.

THE VALLEY OF THE SHADOW.

"Ich weiß nicht was soll es bedeuten
Daß ich so traurig bin"
—*The Lorelei*

But the Pic de Bergonz does not so elect.

During the night the weather has another revulsion of feeling. In the morning it is hysterical, laughing and crying by turns. We come down-stairs booted and spurred for the ascent, and make directly for the barometer in the doorway. Alas, it tells but a quavering and uncertain tale, itself evidently undecided, and holding out to others neither discouragement nor hope. An hour brings no change. The guide looks sagely toward the clouds, as who should know all weather lore, and candidly admits the doubtful state of the case,—which is frank, since for him a lost excursion is lost riches. The sun streaks down fitfully upon the road, and then after a minute the mist sifts over the spot; the mountain-tops appear and disappear among low-lying clouds. We haunt alternately the roadway and the writing-room, restless and inquisitive; but as the morning wears on, it becomes slowly certain that the Pic de Bergonz has taken the veil irrevocably.

The Monné at Cauterets was within our grasp; we sacrificed its certainty to the uncertainty of the more accessible peak. In the mountains, as we are thus again shown, *carpe diem* is a wise blazon. Still, choosing the Monné would have postponed Gavarnie until to-day and thus have forfeited the clear skies of yesterday's memorable trip to the Cirque. It is always feasible to count your consolations rather than your regrets.

It does not rain, so we ramble off about the streets again. There is an eminence near the village on which stand the remains of the old castle of Ste. Marie, and which we are told gives a wide survey over the valley; but we are out with all eminences and refuse to patronize it. We drift again into our little shop of the hempen shoes, with soap for a pretext; the proprietor and his wife are affable and unclouded as ever; and we while off a half hour in another talk with them and some trifling purchases. One learns many lessons in civility in Continental shopping; more usually it is a woman alone who presides, some genuinely winsome old lady often, with white cap and grandmotherly smile. The lifting of the hat as we enter ensures invariably the politest of treatment, and when we depart, it is with the feeling that we have gained another friend for life.

The village stretches itself lengthily about, as many Continental towns do; its limbs, like Satan's,
"Extended long and large,
Lay floating many a rood,"
and two of us later signalize a stroll by becoming *lost*,—lost in Luz. We look helplessly down along the lanes and neat streets for the familiar little porch over the Gave and the open space in front and the overhanging eaves of our hotel. Gone the church, gone the store of the shoes and soap, gone the carriage-shed, the Hotel de l'Univers,—all landmarks gone. It is not until we are driven to the humiliation of actually asking our way, that the alleys are unraveled and show us safely home, into the scoffs and contumely of the unregenerate.

After lunch, the weather is still gloomy, but there is no rain, and we leave Luz for Barèges toward the last of the afternoon, if not in sunshine, at least over a dry road. Some of us are on foot, so but one carriage is needed for the others, and the Widow Puyotte stands smiling at the door as we move away, wishing us fine weather for the morrow's ride on from Barèges over the Col du Tourmalet,—since any further wishes for to-day's weather would be manifestly inoperative.

The Baths of Barèges are on the continuing girdle of the Route Thermale as it extends its way onward from Luz toward Bigorre; they lie about four miles up a short, desolate, east-and-west valley which opens from the hollow of Luz and closes beyond them in a col over which goes the road. These baths are much higher than Luz, and the way is a steady incline throughout. The valley soon shows itself in marked change from the fertile basin we have quitted; it grows bleak and less cultivated; rubbly slopes of shale and slate cover the hills; the vegetation becomes scanter. We are nearing now the Pic du Midi de Bigorre, the summit seen so plainly from Pau, far eastward of the Pic du Midi d'Ossau. It is not as yet in sight from this valley, however, though we are approaching it nearly and though it closely overtops the col which rises beyond Barèges. The road continues desolate, and the dull grey-green pastures hardly serve to relieve its deserted and forlorn squalor. The clouds brood on the hills, the air grows chilly as we ascend, and more than once we sigh half dubiously for the bright parlor left behind at Luz. We move leisurely, almost reluctantly, on, not in haste to reach the climax of this unhospitable avenue; but the four miles shorten themselves unexpectedly, and it seems but a short walk before we are in sight of the Baths of Barèges.

Murray and Madame the Widow had each spoken dishearteningly of Barèges. With their verdict concurred also the few other accounts we had heard of it. Murray stigmatizes it as "cheerless and forbidding," "a perfect hospital," and remarks that "nothing but the hope of recovering health would render it endurable beyond an hour or two." Another marks it curtly as "a desolate village tucked into the mountain side, with avalanches above and torrents below; in summer the refuge of cripples; in winter the residence of bears." No one at Luz was found to say a good word for Barèges, except as to the undoubted cures its waters effect; and on the whole the outlook summed itself up as very far from promising.

In view of this abuse we have been predisposing our minds to extenuate the shortcomings of the place and to extol rather than dispraise it. One does not like to maltreat even a resort when it is down. But as we draw up the hill and see the black surroundings and enter the frowsy, dismal street, the desire to extol vanishes and even the possibility of extenuating becomes doubtful. The carriage pauses, while two of us who have hurried ahead examine the two hotels reputed best; each is equally uninspiring, and the one we finally choose we thereupon immediately regret choosing and regretfully choose the other. Meanwhile the carriage is being circummured by an increasing hedge of idlers and invalids, staring with great and open-minded interest at the arrival of visitors who seemed actually healthy and were coming here uncompelled; and the visitors themselves are glad to vanish from the public wonder into the stone passageway of the hotel.

Within is a large, cobble-paved court around which the hotel is built, and out upon the upstairs veranda overlooking this we are led and assigned to rooms. The rooms are clean, but unadorned and bare, and so seems the hotel throughout. It is not the lack of adornment, however, that dispirits us; Madame Baudot's at

Eaux Chaudes was unadorned likewise, and yet was an ideal of inviting comfort. Here, there seems to be something more,—an inexplicable taint of depression over the hotel, which strangely affects us. We struggle hysterically against it, trying to laugh it off, speculating vainly over the dreary, disconsolate weight which each has felt from the moment of entering the village; and at length conclude to investigate the mystery by a survey out-of-doors.

II.

It takes little time to convince us that Barèges deserves all the abuse it has received. We came unprejudiced and in a sympathetic mood, willing to defend the much-reviled; but we admit to each other that the revilers have only erred on the side of timidity. The pall of the place is unmistakable and wraps us in completely; even a genial party and determined high spirits are slowly forced to succumb. There seems something gruesome about it; the curious burden is not to be shaken off, try as we may.

The village is sorrowfully set, to begin with; the valley here is high and more gloomy even than below; the narrowing hills, grey-black or a sickly green, stand and mourn over their own sterility. Though it is daylight still, the sun has long passed behind them, and the air is chilled and mouldy. The village is merely one long, shaky street crouching in along the side of the mountain; it is lamentably near the torrent, for the rough Gave de Bastan just below is one of the scourges of the Pyrenees, and each spring it tears by and even through the street, and scours down the valley, swollen and resentful, causing discouraging damage along its track. Many of the houses are taken down each fall and re-erected in the summer; and as we walk on through the street, these quavering shanties of pine combine with the jail-like appearance of the heavier stone buildings and the harsh hills and clouds around, all in a strange effect of utter repellence.

But it is the people we meet who intensify the impression. No one visits Barèges for pleasure; its extraordinary springs are the sole reason of its existence, and only those who must, come to seek health in them. Sad-faced invalids, who have tried other baths in vain and have been ordered hither as a last resort; wounded or broken-down soldiers; cripples, who stump their crutches past us down the earthen road,—these are the ones who haunt Barèges, anxious and self-centred and unhopeful. Style and fashion are things apart; there is not a landau to be had in the place, and scarcely a smaller vehicle. In cold or storm, the sick hurry from boarding-house or hotel to the bath-establishment in close-shut sedan-chairs; on fairer days, they limp their own way thither. Talk turns on diseases; there is no fresh news, Barèges is a long ride from the news bearing railway; the discussions begin with this or that spring or symptom and end in a disconsolate game at écarté.

Truly disease is a hideous visitant to the fairness of life,—a hard interruption to its store of joys.

Beyond all this, however, there is a something further about Barèges,—this incubus of depressingness, seemingly the very soul of the spot. Sickness and dreary location will account for it in part; but many have felt that certain subtle spirit pervading a region or even a single house, which in part defies analysis; it is in the air; it overhangs; it may be light and joyous and animating, or forbidding. And Barèges is a striking instance; morbid, abhorrent, funereal, there seems here some influence at work which is not entirely to be accounted for, yet to which it is impossible not to yield.

At the upper end of the street is the long, grim bath-establishment, and we enter its stone corridors and are led about by a noiseless and mournful attendant. Here are rows of waiting sedan-chairs; an office for presentation of tickets; long lines of stone cells, each with its tub or douche or vapor-box; and underground, public tanks of larger size. "I inconsiderately tasted the spring," records a traveler of years ago, "and, if you are anxious to know what it is like, you may be satisfied without going to Barèges, by tasting a mixture of rotten eggs and the rinsings of a foul gun-barrel." Our spirits fall lower and lower in this damp impluvium; never before have we felt so grateful over our limitless good health; we dodge out with relief into the darkening air, and, under the beginnings of a rain-storm, thankfully slip back to the refuge of the hotel.

Certain it seems that if cheerful surroundings are essential to a cure, the waters of Barèges must fail of their full mission.

They accomplish remarkable things, notwithstanding; they are among the strongest of the Pyrenean baths, and are particularly noted for their power in scrofulas and grave skin-disorders, wounds, ulcers and serious rheumatic affections. So healing for wounds are they, that the government sustains here a military hospital for maimed and disabled soldiers. In winter the scene is desolation. The cold is rigorous. Avalanches pour down from the mountains on both sides and often leave little for the spring freshets to do. Modern engineering grapples even with avalanches; wide platforms have been cut in the rocks above the town, on the slopes most exposed, and immense bars of iron set in them and attached with chains. These outworks have proved themselves surprisingly effective in breaking the force of the snowslides; but the scent of danger is always in the air; the ledge of the town is for months deep in drifts; the frailer houses are taken up, the rest closed and stoutly barred; the inhabitants are gone, leaving behind a few old care-takers to hold their lonely revels in the solitudes.

III.

We sit about in the evening in the dim little parlor, and agree once more that Barèges has not been exaggerated. We are united in will to leave this detestable spot to its ghosts of ruin and disease, and to leave it as quickly as we can. Our Luz driver, whom we have judiciously retained to remain with his landau over night, appears respectfully at the door, and is instantly instructed to be ready early in the morning for farther progress; he looks dubious, and warns us of continuing rain; it is nothing; we leave to-morrow in any weather.

"Have you found us a second carriage?" I ask him.

"Monsieur, there is but a *petite voiture*, a small wagonette, up the street, which one could hire; it is small; if monsieur will have the goodness to come out with me to see it?"

So two of us sally forth into the drizzle with the driver, and a few rods up the street turn off into an alley-way, where the wagonette is found under a shed. It *is* small,—deplorably small; the seat will ungraciously hold two persons, and a stool can be crowded in in front for a driver. There is no top nor hood of any sort, and the hotel barometer is still falling steadily.

But we are resolved to leave Barèges.

"Is this the best that one can obtain?" I ask ruefully.

"There is one other, monsieur, close by; but it is yet smaller."

This clinches the matter, and we conclude a bargain with the proprietor for an early departure and hurry back to the dim joys of the hotel reception-room.

IV.

The clouds themselves descend with the drizzle during the night, and we are greeted when we wake by a white opacity of mist and fog filling the hotel courtyard and leaking moisture at every pore. We think shiveringly of the wagonette, but more shiveringly still of Barèges; and resolutely array ourselves for a long and watery day among the clouds.

Our route will continue by the Thermal Road on to Bagnères de Bigorre. There is again a col in the way which we must cross,—the Col du Tourmalet, a shoulder of the Pic du Midi de Bigorre, separating this Valley of Bastan from the greater lateral Valley of Campan. It is a long ride with the ascent and descent,—twenty-five miles at the least; but it can be easily made in the day, and there is a midway halting-place beyond the col for lunch.

Our Luz landau appears promptly on the scene, comfortably enclosed and inviting; and the ridiculous wagonette creeps up behind it, in apologetic and shamefaced comparison. The driver of the wagonette, however, a tough, grizzled old guide, is not shamefaced in the least, but grins broadly and contentedly as he sits there wrapped in his tarpaulin, wet and shiny under the steady rain. The landau soon hospitably receives the favored majority, and disappears into the mist up the street; and the remaining two of us turn to the wagonette,—and turning, involuntarily catch the infection of the old guide's grin. After all, there is a certain zest in discomfort; we clamber in and draw the rough robe around us, unfurl our complicated Cauterets umbrella, and agree that the truest policy is to make little of discomfort and much of its zest.

Old Membielle gathers the tarpaulin about his stool before us, chirrups toward the damp steam which symbolizes a horse, and we move off up the long, soppy street, past its houses and jails and grey bathing-penitentiary,—and out at last from Barèges. Out from Barèges, though into the vast unknown; and our spirits rise higher as the baleful spell of the spot is lifted and left behind.

V.

Barèges is the most convenient point for the ascent of the Pic du Midi de Bigorre. The baths lie almost at the foot of this mountain, and one can make the ascent in about four hours, and descending by another side rejoin the road to Bigorre at the village of Grip, beyond the col before us. We resign the ascent, of course, under stress of barometer; but this climb is assuredly one of the best worth making in the Pyrenees. The Pic is prominently seen from distant points everywhere through the region: it is visible from Pau, from the Maladetta, from the plain of Toulouse. Consequently these points must lie within its own ken. Its huge, shapely dome rises 9400 feet into the air, and standing as it does solitary and apart at the edge of the plain and not buried among rival summits, the view from the top has been solely criticised as too vast for detail and too high for exactness, and commands, it is said, a fifth of all France. The ascent is easy, there being little snow upon the path in the summer; there is a bridle-trail throughout, a small inn higher than half way, and an observatory now erected upon the summit.

We are only intellectually cognizant of this Pic du Midi, however, as we jog on up toward the pass; for the driving fog curtains all the peaks, at times lifting so far as to show the nearer slopes and perhaps the hills ahead, but for the most part enfolding even the road and ourselves in its maudlin affection. We pull steadily on through the morning, over a good road and up through a still dreary region of moist, sparse turf and shaly slopes of slate and rock and profitless débris. The occupants of the landau, as they look down toward us at times from the turn next above, wave dry and encouraging greetings, through the open windows; and we wave back damper but equally encouraging greetings in return, having found that good spirits had fallen to us with unexpected and gratifying ease.

Altogether it has not been in the least a long morning, when we finally reach the crest of the Col du Tourmalet, 7100 feet in elevation, from which begins the descent toward the Campan Valley and Bigorre. This col is not loved by mountaineers during the winter; it is exposed to the full sweep of storms, and is one of the wild passes on which, as the local saying goes, "when the hurricane reigns the son does not tarry for the father nor the father for the son." Before the Route Thermale pushed its way over, it was but a foot-pass, wearisomely traversed in saddle or litter by infrequent travelers or by invalids sentenced to Barèges.

Just at the summit of the col, for a supreme minute, the clouds part at the rear, right and left, and roll away beneath, and we catch for once the long stretch of the desolate Valley of Bastan, with the windings of the road reaching backward and downward along the hills. It is over while we look; the fog writhes and twists down and all is greyness again.

The carriages slip rapidly down the other side, with all brakes set and forty hairbreadth margins recorded for the outer wheels; and, an hour from the col, we are safely at the hamlet of Grip, where the horses and we are doomed to a two hours' halt and a lunch. The first inn, irrationally placed in a patch of field apart from the main road, does not look attractive from the distance, and we drive on to the second. This one, while carefully non-committal in appearance, is at least on close terms with the road, and as there is no third, we cheer us with reminders of Laruns and descend.

It is a creaky little inn, facing a wet, cobbly yard and having the air of being retiring in disposition and somewhat surprised at the advent of visitors. The landlady is away, it appears, and we are received by her spouse, a mild-mannered old man who is not used to being a host in himself but resignedly assumes the burden. The lunch is promised for the near future. The horses are led off, the carriages covered to remain in the road, and the driver and the jovial guide turn to and help with the fire and stabling arrangements in a way which shows that they are entirely at home in the locality.

We stand for a while on the decrepit, covered balcony overlooking the yard, exchanging humorous reminiscences of the ride, and idly commiserating the three fowls and a wet pig which appear below. We are absorbed too in a wooden-saboted farmhand of gigantic proportions who clicks across the cobbles at irregular intervals and exchanges repartee with a milk-maid in the doorway. He has a huge, knobby frame, bulging calves, a colored kerchief turbaning his head, a rough costume throughout, and a fascinating though belying air of desperate and unscrupulous villainy.

But the weather has still its tinge of rawness, and two or three of us go down stairs again and invade the den of the kitchen, where the fire is now under way and the inevitable omelet just in contemplation. The old man acts as extemporary cook. He finds a black and somewhat oily frying-pan, suspends it over the fire to heat, and throws in a handful of salt to draw out the grease. He now looks thoughtfully about for a rag to scour it withal; there is a rag of sooty environment and inferentially sooty antecedents hanging beside a box of charcoals next to the chimney-place; he horrifies some among us by promptly catching it up; gives the pan a vigorous rubbing-out with this carboniferous relic; and certain appetites for omelet fade swiftly away. Their losers speak for a substitution of coffee and bread and fresh milk in lieu of all remaining courses, and beat a hasty retreat from the scene.

The omelet duly appears upon the lunch-table presently set for us in the little room upstairs, and serves at least as a centre-piece, over which to tell the story of its birth; and the coffee, excellent bread, and a huge pitcher of new, creamy milk amply reconcile all abstainers, and fortify us in a feeling of good-tempered toleration even for Grip.

VI.

Bagnères de Bigorre is placed at the opening-out of the broad Campan Valley, some distance out from the higher ranges and about twelve miles on from Grip. The fog passes off as we start again, though it is lightly raining still. In an hour or more we have finished the descent to the floor of the valley, and for the rest of the short afternoon the road runs uneventfully to the northward, for the most part level, and beaded with occasional villages and lesser clumps of houses. Finally, as the light begins to fail behind the clouds, an increased bustle on the road and more frequent houses passed announce the nearness of our destination, and the horses are soon trotting into Bigorre and up the welcome promenade of the main street to the Hotel Beau Séjour.

Past discomforts quickly recede in the warm haze of present satisfactions. We absorb to the full the pleasant glow of the hotel drawing-room, after we have comfortably repaired the ravages of the day. Barèges is a grotesque phantom, and we can hardly admit that tonight there are people still in that shuddering, shivering, banshee-haunted line of hospitals, high in its weird valley, in the cold and in the falling rain. Rayless and despairing their mood must be; escape would seem immeasurably more to be prized than cure. Even the old man of Grip and his rag brighten by comparison, and we agree in viewing our present surroundings as a climax of utter content.

CHAPTER XV.

THE VALLEY OF THE SUN.

"*Baignères, la beauté, l'honneur, le paradis.*
De ces monts sourcilleux"
—DU BARTAS.
"I hear from Bigorre you are there."
—*Lucile.*
An agreeable little city we find about us, the next day. Bigorre is one of the most well-known of the Pyrenean resorts, and has a steady though not accelerating popularity. The tide of ultra summer fashion, has tended latterly toward Eaux Bonnes, Cauterets and Luchon in preference; still, Bigorre, conservative and with it's own assured circle of friends, looks on without malice at its sister spas who have come to wear finer raiment than itself. A number of the English,—some even in winter and spring,—frequent Bigorre almost alone of these Pyrenean resorts, and their liking for it has made it known, beyond the others, in their own country. The streets are shady and well lined; the houses, frequently standing apart in their own small gardens, give a pleasant impression of space and airiness. There are numberless shops, where we can later replenish various needs. The pavements seem to have been built and leveled, by MacAdam himself, as an enthusiast puts it; and everywhere along the side of the walks bound rivulets of mountain water, so dear to these Pyrenean towns.

The mineral springs here are not powerful, but are useful in mild digestive disorders and the like, and afford at least a pretext for an idle summering, as springs will do, the world over. The Establishment is large and well arranged, but getting well is no such stern and serious affair at Bagnères de Bigorre as at Barèges, and here the visitors wisely mingle their saline prescriptions in abundant infusions of pleasure. There are drives and promenades in all directions. The Casino offers concerts and occasional plays and operettas, and a band in the main promenade entertains regularly the listening evening saunterers. Rightly does the town aim still to merit the praise given by Montaigne, who paid it a marked tribute in his writings:

"He who does not bring along with him," observes that great French essayist, "so much cheerfulness as to enjoy the pleasure of the company he will there meet, [at bath-resorts,] and of the walks and exercises to which the beauty of the places in which baths for the most part are situated invites us, will doubtless lose the best and surest part of their effect. For this reason, I have hitherto chosen to go to those of the most pleasant situation, where there was the most convenience of lodging, provision and company,—as the Baths of Banières in France."

The cheery town is large enough to take on something quite akin to a city-like air; it has a population of about 10,000, and in summer the number has its half added upon it by increase of visitors and boarders. The hotels are praiseworthy, though making little display; and a marked attraction of the town is this wide promenade of the main street, termed the *Coustous*,—so called, it is alleged, because anciently the guardians, *custodes*, of Bigorre used here to pace their nightly patrol. The Coustous is doubly lined with arching trees, and has seats and a wide path along the centre; the carriage-ways enclose this, and shops and cafés line the outer walks. A few squares away, another similar promenade broadens out, likewise vivified with trees and shops and booths. Facing this is the bath-establishment before mentioned, and be-

yond, in grounds of its own, the Kursaal or Casino. Cropping up among the houses, stout buildings older than the rest tell of the days when Bagnères was a "goodly inclosed town," the inhabitants of which had a hard time of it against the depredations of Lourdes and Mauvoisin and its other robber neighbors.

For we are among old times again at Bigorre, and many spots in the vicinity are rife with Middle-Age incidents of robbing and righting. This region was the plague-spot of the country for its freebooting fortresses,—Lourdes, Mauvoisin, Trigalet, with their adventurers always ready for a fracas,—the strongholds, as has been said, of those logicians who

"kept to the good old plan
That those should take who have the power,
And those should keep who can,"
and the provinces about them lived in constant worriment. This valley especially suffered from their armed bands; now they raided some exposed hamlet, now made prisoners of merchants or travelers on the highway, anon swooped down here upon Bagnères and made off with money and live stock in gratifying plenty.

And centuries yet preceding this, the valley saw wars on a larger scale, when Cæsar and his Romans, ploughing victoriously through Gaul, came to the Aquitani and crushed them down into the furrows with the rest, after repeated and furious resistance. The Romans knew too of these springs, and there are still remains of the city,—*Vicus Aquensis*,—which they built on this site. In the Museum are Roman relics found while excavating, among them votive tablets recording the donors' gratitude to the nymphs of the springs for cures effected. Clearly, Bigorre is of no mushroom growth, but has been toughened and seasoned by age and warfare into the just reward of its nowaday repose and popularity.

II.

It is Sunday, and there is service in the English chapel, a brief walk away. It is

conducted by the nervous, genial chaplain staying at the hotel, who afterwards greets us cordially at the noon luncheon-hour, and justifies our pleasure at finding a tongue which can return English for English and with fluency. He officiates at Pau during the winter, he tells us, and here at Bigorre during the summer; and so, in a sense, we find, does the hotel proprietor himself, who, with his expansive wife, owns a hotel in Pau as well as here, and conducts the former during the winter months, when the season at Bigorre is ended.

The day is evidently that of some special saint; the population is out in its brightest hues. Saints are in great authority with these people; their recurrent "days" fill the calendar; their ascribed specialties are as various as were those of the minor Greek or Egyptian deities. All is in reverence, be it added; canonization is a very sacred thing with the Catholic peasant. The power even of working ill seems to be, in curious ignorance, at times attributed to certain of these saints; "I have seen with my own eyes," relates a native Gascon writer, M. de Lagrèze, "a woman who, wishing to disembarrass herself of her husband, demanded of a venerable priest, as the most natural thing in the world, that he should say a mass for her to *St. Sécaire*; she was convinced that, this saint, unknown to martyrology, had the power of withering up (*sécher*) and killing troublesome individuals, to accommodate those who invoked his aid."

We take another walk in the afternoon through the streets of the town, and afterward compare international notes once more with our cordial English clergyman. It is renewedly grateful to hear again the mother tongue spoken understandingly by a stranger. The utter and unaccountable absence of our own countrymen's faces and voices from these Pyrenean resorts gives one constantly a touch of regret. One longs occasionally for the crisp American greeting,—the quick lighting-up, the national hand-shake, a comparison of adventures. Saving by two compatriots met in Biarritz, we have found our nation entirely unrepresented in or near the summer Pyrenees.

III.

Bagnères is too far to the northward to be in touch with true mountain expeditions. Its only "star" in this line is the majestic Pic du Midi de Bigorre, which, being itself an outlying peak, is much nearer us than the main range and is often ascended from Bigorre,—a conveyance being taken to Grip and the start on foot or horseback made from that point. There are, besides, a number of lesser mountains about, and drives and longer excursions unnumbered. A rifle perhaps most recommendable, though not always mentioned in the hand-books, is one that will bring us back again for a day to the times of our rascally acquaintance, Count Gaston Phoebus, and his contemporaries. This is to the castle of Mauvoisin before mentioned,—"*Mauvais voisin*,"—"bad neighbor," as it abundantly proved itself to Bigorre. It lies but ten miles away, in a northeast direction; it is reached best by the carriage-road, and the trip can readily be made in a half-day. This was one of the Aquitaine fortresses which with Lourdes, it will be remembered, fell into the hands of the English, about the middle of the fourteenth century, as part of the ransom of King John of France. Raymond of the Sword was appointed its governor, and a right loyal sword did he prove himself to own. But Mauvoisin could not resist siege as Lourdes could. The Duke of Anjou was soon at it, determined to recapture it for the French, and after a stiff course of starving and thirsting, the garrison surrendered and Mauvoisin came back to the French flag.

It was near this spot that a peculiarly savage and yet ludicrous fight once occurred. It was during the same robberesque period,—about the middle of the fourteenth century; and Froissart gives us an animated account of it; he was on the way to Orthez through this very region, and his traveling companion tells him of the event as they pass:

A party of reckless men-at-arms, bent on mischief and plunder, had sallied out from Lourdes, it seems, on a long foray.

They were a hundred and twenty lances in all, and they had two dashing leaders, Ernauton de Sainte Colombe and Le Mengeant de Sainte Basile,—the latter well called the Robin Hood of the Pyrenees. They were all men whose very breath of life was in thieving and combat. The band had "lifted" an abundance of booty; they had exploited the country as far even as Toulouse, "finding in the meadows great quantities of cattle, pigs and sheep, which they seized, as well as some substantial men from the flat countries, and drove them all before them."

The Governor of Tarbes and other knights and squires of Bigorre heard of this mischief and determined to attack the marauders. They assembled at Tournay, a town not far from Bigorre and close by Mauvoisin, and counted up two hundred men. Among them was our athletic celebrity, the Bourg d'Espaign, the same who carried the ass and wood upstairs, that Christmas Day at Orthez. He was a regiment in himself, "being well formed, of a large size, strongly made and not too much loaded with flesh; you will not find his equal in all Gascony for vigor of body." At Tournay they prepared to lie in wait and spring on the thieving band as it returned.

The Lourdes roughs had wind of the ambush on their homeward way. They were quite as ready for a fight as a foray, but prudently divided their numbers: one detachment was to drive the booty around by the bridge half-way between Tournay and Mauvoisin and thence on through by-roads; while the main band was to march in order of battle on the high ground and so draw the attack. Both sections were later to meet at a point beyond, from whence they would soon be safely at Lourdes. "On this they departed; and there remained with the principal division Ernauton de Sainte Colombe, Le Mengeant de Sainte Basile, and full eighty companions, all men-at-arms; there were not ten varlets among them. They tightened their armor, fixed their helmets, and, grasping their lances, marched in close order, as if they were instantly to engage; they indeed expected nothing else, for they

knew their enemies were in the field."

The Bourg and his friends scented the stratagem in turn, and promptly divided themselves likewise. He himself with one division guarded the river passage, which they suspected the cattle and prisoners would be sent around to cross. The other division, under the Governor of Tarbes, took the high ground.

At the Pass of Marteras, not far from the castle, the governor's division met the main body of the enemy. "They instantly dismounted, and leaving their horses to pasture, with pointed lances advanced, for a combat was unavoidable, shouting their cries: 'St. George for Lourde!' 'Our Lady for Bigorre!'"

Now it is to be remembered that fighters in those days were often cased in armor from crown to sole,—a preposterous armor, burdensome and unwieldy, but almost utterly invulnerable. Sword-blows might dint it for hours without doing damage; the danger in battle lay chiefly in simple over-exertion. This gives the ludicrous point to the demure narration made to Froissart by his companion:

"They charged each other, thrusting their spears with all their strength, and, to add greater force, urged them forward with their breasts. The combat was very equal; and for some time none was struck down, as I heard from those present. When they had sufficiently used their spears, they threw them down, and with battle-axes began to deal out terrible blows on both sides. This action lasted for three hours, and it was marvelous to see how well they fought and defended themselves. When any were so worsted or out of breath that they could not longer support the fight, they seated themselves near a large ditch full of water in the middle of the plain, when, having taken off their helmets, they refreshed themselves; this done, they replaced their helmets and returned to the combat, I do not believe there ever was so well fought or so severe a battle as this of Marteras in Bigorre, since the famous combat of thirty English against thirty French knights in Brittany.

"They fought hand to hand, and Ernauton de Sainte Colombe was on the point of being killed by a squire of the country called Guillonet de Salenges, who had pushed him so hard that he was quite out of breath, when I will tell you what happened: Ernauton had a servant who was a spectator of the battle, neither attacking nor attacked by any one; but seeing his master thus distressed, he ran to him and wresting the battle-axe from his hand, said: 'Ernauton, go and sit down! recover yourself! you cannot longer continue the battle.' With this battle-axe, he advanced upon the squire and gave him such a blow on the helmet as made him stagger and almost fall down. Guillonet, smarting from the blow, was very wroth, and made for the servant to strike him with his axe on the head; but the varlet avoided it, and grappling with the squire, who was much fatigued, turned him round and flung him to the ground under him, when he said: 'I will put you to death if you do not surrender yourself to my master.'

"'And who is thy master?'

"'Ernauton de Sainte Colombe, with whom you have been so long engaged.'

"The squire, finding he had not the advantage, being under the servant, who had his dagger ready to strike, surrendered, on condition to deliver himself prisoner within fifteen days at the castle of Lourde, whether rescued or not.

"Of such service was this servant to his master; and I must say, Sir John, that there was a superabundance of feats of arms that day performed, and many companions were sworn to surrender themselves at Tarbes and at Lourde. The Governor of Tarbes and Le Mengeant de Sainte Basile fought hand to hand, without sparing themselves, and performed many gallant deeds, while all the others were fully employed; however, they fought so vigorously that they exhausted their strength, and both were slain on the spot.

"Upon this, the combat ceased by mutual consent, for they were so worn down that they could not longer wield their axes; some disarmed themselves, to recruit their strength, and left there their arms. Those of Lourde carried home with them the dead body of Le Mengeant; as the French did that of Ernauton to Tarbes; and in order that the memory of this battle should be preserved, they erected a cross of stone on the place where these two knights had fought and died."

At the bridge, a few miles away, the other sections met, and belabored each other as vigorously as did those at the pass. The Bourg d'Espaign performed wonders: "he wielded a battle-axe, and never hit a man with it but he struck him to the ground. He took with his own hand the two captains, Cornillac and Perot Palatin de Béarn. A squire of Navarre was there slain, called Ferdinand de Miranda, an expert man-at-arms. Some who were present say the Bourg d'Espaign killed him; others, that he was stifled through the heat of his armor.

"In short, the pillage was rescued and all who conducted it slain or made prisoners; for not three escaped, excepting varlets, who ran away and crossed the river by swimming. Thus ended this business, and the garrison of Lourde never had such a loss as it suffered that day. The prisoners were courteously ransomed or mutually exchanged; for those who had been engaged in this combat had made several prisoners on each side, so that it behooved them to treat each other handsomely."

"Such," laughs Johnson, "was a fight of men-at-arms in the Middle Ages,—derived from the graphic description of Froissart, in whose narrative there always runs an undercurrent of sly humor when portraying the military extravagances of the age. And it is impossible to avoid the contagion; for who can picture in any more serious style a hurly-burly of huge, iron-clad, suffocating, perspiring warriors, half blinded with helmet and visor and scarce able to stir beneath the metallic pots encompassing them around; belaboring and hustling each other about with weapons quite unequal to reach the flesh and blood within, till, out of breath and blown with fatigue, they sate down as coolly as they could and refreshed themselves; then getting up again, again drove all the breath out of their bodies,—and all without doing the least mortal harm, unless somebody died of the heat or was smothered to death in his own armorial devices."

IV.

This Le Mengeant, the worthy killed in his armor, as above recorded, at the Pass of Marteras, had been the hero of more than one bedeviling exploit during his career thus untimely cut off. One I cannot forbear giving, told in these Chronicles and retold with charming gusto by the writer above mentioned. Le Mengeant, it would seem, had evidently "a strong notion of the humorous in his composition. One time, he set out, accompanied by four others, all with shaven crowns and otherwise disguised as an abbot and attendants going from upper Gascony to Paris on business. Having reached the Sign of the Angel at Montpelier, a suitable hostelry for such holy men, they soon gained much credit for their saintly deportment and conversation; insomuch that a rich man of the city, Sir Béranger, was fain to avail himself of their company and ghostly comfort by the way. We say nothing of the generosity which prompted the holy father to offer Sir Béranger an escort free of all expense, so much was he captivated by that gentleman's charming society. One can imagine the sly winks and contortions interchanged by this pious party as the victim fell into the trap. But no amount of imagination can ever do justice to the features of Sir Béranger, when, three leagues from the city, the right reverend prelate and his apostolic brethren threw off the mask with peals of un-canonical laughter, led the wretched cit off to Lourdes through crooked by-roads, and there extracted from his disconsolate relatives five thousand francs of ransom,—which they, holy men, doubtless devoted to the purposes of their order. There is a story for a rhymer Sherwood forest could not beat!

"It is but proper to set society right as to those gallant days of chivalry, when knights fought for the love of ladies' eyes and glory that lived for ever. More practical men are hardly to be found in business to-day, for they never lost sight of that grand maxim, to 'get money.' 'Quærenda pecunia primum, virtus post nummos' was a motto each knight might have much more truly borne upon his shield than the charming bits of brag and sentiment cunningly designed for that purpose by accommodating heraldry. Money they got, honestly if they could, but they got it; and to do them justice they spent it right jovially, as all such gallant spirits do when they are disbursing what does not belong to them. After all, time only alters the characters in the Drama,—the plot is pretty much the same; and with a suburban villa for a château, a face of brass for a coat of iron, and a steel pen for a steel sword, your gallant knight of to-day storms his bank or plunders his neighbors from an entrenched joint-stock fortress or leads on his band to surprise the public pocket from some tangled thicket of swindling,—just upon the same principles as our old Pyrenean friends."

CHAPTER XVI.

THE INTERLAKEN OF THE PYRENEES.

"Perle enchâssée au sein des Pyrénées
Par l'ouvrier qu'on nomme l'Éternel,
Je te prédis de belles destinées;
L'humanité te doit plus d'un autel.
Car l'étranger dans ta charmante enceinte
Trouve toujours, suivant son rang, son nom,
Le bon accueil, l'hospitalité sainte,
Que sait offrir l'habitant de Luchon."
—Local Ode.

We now prepare for the last and longest drive on the Route Thermale,—that from Bigorre to Luchon. The distance is forty-four miles; the journey can be made in one long day, but owing to the amount of work for the horses "against collar," it is wiser to break it into two. This can be done at the village of Arreau, the only practicable resting-place between. There are two severe cols to cross on this trip, one on this side of Arreau, the other beyond; the first is the most noted of all the Pyrenean cols for the immense and striking view it commands. This pass, the *Col d'Aspin*, is but a morning's drive from Bigorre, and is often made an excursion even by those not going to Luchon. Another mode of reaching Luchon from Bigorre is by rail, both places being at the end of branches from the main line. But the charm of mountain travel is in these magnificent roads, and few loving this charm would wisely sacrifice it to a mere gain in time.

Allotting, then, two days for the journey, we are not impelled to drive off from Bigorre at any unseasonably early hour. In fact it is verging upon noon when the start is made. Our Tourmalet conveyances have long since gone back, and we have a fresh landau and victoria duly chartered, with two strong and capable-looking drivers. For the first half hour or more the road retraces its steps down the valley toward the foot of the Tourmalet, only breaking off at the village of Ste. Marie. Through this we had passed in the late afternoon rain of the drive from Barèges, and here our present road strikes away from the Barèges route and directs its way toward the Col d'Aspin.

The Vale of Campan, in which we are running, has long had its praises appreciatively sung. It is fertile and smiling, but we decide that it does not vie with the Eden of Argelès. The remembrance of that happy valley under the full afternoon sun, as we saw it in driving to Cauterets, diverse in its sweet fields and silenced fortresses, will long hold off all rival landscapes. The road twines on between pastures and rye-fields, as we approach again nearer and nearer the mountains, and after an easy two-hour trot, we are drawn up before the little inn of Paillole, the last lunching-station before crossing the col. Here is found the tidy air of nearly all these little hostelries, and our confidence in them, born at Laruns and nowhere as yet injured save by the demon kettle-rag of Grip, finds nothing here to further cripple it in any way. There is an old man at hand to greet us, as at Grip, but his wife is by, as well, and her alert, trim manner is alien to all sooty napery. It is always unfair to carry over a suspicious spirit from past causes of suspicion; and we prudently refrain from tampering, by reminiscence, with present good impressions.

Pending the preparation of the repast, we wander out about the grounds. The Campan Gave is sufficiently wide to be called a river, and flows at the rear of the hotel kitchen-garden in a broad, rock-broken bed. It is pleasant to stand by its cool, firm rush, and grow alive to the sound of it and to the pushing of the wind and to the white and blue of clouds and sky framing the sunshine. Cities and city life fall so suddenly out of sight, as an unreal thing, in the presence of these rustlings of Nature's garments.

From this winning little olitory plot here at the side of the house by the river, we can see under an arbored porch the kitchen itself, open to the world. The old woman is at work within, as we can also see, at the needful culinary incantations; and assisting her with single-minded but safely-controlled zeal is her husband the landlord, aproned for the occasion.

But nearer by, close to the stream, our host has a flooded trout-box, and he presently comes stumbling out to it along some rough boards thrown down for a path. He unlocks the padlock, opens the lid, and we group around to witness the sacrifice,—innocent speckle-sides butchered to make a Pyrenean holiday. There is no fly-casting, no adroit play of rod and reel; the old gentleman plunges in his bare arm, there is a splashing and a struggle, and his hand has closed over a victim and brings it up to the light,—a glistening trout, alive, breathless, and highly surprised and annoyed. He takes the upper jaw in his other thumb and forefinger and bends it sharply backward; something breaks at the base of the skull and the fish lies instantly dead. This painless mode of taking off is new to us, and we concur in approving its suddenness and certainty. And so he proceeds, until the baker's dozen of trout lie on the boards at his feet. Then he closes and locks the box, bows to the spectators, and retires with the spoils; while we go back to our communings with the river and the garden.

II.

It is a trifle later than it should be when we finally start afresh; and newly-come clouds are moping about the mountains and banking up unwelcomely near the hills of the col ahead. The ascent begins at once in long, gradual sweeps, and for an hour as we ride and walk progressively higher, the view of the valley behind lessens in the haze, and the clouds in front become thicker and thicker. There is then a straight incline toward the last, of a mile or more; the notch of the col is sharp-cut against the sky just ahead, and we hurry on to gain a shred at least of the vanishing view before it is too late. In vain; we are standing upon the Col d'Aspin,—a herd of cloud-fleeces wholly filling the new valley ahead and now whitening also the Campan Vale behind us.

This is not such an irremediable disappointment as might appear. We resolve now and here to outgeneral circumstances. The view from the Col d'Aspin is unquestionably too fine to be lost, and we decide to return from Luchon to Bigorre by this same route, instead of leaving by rail. Thus we shall recross this col; and vengeful care shall be taken to await a flawless day for the crossing.

So we get into the carriages again and speed off down the long slopes which lead into the Arreau basin, grimly regarding the clouds and promising ourselves recoupment to the full. By the road, it is five miles before the carriages will be on level ground again, and three miles thence to Arreau. The drivers point out a short-cut down the mountain, and some of us are quickly on foot, crossing the road's great arcs with steep descent, stepping lower and lower over pastures and ploughed ground and through reappearing copses and thickets, until we are at last upon the road again in the floor of the valley. Here at a stone bridge the party finds us, and soon after, all are bowling into Arreau and traversing its one long street to the low door of the Hotel d'Angleterre.

There is naught of the pretentious about the Hotel d'Angleterre. It is listless and antique and not worldly wise, but we very soon find that it is in good order and quite able to entertain Americans unawares. There is a stone hallway with a large, square staircase in the centre; upstairs, the rooms, though low-ceiled, are commodious and airy; and we find a tolerable reception-room below, near the entrance. In the rear is a charming garden of terraces and rose-beds and flat-topped trees and odd nooks for café-tables; and later in the evening a neat service of tea and tartines brightens our pathway to the wider gardens of sleep.

III.

Arreau, as we find it in the morning, has little more to show than the long street through which we drove on arrival. Age-rusted eaves overhang the white-washed walls of the houses; there are queer, primitive little shops and local *cabarets* or taverns, the latter sheltering their outside benches and deal tables behind tall box-plants set put in stationary green tubs upon the pavement. Midway down the street is a venerable market-shelter, a roomy structure consisting simply of a roof and countless stone pillars. Its parallels may not infrequently be seen elsewhere in Europe,—as at Lucerne and Annécy and Canterbury; there is no side-wall, no enclosure; all is public and out of doors, a habit of many years back, and on market-days it is the centre of interest for the entire district. There is little to tempt, in the stores; beyond dry tablets of Bayonne chocolate and some time-hardened confectionery sold in a musty little shop below the church, we find nothing to buy combining the interest and lastingness of a proper memento. Arreau is in short an old-fashioned town in all particulars, unawakened even by the thoroughfaring of the Route Thermale.

The church, with its sculptured arms and round chancel, is another work of the Templars,—one of several in this

valley, for the territory was once assigned by a Count of Bigorre to their order, and one town in the district, Bordères by name, was even erected by them into a commandery. On the destruction of the order in 1312, nearly all the Templars throughout the county of Bigorre, with their commander, Bernard de Montagu, were seized, and were executed at Auch and their possessions confiscated. Afterward, the valley passed to the Counts of Armagnac, whose wickedness and family pride were intense enough to have prompted that most transcendent of boasts, "In hell, we are a great house!" and who waged more than one stiff feud with Béarn and the Counts of Foix.

We drive off toward Luchon after the survey, not leaving a final farewell, since we shall pass through once more in returning to cross again the Col d'Aspin. The col before us now, cutting off the Arreau valley from that of Luchon, is the *Col de Peyresourde*, the last of the throes of the Route Thermale; and up the sides of the mountain the carriages unceasingly climb during the forenoon until the crest is reached. From this the road lowers itself again by the usual complicated zigzags. The dauntless Highway of the Hot Springs here completes its work and allows itself a last well-earned rest along the smoother valley, until by two o'clock we see it find its final end in the broad avenue leading into Luchon.

IV.

Luchon is easily the queen of all these beautiful Pyrenean resorts. We very soon concur in this. I have called it the Pyrenees Interlaken, and this perhaps describes it more tersely, than description. It is in fact surprisingly like Interlaken; its broad, arbored highways or *höhewegs*, its rich hotels, its general enamel of opulence and leisure, suggest the charm of that Swiss paradise at every turn. Only the great glow of the Jungfrau is missing; but one need not go far, as we shall later see, to view almost its full equal.

"It is not possible to be silent about Luchon," declares the enthusiastic essayist who described so appreciatively the fair valley of Luz, "Luchon is a capital. No other place in the world represents beauty and pleasure in the same degree; no other town is so thoroughly typical of the district over which it presides. One can no more imagine the Pyrenees without Luchon than Luchon without the Pyrenees; neither of them is conceivable without the other; together, they form a picture and its frame. A region of loveliness, amusement and hot water needed a metropolis possessing the same three features in the highest degree; in Luchon they are concentrated with a completeness of which no example is to be found elsewhere. No valley is so delicious; nowhere is there such an accumulation of diversions; nowhere are there so many or such varied mineral springs. If it be true that a perfect capital should present a summary of the characteristics and aspects of its country, then Luchon is certainly the most admirable central city that men have built, for no other represents the land around it so faithfully as Luchon does. Neither Mexico nor Merv, nor Timbuctoo nor Lassa, nor Winnipeg nor Naples, attain its symbolic exactness."

We find super-luxurious quarters at the Richelieu, one of the handsomest of the handsome hotels, and groan at the narrowing limitations of the calendar. Before us is a wide, leafy park, with rustic pavilions, and an artificial lake enlivened with swans; these grounds are a constant pleasure; you stroll under the trees and listen to the music and see all humanity unroll itself along the paths about you. Here stands the Establishment, a low, many-columned building, whose effect from without is unusual and pleasing. Within, the noticeable feature is the great entrance stairway and hall, the latter with the proportions, of a Roman church and adorned with wall-paintings in large panels. Beyond, still in the park, is a graceful rustic kiosque, where other than sulphureous drinks are dealt out and where many people contrive to linger in passing. Here, in the mellow afternoon, Luchon is unfurling itself, as we saunter along; the broad space abutting on the Establishment is the focus of the throng, silk-sashed children are playing, boy's selling bonbons or the illustrated papers, fashionable French messieurs and mesdames and mesdemoiselles taking the air and portraying the modes.

We turn to the right, and emerge from the park, into the main promenade of the town. This is the Allée d'Étigny. It sets the type of these noted Luchon streets,—unusually broad, overhung with a fourfold row of immense lime-trees, and bordered with hotels and with enticing and polychromatic shops and booths quite equal to those of Interlaken. These wide Allées give to the village one of its individual charms. There are several of them,—among others, the Allée de la Pique and the Allée de Piqué, starting one from each end of the Allée d'Étigny; these meet in an irregular figure, edged by villas and *pensions*, and everywhere green and shaded. Others lead out along the streams. This plenitude of shade is another of the place's attractions; foliage is nowhere more abundant; trees stock the park, the streets, all the avenues of approach,— their cool canopy gratefully filtering the July sun.

The D'Étigny is clearly the chief of the Allées, and we make slow progress past its tempting booths and flower-stalls and solider emporiums. Promenaders are out in force; carriages are rolling forth from the town for a late afternoon drive or returning from an earlier; the omnibuses come clattering up from the arriving train; we have scarcely found such a joyous stir south of the boulevards of Paris.

It is of its own kind, this midsummer fashion, and, whether in its beach or mountain homes, as worthy to be absorbed and appropriated in its turn as the antiquity of Morlaäs or the silence of the Cirque. We enjoy it unresistingly, as we idle down the bright street, eyes and ears alert to its beauties and its harmonies.

But there is the seamy side to Luchon, as to many things on earth: you go but a few paces from these opulent Allées and you find poverty. Frowsy women stare at us from rickety houses in the old part of the town; children, no longer silk-sashed but dirt-stained and ignorant, play in the mud-heaps; patient old tinkers and cobblers are seen in the dim shops at work. The very poor rarely gain by the growth of their neighbors. These in Luchon seem not to feel envy, but they have no part nor heart in the pride of civic progress around them. They keep on along their stolid, uncomplaining ways, having long ago faced the fact that they were immovably at the bottom of Fortune's wheel, and having forgotten since even to repine over it.

Turning off into the second Allée of the triangle, we find ourselves presently in view of the Casino, which stands back in a park of its own, set in trees, and possessing a theatre and concert-room, drawing-room or conversation-hall, and the usual café and reading-apartments. There is opera every second night and a small daily entrance-charge to the building, which may be compounded by purchasing a ticket for the month or the season.

The remaining avenue crosses back to the beginning of the first, ending with a long building given up to a species of universal bazaar, whose divisions and stands, festooned with crimson cambric, display confectionery, worsted goods, paper-weights of Pyrenean marbles, and nick-nacks of high and low degree. Opposite is a large store comfortably called "Old England"; it augurs the presence and patronage of at least a few of the British race at Luchon, and offers a homelike stock of Anglo-Saxon goods. The walk has brought us out once more at the corner facing our hotel, and the hour for table-d'hôte strikes elfinly on the ear.

V.

Luchon owes much to one man. This was a certain Intendant of the province and of Bigorre arid Béarn, who lived about the middle of the last century and was the most practical and enterprising governor the region ever had. The Luchonnais honor the name of the Baron d'Étigny. He believed in his Pyrenees; he believed in their future, and set himself to speeding it with all his heart. He not only expended his salary but his private fortune; he wrought extraordinary changes in facilities both for trade and travel, and, curiously enough, made an extraordinary number of enemies in doing so. Towns and districts were spurred up to their duty; tree-nurseries established, agriculture stimulated, sheep and merinos and blooded horses imported for breeding; lawlessness found itself, suddenly under ban; and in especial, paths and roads were cut through the country in all directions, two hundred leagues of them, opening up to trade and fashion spot after spot only half accessible before. Thus Eaux Chaudes, Cauterets, St. Sauveur, Barèges, Luchon, previously gained only by foot-ways, were by D'Étigny made accessible for wheeled vehicles; uncertain trails were made over into good bridle-paths; and routes also over some of the cols were begun which have been since gathered up into the sweep of the Route Thermale.

On Luchon particularly, D'Étigny's kind offices fell; and Luchon resented them the most acridly. But the fostering hand was quite able to close into a fist. D'Étigny pushed his plans firmly, despite opposition. Pending the construction of a road from Montréjeau opening full access to the valley, the town itself was taken in hand. The main street, now the Allée d'Étigny, was projected; the springs,—from which the town was then some little, distance away,—were rehabilitated; and to replace the rough path leading to them he proceeded to level the ground between and open three additional avenues, each planted with quadruple ranges of trees. But this last innovation wrought trouble; it focused the growing opposition; every chair-carrier and pony-hirer in Luchon, together with every owner of the lands condemned, spitefully resented the opening of the new routes. Combining with the neighboring mountaineers, they rose one night and utterly demolished all three of the avenues, uprooting the young trees, leaving the ways strewed with débris and wholly impassable.

D'Étigny calmly built them up anew, and with increased care.

They were demolished again.

Even the Intendant's patience failed then. He built the roads the third time, but in addition to trees he studded them with troops.

They were not molested after that. Their enemies found they had a man against them who meant what he said and was prepared to stand by it. Eventually they veered around even into respect; Luchon in the end grew to rejoice in her Allées unreservedly; they stand to this day, and D'Étigny's name is all but canonized under the lindens which once heard him vigorously cursed.

VI.

Luchon is undoubtedly over-petted. The belle of the spas is a trifle spoiled. The inblowing of fashion has been fanning her self-appreciation for years. Prices are crowded to the highest notch, for the season is short and one must live; the hotels are expensive, though *pensions* and apartment-houses mitigate this; the cost of living is high for the region, though always low when judged by home standards; articles in the shops are chiefly of luxury, and even carriages and guides are appraised at advanced rates. It is the extreme of French fashion which comes to Luchon. Eaux Bonnes and Cauterets are close rivals, but Luchon is the queenliest of the triplet. As a consequence, the place shows a touch of caprice, of vanity, even of arrogance; prosperity is a powerful tonic, but sometimes its iron enters into the soul.

Notwithstanding, the bright little town ends by enchaining us completely. During the days we pass in its Allées and vallées, we come to agree that there could be fewer more captivating spots for a summer wanderer, singly or *en famille*, seeking a six weeks' resting-place in the mountains. It will grow at length into the recognition of the English and Americans, now so unaccountably unknowing of this mountain-garden; the prediction lies on the surface that in time it must open rivalry almost with that much-loved Interlaken it so happily resembles.

The finishing charm of Luchon is its nearness to the great peaks. Ice and snow are but scantily in sight from the valley itself, but a short rise upon any of the surrounding hills shows summits and glacier fields on all sides but the north, and more ambitious trips quickly place one among them. The range culminates in this region; from east and west it has been gradually rising to a centre, and south from Luchon it finds its climax, attaining in the bulky system of the Maladetta to its full stature of over eleven thousand feet. This mountain mass is the lion of the Pyrenees. It lies in Spanish territory, on the other side of an intervening chain; but from a noted port in the crest of the latter, three hours from the town, the eye sweeps it from base to brow, and its ascent is made from the Luchon valley as headquarters.

There is a peculiar attraction in the proximity of the highest mountain of a range. But if Luchon in this resembles Chamouni, in all other respects it holds its parallel with Interlaken. Here, as there, other groups of important peaks are scattered within reach of attack; explorations on the higher glaciers are facile; the Vallée du Lys is its Lauterbrunnen, the Port de Vénasque its Wengern Alp. Within reach of the idler majority, there is a walk, a drive, or a point of view for each day of the month. The roads now pierce every adjoining valley, and paths climb up to all the summits that fence them in.

VII.

A day or two pass uneventfully over us as we linger under the trees at Luchon, and then we shake off the spell, to look for its mountain neighbors. One of the peaks from which the panorama of the Maladetta chain can be best seen is the *Pic d'Entécade*, a noted point for an object-lesson of the mountains' relief. Some of us accordingly resolve to ascend it. We have at last begun to recognize the truth of a truism,—that of early rising among the mountains. Always given in all "Advice to Pedestrians," in all "Physicians' Holidays," in all handbooks and guides, it had worn off into a commonplace, founded chiefly, it seemed, on *a priori* health-saws and on repetition. But there is reason, we find, in this worthy acquaintance, and a reason quite apart from health-saws, for it is a weather reason. The great proportion of these Pyrenean days, barring the rainy ones, run a uniform career: gold in the morning, silver at noon, gold again at night. The early mornings are brilliantly cloudless; by nine or ten o'clock the horizon whitens,—it is the dreaded *brouillard*; faint cloud-balls are taking shape; they roll lightly in, bounding like soap-bubbles along the peaks, finally clinging softly about them; and by noon, though the zenith holds still its rich southern blue, the circle of the hills is broken, the higher summits thickly hung with misty gauze. In the late afternoon, the breeze dislodges the intruders, and softly polishes the rock and ice of the peaks until at dusk they are free again from even a shred of vapor.

Thus, even on fine days, a fine view is rare unless it is an early one. We deplore this unhappy trait of the weather and deeply resent its arbitrariness. But resentment is fruitless under a despotism. And there is after all a certain glow of superciliousness in being up early; the feat once accomplished, it brings its own reward; one feels a comforting disdain for the napping thousands who are losing the crisp, unbreathed freshness in the air and on the mountains; one speedily ceases regretting the missing forty winks, as he opens eyes and lungs and heart to the spirit of the morning.

We accordingly arrange for an early start, not precisely resigned, but resolved nevertheless. The guide, as instructed, knocks at our doors in the morning, just before six o'clock. We hear the fatal words: "It makes fine weather, monsieur;" we awake, imprecating but still resolved; we call out a response of assent, still imprecating; nerve ourselves to rise,—struggle mentally to do so,—struggle more faintly,—yield imperceptibly,—forget for an instant to struggle at all,—and in another instant we are restfully back beyond recall in the land of dreams.

Our resentment was stronger than we knew.

When the carriage finally carries us out from the town, it is the fifth hour at least after sunrise and more than three after our time for starting. We should have had half of the Entécade beneath us, and are but just quitting Luchon. The inevitable thin lines of mist are already cobwebbing the horizons; but there is a good breeze abroad to-day and the clouds are not resting so quietly in the niches as usual. So we comfort us greatly, and the horses urge forward up the valley, themselves seemingly full of hope that the day is not lost.

The base of the Entécade is six miles from Luchon. For some distance the road runs up the Vallée du Lys, whose continuance merits a separate excursion. Then we turn off, under the old border-tower of Castel Vieil, and soon the carriage is dodging up a cliffy hill, the road hooded with beeches and pines and playing majestic hide-and-seek with the sharp mountains ahead. It is only an hour and a half, and we are at the Hospice de France. Here the road ends. The horses stop before the plain stone structure, low, heavily built, and not surpassingly commodious, and we alight to prepare for the climb. The building is owned by the Commune of Luchon, which rents it out under conditions to an innkeeper; and its object, like that of the St. Bernard, is to serve as a refuge for those crossing the pass near which it lies. There are no monks in it, however; it is simply a rough mountain *posada*, offering a few poor beds in emergencies, and finding its chiefer lifework in purveying to the Luchon tourists.

The hospice is situated in a deep basin of mountains open only on the Luchon side. Directly in front of it, high above us, is located the pass referred to,—the *Port de Vénasque*: the notch in the chain from which the Maladetta is so strikingly revealed. It is itself another noted excursion from Luchon. A great sweep of rocky ridges rises to it, not perpendicular but sharply inclined. There is a savage black pinnacle shooting up on the left, remarkable for its uncompromising cone of rock, its rejection of all the refinements of turf and arbor and even of snow. This is the *Pic de la Pique*. On the right starts up another summit, sharp also, though less precipitous; and the short ridge between the two has in it the notch, itself not to be seen from below, which constitutes this pass, the gateway into Spain,—the Port de Vénasque.

This is one of the most used of all these mountain portals; hundreds of persons cross it annually, herdsmen, mule-drivers, merchants with their small caravans of horses, Spanish visitors coming to Luchon, French tourists seeking the view of the Maladetta,—and most often of all, despite surveillance, the shadowy contrabandista, whose vigilance is greater than the vigilance of the law and the custom-house. We can plainly trace the path as it zigzags upward over the snow and débris, and can outline its general course until it vanishes into the break in the ridge. The line of the ridge itself is just now cut out clearly against the sky, but soft puffs and ponpons of cloud are loitering near it with evident intentions.

But our present quest is the Entécade. This mountain stands farther to the left in the circle of the basin; its own flanks hide its summit from the hollow, so we go forth not knowing whether into the blue or the grey. Impedimenta are abandoned, sticks are grasped, and the guide leads to the assault.

The path turns to the rear of the hos-

pice and crawls up a green slope, commanding finely the black sugar-loaf of the Pic de la Pique opposite. As we advance, the mist has finally closed in upon the crest of the Vénasque pass at its right; the ridge is completely hidden, and we turn and look ahead, somewhat solicitous for our own prospects. Before us, up the mountain, long streamers of hostile vapors are swinging over the downs, trailing to the ground and at times brushing down to our own level; but the wind keeps hunting them off, and so far their tenure is hopefully precarious. There is scarcely a tree above the hospice; we have left the line even of pines.

An hour passes. We come to a table-land stretching lengthily forward, covered with the greenish yellow of pastures, and alive with cattle browsing on a sparse turf. The way winds on among the herds; we form in close marching order, with the guide in front and spiked staffs ready for use; for these neighbors are a trifle wild and not used to strangers. They feed on unconcernedly, jangling their bells, but one or two of the bulls cast inquiring glances upon us, and we prudently retire to our pockets the bright red sashes bought in Cauterets until we have passed the zone of porterhouse.

In this plateau is a boundary-stone, and we pass anew into Spain,—stopping to cross and recross the frontier

several times, with grave ceremony, and to the unconcealed mystification of the guide. The path slopes up again, passes a dejected little mountain tarn, and another half hour brings us to the final cone, the summit just overhead. The mists are still whirling down, but as often lift again; the Pic de la Pique has disappeared under a berret of cloud, but other and greater peaks beyond it are still cloudless; so, as we push on up the last slope of rock and scramble upon the summit, we see that the panorama is not gone after all and that the climb will have its reward.

For the view is a wide one from the Pic d'Entécade. The summit, 7300 feet above the sea, is an island in a circle of valleys. The hospice basin has dwindled into insignificance. Behind is the trough of the Luchon depression, its floor invisible but the main contour traceable for miles. The Valley of Aran, which opens out below us on the east, shows the fullest reach in the view; its entire course lies under the eye, and the lines of rivers and roads are marked as on a map, while we count no less than fourteen villages spotting its bottom and sides. Beyond and about roll the mountains, in swells and billows of green, roughening into grey and the finishing white.

But it is their culminating summit at the right that at once absorbs attention; it is the monarch of the Pyrenees; we are looking at last upon the Maladetta. It stands in clear view before us, well defined though distant. It is rather a mass than a mountain; it shows no accented, unified form; the wide crests rise irregularly from its wider shoulders of granite and glacier, and fairly blaze for the moment in the break of sunlight.

At nearer quarters, as from the Port de Vénasque, the true dimensions of the Maladetta are better realized. There one sees it from across a single ravine, as the Jungfrau is seen from the Wengern Alp. But here from the Entécade also, we can seize well its proportions,—

"In bulk as huge
As whom the fables name of monstrous size,
Titanian or Earth-born, that warr'd on

Jove."

The highest point of the Maladetta, the Pic de Néthou, is 11,165 feet above the sea. The mountain has always been regarded superstitiously; the name itself,—*Maladetta, Maudit*, the Accursed,—tells of the traditions of the mountaineers. For long, no one dared the ascent. Ramond finally attempted it in 1787, but failed to gain the highest point. In 1824, a party renewed the attempt, and were worse than unsuccessful, for one of the guides, Barreau by name, was lost,—precipitated into a crevasse almost before the eyes of his son,—and the body was never recovered. This added to the evil repute of the mountain; years passed before the cragsmen would have anything further to do with it. It was not until 1842 that M. de Franqueville, a French gentleman, accompanied by M. Tchihatcheff, a Russian naturalist, and by three determined guides, successfully gained the summit,—taking four days and three nights for the enterprise. Since then the ascent has a number of times been made.

This mountain is said to give forth at times a low murmuring sound distinctly audible.

"There is sweet music here that softer falls
Than petal from blown roses on the grass,
Or night-dews on still waters between walls
Of shadowy granite in a gleaming pass.
"

"One of the most impressive features of the scene on the ridge of Vénasque on this memorable morning," so relates one E.S., a traveler of sixty years ago, "was the peculiar, solemn noise emitted from the mountain. The only sound which broke upon our silence while we stood before it without exchanging a word, was an uninterrupted, melancholy mourning, a sort of Æolian, aerial tone, attributable to no visible or ostensible cause. The tradition of the Egyptian statue responding to the first rays of the morning sun came forcibly to my recollection. In her voice, this queen of the Pyrenees 'Prince Memnon's sister might beseem,' and superstition if not philosophy might have persuaded some that this sudden glare of brightness and warmth, glistening with increasing intenseness on every ridge and eastern surface, might call forth some corresponding vibrations, and therefore that the plaintive tones we heard were in fact a sort of sympathetic music,—the Maladetta's morning hymn."

Far to the west, over other ranges, the guide points out the glaciers of Mont Perdu and the Vignemale. We are looking off also from this point upon the beginnings of Aragon and of Catalonia; there is nothing smiling about Spain as seen from the Entécade; sterile hills solely heap themselves to the horizon.

We linger on the small knoll, a few feet only in width, which caps the mountain beneath us. Clouds scud over the summits and pass on, and turn by turn we have seen the full view. Finally they come streaming in more resolutely, and eventually defeat the breeze; then we turn downward at last, at a brisk pace, race down the slopes and re-enter France; and warily recrossing the long pasture of the corniculates, hasten on until the hospice appears in sight once more below.

It is far past mid-day now, and we are more than ready for suggestions of alimentation. There is a sheltered table with benches just out of doors before the hospice, and here we seat ourselves, flanked by with two massive dogs, and soon are discussing a nondescript repast which is too late for lunch and too early for dinner but which is remarkably appetizing in either view. An hour later, we are again in Luchon, greeted by the deferential head-waiter of the Richelieu, whose starchy bosom expands with hourly welcome for each who comes or who returns.

VIII.

There are divers other trips near Luchon which should be taken by the time-wealthy. It is a centre of more excursions than any of the other resorts; to count those which are *très recommandées* alone needs all the fingers.

There is the much praised drive into the Vallée du Lys, with its white cascades, its "Gulf of Hell," its fine view of the ice-wastes of the Crabioules. There is the ascent to Superbagnères, an easy monticule overshading Luchon, whose view is ranked with that from the Bergonz. There is the day's ride through the Valley of Aran, which opened out below us from the Entécade,—a truly Spanish valley, though in France; its natives, its customs, its inns, all Hispanian, and unwontedly unconventional. There is the ride and climb to the Lac d'Oo, a mate of the trip from Cauterets to the Lac de Gaube. And for a longer jaunt, one can remount to the Port de Vénasque and pierce down upon the Spanish side to the village of Vénasque itself, returning next day by another port and the Frozen Lakes. Or this trip can be prolonged by making the tour of the Maladetta, passing on from Vénasque entirely around that mountain system and returning within the week by still another route to Luchon. The views on this last tour are described as remarkable, though it is a trip seldom made; the accommodation is doubtless uncomforting, but the tour, in outline at least, strongly resembles the tour of Mont Blanc, which ranks with the finest excursions in the Alps.

In short, there is a bewilderment of alternatives, each of the first rank in interest and heavily endorsed. Luchon is as easily the belle of the spas in location as in beauty; and one might strongly suspect that the charms of its climbs cure quite as many ills as its springs. Good as the waters may be, one does not become well by drinking merely, and sitting in wait for health; it needs precisely the invigoration of these tempting outings to quicken languid pulses and inspire sluggish systems.

Even in winter, many of these Pyrenees mountain-trips are entirely practicable. The Cirque of Gavarnie is reputed a double marvel under a winter robe, when its cascades are stiffened into ice and the eye is lost in the sweep of the snow-fields. Cauterets is hospitable throughout the winter, and so are both of the Eaux. Even the Vignemale has

been ascended of a February, and the more ordinary excursions can be undertaken in all seasons. One cannot help thinking that the invalid of Pau's winter colony could better tell over the benefits of this Pyrenees climate if he would but test it,—if he would seek its pure, sharp, aromatic stimulus in in-roads upon the mountains themselves, in place of his mild promenadings along the Terrace in view of them with a heavy fur coat on his back and another on his tongue.

The mountains are nearer him, besides, than they formerly were. They have been opened to approach. Once there was no Route Thermale over the cols; no facile pass to Vénasque or the Lac de Gaube; no iron bars in the difficult spots en the Pic du Midi d'Ossau. That day is gone by. Parts at least of the wild mountains are tamed; danger has been driven back, hardly the daunt of difficulty remains. D'Étigny and Napoleon and the Midi Railroad have smoothed all the ways; there is no longer reason to dread the lumbering diligence, the rough char-roads, the pioneer cuttings through the pine-brakes. The buoyant mountain trips we have touched upon, and more, are within almost instant call of every dispirited Pau valetudinary, and of farther travelers as well. They have but to go forth and meet them.

That this is becoming known is shown by the yearly increasing tide of visitors. The cultured modern world enjoys reading the book of nature,—especially so, provided some one has cut the leaves.

IX.

In the evening, we repeat the stroll down the Allée d'Étigny. The lights twinkle brightly down upon the street; the shops are open, the hotels lit up, the cafés most animated of all. Here on the sidewalks, around the little iron tables, sits Luchon, sipping its liqueurs and tasting its ices. It is the café-life of Paris in miniature,—as characteristically French as in the capital. To "*Paris, c'est la France*," one might almost add, "*le café, c'est Paris*." France would not be France without it. It is its hearthstone, its debating-club, the matrix of all its national sentiments.

There is an "etiquette" of Continental drinks. By the initiate, the code is rigorously observed; each class of beverages has its hour and reason, and your true Frenchman would not dream of calling for one out of place and time. In the cafe-gardens of the large hotels you will see the waiters' trays bearing one set of labeled bottles before dinner and another after; one at mid-day, another in the evening. There is also a ritual of mixing; syrups and liqueurs all have their chosen mates and are never mismated.

From, an intelligent waiter in Lyons, a double fee extracted for me on one occasion some curious if unprofitable lore on the subject, since expanded by further queryings. The potations in-demand divide themselves, it appears, into two main classes: *apéritifs* and *digestifs*. The former are simply appetizers, usually of the bitters class, and are taken before meals. The latter, as their name shows, come after the repast, for some supposed effect in aiding digestion. These liquors are often, exceedingly strong, but it is to be remembered that the quantities taken are minute; when brought not mixed with water or syrups, a unit portion might hardly fill a walnut shell.

The favorite *apéritifs* are:

Absinthe,	mixed with	Orgeat	a
Bitter,	"	"	Curaçao	"
Vermouth,	"	"	Cassis	"
"	"	"	Curaçao	"
"	"	"	Bitter	"
"	"	"	Gomme	"
Amer Picon,	"	"	Curaçao	"
"	"	"	Grenadine	"
"	"	"	Sirop ordinaire	

Madeira, Malaga, Frontignan, Byrrh, Q Ratafia, unmixed,

After meal-time come the *digestifs*:

Price.

Curaçao	unmixed,	60
Fokyn,		
Maraschino,	"	60
Kümmel,	"	30
Kirschwasser,	"	50
Chartreuse,	" (yellow or green,).	60 or 80
Anisette, with seltzer,		80
Menthe, (Peppermint,) unmixed, or with seltzer,		50
Mazagran, or goblet of black coffee, with water,		40
Café noir,	or small cup of black coffee,	35
"	with Cognac,	50
Limonade gazeuse,		40
Bière, bock or ordinaire,		30

Later in the evening, the ices come into play; returning from concert or promenade, one can choose from the following to recruit the wasted frame:

		Price.
Sorbet	au Kirsch,	80
"	" Rhum,	80
"	" Maraschino,	80
Bavaroise	au lait,	60
"	à la vanille,	70
"	au chocolat,	70
Glace vanille or other flavors,		50 and 75
Café glacé,		50
Grock or Punsch.		60

And last, the inevitable

Eau sucrée, with orange-flower, 35

The above sketchy division may perhaps add to the visitor's alien interest in Continental café-life, showing something of its system and rationale. These elaborate and varied concoctions, noxious and innoxious, are not, it must be understood, tossed off in the frenzied instantaneity of the American mode; before a tiny glassful of Curaçao or sugar and water, the Gallic "knight of the round table" will sit for hours in utter content, reading the papers, talking, smoking, or clicking the inoffensive domino. Intoxication is almost unknown in the better cafés; their patrons may sear their oesophagi with hot Chartreuse, derange the nerves with Absinthe, stimulate themselves hourly with

their little cups of black coffee and brandy; but they never get drunk. Frenchmen are temperate, even in their intemperance. An English gin-mill and probably an American bar causes more besotment than a dozen French cafés.

CHAPTER XVII.

OUT TOWARD THE PLAIN.

"How the golden light
On those mountain-tops makes them strangely bright."
—*The Pyrenees Herdsman.*

We revolve an unhappy fact, as we ramble on along the brilliant Allée, this clear summer evening. We are no longer among the time-wealthy. With Barcelona and the Mediterranean in prospect, we cannot draw further in Luchon upon our reserve of days. The evening is flawless; the stars blaze overhead like the burst, of a rocket; the promise of the morrow is beyond doubt, and the Col d'Aspin is yet to be reconquered. We come back across the park to our pleasant rooms in the Richelieu; and a conclave ends in a summons to a livery-man and the order for carriages for a to-morrow's return to Bigorre.

Early rising is therefore enforced, without regard to resentment, the next morning, for we are to drive through within the day, not making a night's break as before at Arreau. There are thus the two hard cols to cross, one in the forenoon, the other in the afternoon; and the horses must have a long mid-day rest to accomplish the task. So the Allée-d'Étigny is just taking down, the shutters, as we prepare to drive away from the hotel; the dew is still dampening the walks; domestics are scouring entrance-ways and windows, a few early guides and drivers look wistfully at the departing possibilities. We are unfeignedly sorry to leave Luchon. But we exult in compensation over an unclouded day for the Col d'Aspin.

By the usual mysterious Continental system of telegraphy, the fact has spread that we are going, and even at this unseasonable hour the entire working force of the Richelieu, portier, waiter, head-waiter, maids, buttons, boots and bagsman line up to do us reverence. We pass from hall to carriages through a double row of expectants. It is a veritable running of the gauntlet, save that in running it we give rather than receive. Unlike recipients in most other parts of Europe, however, the servants here have the air of expecting rather than of demanding, and take what is given more as a gift than as a right. So we depart in the comfortable glow of benefaction, rather than in the calmer consciousness of indebtedness baldly paid.

We reach the foot of the first col, the Peyresourde, with views at the left of the distant glaciers above the Lac d'Oo, wind up to the crest as the morning wears on, and by noon have scudded down by the other side and are again at Arreau. It is a fête-day throughout France, and as we drive into the town we find the plain little street transformed into a bloom of flags and flowers and tri-colored bunting. On every side, as we stroll out later from the inn, the shops and houses are fluttering the red, the white and the blue, colors as dear to the American eye as to the French. Boughs and garlands festoon the archways; the neighborhood has flocked to the town in holiday finery, the *cabarets* or taverns are driven with custom, the nun-like town is become a masquerader. The scene is so different from that of the cold, grey morning on which we left for Luchon, that we vividly see how impressions of place as of person may change with the change of garb and mood.

The air is warm, even sultry, but not oppressive. In fact, the thermometer has not throughout the tour given any markedly choleric displays of temper. The Pyrenees, lying as they do so far toward the south, had held for us vague intimations of southern heat: linked closely in latitude with the Riviera and with mid-Italy, we had half feared to find them linked as well with Mediterranean and Italian temperatures, and so far ill adapted for summer traveling. But the fear was uncalled for. The weather has, on infrequent days, been undeniably warm, but no warmer than the summer heat of the valleys of the Alps or the Adirondacks. In fact, as a matter of geography, the Pyrenees lie in the same northerly latitude as the Adirondacks themselves. In point of elevation above the sea, the belt, even in its lowlands, is everywhere higher than the neighboring parallels of Nice or Florence; the air is fresher, shade and breeze are more abundant, as always among mountains; our trip, aiding, to verify this, convinces us that apprehensions as to excess of heat will here find gratifyingly little fulfilment.

II.

We beguile the three hours' wait with a lunch, a walk, and an idiot beggar with an imposing wen or goitre. This creature crouches persistently by the carriages while the horses are reharnessed and we are taking our places. The form is misshapen, the face distorted and scarcely human; we can get no answer from the mumbling lips save a sputter of gratitude for our sous; it is cretinism, hideous, hopeless, a horror among these beautiful valleys, yet as in the Alps pitifully common.

In the presence of this frightful disease, destroying every semblance of fair humanity, one can see some reason also for the belief in witchcraft and diabolism once so intense in the Pyrenees. If the body and mind of an "innocent" can thus come to part with the last vestige of its holy lineage, the soul of a "wicked" might with good reason seem to be capable of growing into full fellowship with the devil himself. So late as 1824, not far from this spot, they nearly burned an old woman for alleged sorcery; and in 1862, one was actually so burned, in the town of Tarbes, a few leagues away. This superstition of witchcraft has here been strong in all eras, but it is at last becoming extinct; cretinism, as anachronous and as horrible,—a fact, not a superstition,—remains unaccounted for and unlessened.

III.

By four o'clock, we are at the base of the Col d'Aspin and commence on the long curves that lead to its top. The valley behind extends as we rise; new breaks and depressions appear, branching off right and left on all sides. After a half hour, peaks begin to peep over the hills at our rear; they come up one by one into sight, each whiter and sharper than the last, until the southern line is a serrate row of them, gradually lifted wholly above the nearer hills. The promised panorama is truly taking shape. We near at length the crest of the col. The Pic du Midi de Bigorre will loom up beyond it, unclouded to-day, the drivers assure us, and we watch for a glimpse at last of that mythical peak, which we have skirted in cloud from Barèges to Bigorre and never yet once seen. We are just below the top of the col; twenty feet farther will place the carriages on the summit, when lo a huge rounded dome begins to rise slowly up beyond the edge, and as we advance lifts itself into the full form of the long sought Pic,—ten miles away to the west, yet looming out as clearly as if but across the valley. It stands alone against the horizon; there is no summit near to rival it; the sides are dark and steep and almost snowless; the summit is looking down upon Gavarnie,—upon Pau,—upon the wide march of the plains of France,—as upon us on the Col d'Aspin, eying us with its stony Pyrenean stare.

Behind, the southern view is now in its entirety. The full line of the Arreau and Luchon depressions is traceable, and of all their tributaries as well; the giant humps of the hills marshaled to form their walls. The separate pinnacles beyond them are countless. The chief array is compacted directly south, a fraise of bristles numbering the white Crabioules, the Pic des Posets, the Monts Maudits,—and at the left the summits of the Maladetta, a "citadel of silver" in a sky of gold, its glaciers fierce against the late afternoon sun.

At the right above the col is a wider point of view; we ascend for some twenty minutes over the pastures to the top, led by a herd-boy. The view now sweeps a new quarter of the horizon,—

that of the northeast; and the full plain of Toulouse is spread at our feet, shading off in the far distance into a faint hazy transparence where a few soft clouds seal it to the line of the sky.

"Not vainly did the early Persian make His altar the high places and the peak Of earth-o'ergazing mountains."

The Dark Ages were strangely dark in one respect: they had forgotten the admiration for Nature. Save as to unaccustomed manifestations,—quakes and comets and like portents,—they seem to have noticed little of her higher or more unfamiliar moods. The sensation of the sublime was not in their range of emotions; it is distinctively a modern growth. Froissart traveled through this region on his way to Orthez; the Pyrenees peaks were in sight before him, day after day, near and distant; and they shone upon him for weeks from the hills about Gaston's castle. Not once does he mention their presence to admire it. Scarcely once do other writers of his or neighboring centuries notice even their existence, except as hunting-grounds or boundary-lines; "*le spectacle des Alpes ne dit rien à Racine, et l'aspect des glaciers fait froid à Montaigne.*" All the historian's of the time of Henry IV speak of his having been born in "a country harsh and frightful,"—"*un pays aspre et affreux.*" Even the early troubadours and trouvères, poets and rhapsodists, loving to admire and enlarge and extol, are silent concerning the mountains. Despourrins, the poet of the Pyrenees, sang of love and lyric inspiration; but he rarely looked up to seek the higher inspiration of their hills and snows. It is inexplicable that the power of the sublime should have been withheld from the age of romance and poetry and nearness to nature, and bestowed in growing measure upon our commercial and unenthusiastic era. It is not all wholly prosaic, after all, this nineteenth century of ours, when it has so ardently this high emotion, scorned by its intenser predecessors.

As we descend to the carriages, facing another tall Pic which shoots up from the farther side of the col, the sun has neared the clouds in the west; it strikes the far-off Maladetta glaciers with a light no longer white, but rose-tinted; the snows glow softly under it like fields of tremulous flame; the mountains gleam almost as something supernal, as we take a final gaze before turning away down the valley.

IV.

It is the last of our midsummer drive through, the Pyrenees. We realize it almost suddenly, and with regret. We seek to absorb and enjoy every minute as we drive down the long hills and on through the Vale of Campan in the evening light toward Bigorre. It is a chaotic, delightful array of memories that our minds are whirling over and over in their busy hoppers,—incidents and scenes, grains of legend, kernels of history, gleanings of quick, nearer life,—all the intermingled associations now sown for us over the region.

Instinctively we summon up recollections of the Alps for comparison with the mountains we are leaving. And the comparison is not found to be entirely a sacrilege. The Alps are first and preeminent among European mountains; the repose of their immensity, the sense of power, the indefinable, spell they exert, lesser ranges cannot in general features attempt to rival. But this is not to say that a lesser range, is a wholly inferior range,—that even in this effect of immensity, of power, it may not at certain points bear almost full comparison. The Pyrenees, we agree, are far from lacking material for a parallel. As we think of the briefly glimpsed cliffs of the Pic du Midi d'Ossau, or of the ice-fields seen about the Balaïtous, the Vignemale, the Taillon, the Crabioules, we set them in thought almost against the crags of the Mont Cervin, or the Eismeer and the glaciers of the Bernina. We instance, as Alpine impressions, the prospects, among others, from the Aubisque and the Entécade; the snow-peaks, named and unnamed, in their sight, the heights and depths revealed by the view. We traverse again the gorges leading to Eaux Chaudes and Cauterets, and the winding road through the Chaos; we confront the amazing wall of the Cirque of Gavarnie, which has nothing of its own order in Switzerland that is even commensurate; we rehearse the account of the scaling of Mont Perdu and of the outlook from its summit, as first recorded by Ramond nearly a century since, when he finally succeeded in that initial ascent; we recall the descriptions of the illimitable desolations of the Maladetta fastnesses, more recently explored by Packe and Russell; and while these are single effects, and those of the Alps are beyond count, they are in character not to be excluded from almost equal rank. And over all the lowlands we throw that luxuriance of vegetation and of foliage, and a certain softness and richness of landscape, which cannot be found nearer the north, and which, in the contrast with the snow-peaks in sight beyond adds so strangely to the height and aloofness of the latter,—as in the view of the Pic de Ger from Eaux Bonnes, and the wider sweep from the Pau Terrace or the Col d'Aspin behind us. In fine, as genial Inglis long ago made summary, "the traveler who is desirous of seeing all the various charms of mountain scenery, must visit both Switzerland and the Pyrenees. He must not content himself with believing that having seen Switzerland he has seen all that mountain scenery can offer. This would be a false belief. He who has traversed Switzerland throughout has indeed become familiar with scenes which cannot perhaps be equaled in any other country in the world; and he need not travel in search of finer scenes of the same order. But scenes of a different order,—of another character,—await him in the Pyrenees; and until he has looked upon these, he has not enjoyed all the charms which mountain scenery is capable of disclosing to the lover of nature."

V.

Lights twinkle out everywhere over the valley, as we roll on toward Bigorre; every village and hamlet we pass is aglow with colored lanterns and varied illuminations, and all the Pyrenees seem to be keeping high holiday. Stalwart songs are resounding from porches and through the windows of the local cafés when the carriages reach Ste. Marie; we respond with the notes of *America*, as we drive out from the village, and catch an answering cheer in return. Everyone is determinedly happy, but happy or not, they have always a good word for our country. Other songs and scenes are caught as we whirl on over the valley-road and through the settlements; peasants peer at us from the wayside or from the occasional chalets near by, with pleasant salute and good wishes. At last, and with real regret, we have reached our destination; Bagnères de Bigorre is before us, and we are speeding into its streets.

It is here that we find the climax of the fête. The entire Promenade des Coustous is a blaze of light. Arches have been erected, rows of tiny glass lamps swing across from the trees, flags and bunting stream out over the music-stand and the hotels and shops on each side. The place is a mass of people; the bordering cafés are thronged; the band is playing clearly above the hum and buzz, and as we enter the street it happens to be just striking the signal for the *Marseillaise*. In an instant, the thousands of throats join in the sound; the roll of song deepens to a diapason; the solemn, forceful march of the melody is irresistible; all France seems to be joining with prayer and power in her loved anthem.

Quickly we have greeted our welcoming hostess once more, congratulated the drivers for their good day's work, and hurried out to the Coustous,—there to sit and sip ices and steep in the exhilaration of the festival until far into the night.

And so ends our mountain faring; and when, the next day, we turn to the morning train for Toulouse and the open plain, it is with anticipation still, yet with an unrepressed sigh at leaving these mountains and laughing valleys of the Pyrenees, of whose charms we had once so inadequately known.

FOOTNOTES

[1] *Voyage aux Pyrénées.*

[2] INGLIS: Switzerland and the South of France.

[3] INGLIS.

[4] *Tour Through the Pyrenees*; translated by J. SAFFORD FISKE, New York: Henry Holt & Co.

[5] LAGRÈZE: *La Société et les Moeurs en Béarn.*

[6] MISS PARDOE: *Louis XIV.*

[7] It is said that the Basque nomenclature of domestic animals is almost entirely Finnish.

[8] VINCENT: *In the Shadow of the Pyrenees*. New York: Charles Scribner's Sons.

[9] Ganelon was the traitor and Roland's own step-father. The lines quoted are from the late version by JOHN O'HAGAN, outlined in an article in the *Edinburgh Review* to whose appreciative commentary much indebtedness is acknowledged.

[10] *Peninsular War.*

[11] FIELD: *Old Spain and New Spain.*

[12] *Gave* is the generic name among the Pyrenees for a mountain stream or torrent.

[13] In 1620.

[14] Anciently written Ortayse, afterward Orthès.

[15] The genuineness of the present shell has frequently been questioned; but the testimony of LAGRÈZE has now fairly established the story of its preservation.

[16] ELLIOTT: *Old Court Life in France.*

[17] *Tour Through the Pyrenees.*

[18] "The colonel," continues Perefix, "sensibly moved with this behavior, replied with tears in his eyes: 'Ah, Sire! in restoring to me my honor you take away my life; for after this I should be unworthy of your favor if I did not sacrifice it to-day for your service. If I had a thousand lives I would lay them all at your feet.' In fact he was killed upon this occasion."

[19] See Frontispiece.

[20] Now the frequented watering-place, Bagnères de Bigorre.

[21] The translation made in 1523 by John Bourchier, Lord Berners, at the request of Henry VIII. The one I have elsewhere quoted from is that of Thomas Johnes.

[22] "*Nous jugeons que l'immaculée Marie, mère de Dieu, a réellement apparu à Bernadette Soubirous, le 11 Février, 1838, et jours suivants, au nombre de dix-huit fois, dans la grotte de Massabielle, près la ville de Lourdes; que cette apparition revêt tous les caractères de la vérité et que les fidèles sont fondés à la croire certaine.*"

[23] Puy—St. Pé—is a shrine near Lourdes.

[24] Marguerite of Angoulême is often, even by historians, designated as Marguerite of Valois. It is better to preserve the distinction in the names. Marguerite of Angoulême was the wife of Henry II of Navarre; the name Marguerite of Valois more properly designates the wife (known also as Margot) of Henry IV, their grandson.

[25] "*Encores que l'air chault de ce pays devoit ayder au roy de Navarre, il ne laisse pas de se ressentir de la cheute qu'il prist; par le conseil des médecins à ce moys de may s'en va mettre aux Baings de Caulderets, où il se foit tous les jours des choses merveilleuses. Je me deslibère, après m'estre repousée ce caresme, d'aller avecques luy, pour le garder d'ennuy et foire pour luy ses affaires; car tant que l'on est aux baings, il fault vivre comme ung enfant, sans nul soucy.*"

[26] From *Roadside Sketches*, by Three Wayfarers.

[27] "This woman," naively adds the writer, "irritated at the refusal of the priest, showed that she could dispense with saintly help in the matter altogether: she killed her husband herself, with a gun."

[28] "*Edinburgh New Philosophical Journal*, No. XVI; *The Peculiar Noises Heard in Mountains.*"

[29] A centime is one-fifth of a cent.

***

Lightning Source UK Ltd.
Milton Keynes UK
UKOW06f0354170514

231847UK00011B/516/P